FIGHTER PILOTS OF THE RAF

FIGHTER PILOTS OF THE RAF

1939-1945

CHAZ BOWYER

WILLIAM KIMBER · LONDON

First published in 1984 by
WILLIAM KIMBER & CO. LIMITED
100 Jermyn Street, London, SW1Y 6EE

© Chaz Bowyer, 1984

ISBN 0-7183-0519 1

Photoset in North Wales by
Derek Doyle & Associates, Mold, Clwyd
Printed and bound in Great Britain by
The Garden City Press, Letchworth, Herts.

Contents

List of Illustrations

Introduction

To the layman the generic label 'fighter pilot' conjures up many characteristics – dashing, extrovert, steely-eyed, rock-jawed, even romantic killer; all facets engendered by an Everest of pulp and journalistic fiction, sensation-seeking yellow press, and/or sheer propaganda. Rarely do such descriptions apply to the men who actually fought from the cockpit of a fighter aircraft in war. As in any community of Servicemen with a common *raison d'être*, fighter pilots came in all sizes, shapes and characters, with origins ranging from humble artisan to 'blue-blood' aristocracy, from elementary schoolboy to university graduate, from fearless oaf to ultra-sensitive aesthete. In other words, there was (is) no pattern from which all fighter pilots can be said to have derived. Each is a distinct individual, with individual attitudes, reasoning, reactions, motivations, albeit having received a parallel form of training and inculcation to his 'trade' in common with all other fighter pilots within his particular air service initially. Yet, in one sense, that very individuality was the true essence of any successful fighter pilot. During both the 1914-18 and 1939-45 wars especially, the fighter pilot, once combat was joined, was virtually on his own, needing an instinctive aggression, single purpose, and unforced ability to conquer all odds if he was to survive and fulfil his duty.

Resulting from the wide publicity and indeed glamorisation applied to certain fighter pilots during the 1914-18 conflict, when the entire specious status of the 'ace' fighter pilot was born, the equivalent generation of fighter crews during the 1939-45 war inherited, albeit unconsciously, the same heroic image in the lay mind. Thus a relative handful of World War Two fighter pilots received unsought plaudits on an international scale as 'aces' – in the context of having accumulated a number of claimed aerial

9

combat 'victories' – and were honoured and fêted accordingly. Though such publicity was rarely of the individual's choosing, it inevitably over-shadowed the feats and prowess of the majority of other fighter pilots who displayed equally high courage and determination to those who, however unwittingly, basked in the limelight of public acclaim. This silent majority comprised the true spine of any fighter force; men who flew and fought with a fervour matching that displayed by their more famed colleagues, and who, speaking statistically, made the greater sacrifices.

My purpose in this book is primarily to give overdue recognition to those unknowns, but also to demonstrate the diverse *types* of men exemplifying the fighter pilots of the Royal Air Force during the 1939-45 struggle against German Nazidom and Italian fascism. In deference to further volumes already in preparation about pilots who served mainly in the Middle and Far East war theatres, Coastal Command, *et al*, I have deliberately restricted my selection of subjects herein to a cross-section of fighter pilots who fought their particular war mainly, if not exclusively, in the Northern European theatre. Of the men featured here some were indeed aces in the popular lay conception of achieving relatively high scores, but I would emphasise to the reader that pure 'acedom' has *not* been my criterion for inclusion. In the present era of computerised technology the role of the fighter pilot *per se*, as exemplified in the following pages, no longer exists in the RAF. The modern equivalent is very much more a highly skilled, professional segment of a superbly constructed weapons system. Yet let it never be forgotten that such a segment remains a human individual, not a robot, requiring all and possibly even more of those singular characteristics which comprised the fighter pilot of yesteryear. Whatever else may change, the essential human spirit remains.

Chaz Bowyer
Norwich, 1984

CHAPTER ONE

Background

While the prime purpose of this book is to highlight the lives, deeds, attitudes, characteristics – and in certain cases, self-sacrifices – of a tiny selection of individual men who flew to war in fighter aircraft, such accounts must be set against the overall contexts of the aircraft they were given to fly, the tactics currently employed, and particularly the state of the organisations they belonged to at their various stages of the aerial conflict. Even the finest human spirit is hampered when given inferior equipment or faulty intelligence with which to undertake any assigned task or duty. Equally, even the finest equipment and/or supportive organisation is of relatively small value without a matching human willpower and determination to utilise such ironmongery to its greatest advantage. Since the men described in this volume flew most, if not all, of their operations in the Northern European theatre of war, their parent organisation was RAF Fighter Command for the most part of the war; thus a progressive account of that Command is relevant here as a backdrop to the actions, prowess, problems, and circumstances integral with each man's story.

Originally created as a separate entity on 14 July 1936, RAF Fighter Command faced the prospect of all-out war with Nazi Germany in September 1939 with an overall strength far below the minimal requirement of 53 first-line squadrons officially mooted then as essential for the metropolitan defence of the United Kingdom – the primary role or *raison d'être* of the Command from its outset. Its true operational strength on 1 September 1939 comprised 37 first-line squadrons, 14 of which were recently-mobilised non-regular squadrons of the Auxiliary Air Force (AAF), the so-termed, pre-war 'Week-end Air Force'. Of the overall total, 17 squadrons were flying Hurricane I

11

fighters, 12 were equipped with Spitfire Is, but no less than six were flying stop-gap Blenheim If 'fighters' i.e. Blenheim I bombers modified to carry a four-gun pack bolted under their bomb bay doors. Among them the 37 squadrons held the following aircraft totals:

Hurricane I	347 (400)
Spitfire I	187 (270)
Blenheim If	111 (111)
Gladiator	76 (218)
Gauntlet	26 (100)

The bracketed figures here were the *total* aircraft of each type held on actual aircraft strength by the RAF that day. Thus, of its complete stock of 1,099 fighters, the RAF's front-line squadrons actually possessed 747 machines; some 30-odd per cent of which were outmoded biplanes or roughly converted bombers. Though unknown precisely to the contemporary RAF or government hierarchy, the German Luftwaffe's aircraft strength on that same date totalled 4,704, of which 2,069 could be realistically described as first-line bomber or attack machines.

In the context of pure metropolitan aerial defence of the UK, these theoretical odds against Fighter Command were offset during the opening months of the war by the simple fact that only certain German bombers possessed the range needed actually to attack Britain from their contemporary bases in Germany itself, and even then would be unescorted by the Luftwaffe's standard fighters, the Messerschmitt Bf 109E, or its twin-engined stablemate Bf 110.

Nevertheless, Fighter Command's already understrength inventory of fighters based in Britain was further reduced immediately upon the declaration of war, when four Hurricane squadrons were sent to France in direct tactical support of the British Expeditionary Force (BEF), and the Fighter Command chief, Hugh Dowding, was instructed to bring a further six squadrons to a mobile state, ready for further possible reinforcement of the BEF. Thus, at a stroke, Dowding was left with virtually half the required minimal strength in squadrons to fulfil his Command's foremost duty – defence of the United Kingdom.

Perhaps fortunately for Fighter Command, and indeed Britain, the first seven months of war proved low-key in terms of aerial activity, with only sporadic incursions by small numbers of German bombers over Britain, all of which were promptly opposed by the RAF fighters in the immediate areas concerned. In November 1939 Dowding was ordered to despatch two more fighter squadrons to France, while normal day-to-day attrition in aircraft already based on the Continent, due mostly to accidents or technical defects, meant a minor but constant drain on Dowding's reserves for fresh replacement aircraft.

However, pure aircraft strength, though obviously of great importance, was not Hugh Dowding's prime concern at that period. Of greater concern was the question of trained pilots to fill their cockpits. At the beginning of hostilities the bulk of RAF fighter pilots were men serving long or short-term service engagements, thoroughly trained, and with a dedicated professional attitude to their trade. Training of war-enlisted future pilots, though already underway, could not even begin to produce significant numbers of trained men much before mid-1940. Even then it would be some months before such 'sprogs' could be regarded as truly fit for firstline operations, needing to be guided and generally inculcated in their future role by the hard core of experienced regulars.

This premier worry for Dowding was swiftly exacerbated in the spring of 1940 when, on 9 April, Germany launched its invasion of Norway, and occupied neutral Denmark. In early May, accordingly, Fighter Command sent two squadrons for aerial support of British army and naval forces in Norway. Within mere weeks both squadrons had been decimated or lost at sea. Meanwhile, on 10 May 1940, Hitler set in motion his invasion of the Low Countries and France with a massive triple-blow advance westwards. Within 48 hours Fighter Command despatched four more fighter squadrons to France, while on 13 May a further 32 Hurricanes and pilots were flown across the Channel to boost RAF opposition to the German juggernaut. From dawn on 10 May the resident fighter pilots in France commenced virtually non-stop operations against the invading Luftwaffe throughout the hours of daylight, flying five, six, even seven sorties each day. Combat was joined on every sortie, swift and savage, with casualties mounting rapidly on both sides.

Examples of this fierce fighting pace were 501 Squadron AAF which, within an hour of arrival in France, began operations and claimed 18 victims within 48 hours; while No 1 Squadron, between 10 May and 24 May, claimed over 100 victories before the surviving original pilots were repatriated to England and replaced by fresh men. Yet another of the first four units sent to France in September 1939, No 87 Squadron, claimed some 80 victories during ten days' incessant action in May 1940 – but lost nine pilots killed and five others wounded.

As the BEF was forced back towards the Channel coast, the RAF maintained its fierce opposition without pause, but on 26 May Operation Dynamo – a general evacuation of the BEF and Allied troops centred round the coastal town of Dunkirk – began. Aerial protection for Dynamo immediately became the responsibility of AVM Keith Park, commander of No 11 Group, Fighter Command, who had at his disposal merely 16 squadrons at most on any given day, based in south-east England, totalling at best some 200 fighters. These Park was only able to use in single squadron patrols over Dunkirk and its inland approaches, but from 26 May until the end of Dynamo on 4 June Park's fighter crews flew at maximum intensity, accumulating a total of 2,739 individual sorties. In that period the squadrons lost more than 100 aircraft to enemy action, but the more significant losses were human casualties. Of the fighter crews, 57 were killed in action, one died in a flying accident, 13 others were wounded, and eight more became prisoners of war (one subsequently dying in captivity). Claims, made in all good faith, for combat victories over the Luftwaffe totalled 282 destroyed and a further 180 either probably destroyed or at least damaged; though postwar discovery of Luftwaffe records revealed the admitted losses of some 100 German aircraft to RAF actions over or near Dunkirk itself. Of the RAF's losses, the most worrying facet for Fighter Command was the high proportion of leading pilots lost – some two dozen squadron, flight, or section leaders i.e. almost half the total. Such men were sorely needed and, at that early stage of the war, virtually irreplaceable in the short term.

For the great majority of fighter crews involved in the Dynamo operations this had been their first combat blooding in engaging the Luftwaffe, and indeed many future outstanding fighter pilots, men like A.G. 'Sailor' Malan, Robert Tuck, Douglas Bader, and many others, claimed their first combat victories high above Dunkirk's bloody beaches. It was also the first real clash between RAF Spitfires and their German counterparts, Bf 109s, outside British territorial waters; until Dunkirk (and indeed during Dynamo) such combat clashes had been borne in the main by Hurricane squadrons.

By 18 June 1940 the final stragglers from France had returned to England, and Hugh Dowding took stock of his losses and strength. From 10 May to 4 June 1940 a total of 432 Hurricanes (mainly), Spitfires, and other fighters had been lost – roughly equivalent to 20 squadrons – while the overall *blitzkrieg* period boosted this figure to 477, apart from 32 more fighter aircraft lost in the ill-fated Norwegian venture earlier. Fighter Command's next immediate problem was the fact that the Luftwaffe now occupied air bases all along the northern European coastline, particularly in France, which meant that German bombers *and* fighters were now within fighting range of southern England; a situation emphasised in the weeks following Dynamo, when clashes between British and German aircraft over the Channel waters led to RAF claims for at least 56* Luftwaffe aircraft shot down, but at a cost of 28 RAF fighters, with 23 of their pilots killed or wounded.

The much-publicised Battle of Britain which followed shortly after France's collapse in mid-1940 needs little elucidation here, bearing in mind the mini-mountain of published literature on that crucial struggle since 1940. Bare factual details of the overall Battle cannot do justice to the courage, effort, and determination overtly displayed by the air and ground crews of Fighter Command in that fateful summer and autumn, though it should be borne in mind that while the RAF's fighter pilots were the true

* This figure is extracted from German documentation; RAF claims at the time were much higher.

cutting edge of the aerial defences, they were by no means the only men involved in contributing to the ultimate victory. As the fighter 'Few' maintained their dawn-to-dusk challenge to the incoming Luftwaffe formations, their undaunted efforts were matched each night by the crews of Bomber Command, attacking vital enemy invasions ports *et al* along the Channel coast and penetrating deeper inland to Germany itself, while Coastal Command, Balloon Command, and the myriad forms of ground defences each played their part in nullifying the constant threat of German invasion of England.

The *official* parameters of the Battle of Britain, later decreed by the Air Ministry, were from 0001 hours on 10 July 1940 to 2359 hours on 31 October 1940; an arbitrary limitation imposed by the bureaucratic requirements of the Whitehall 'Paper Factory' (for reasons which continue to baffle logic ...), but which, for merely one example, takes no account of the fighting over the Channel convoys etc in June and early July. It should be added that the contemporary Luftwaffe never recognised the Battle of Britain as a distinct battle *per se*, but simply as various phases of a longer, wider attempt to crush Britain by aerial assault, both by day and by night, and *including* the concentrated nightly *blitzkrieg* on Britain throughout the winter months, 1940-41. The air strength available in the three *Luftflotten* tasked with paving the way for a German invasion of southern England stood at 1,610 bombers and 1,155 fighters on 20 July 1940, though realistically only 944 bombers and 824 fighters were actually fit for immediate operations. On that same date RAF Fighter Command could barely muster 600 fighters, even including such designs as Defiant two-seaters and converted Blenheim Is which would clearly be outmatched in combat with Messerschmitt Bf 109s. For Hugh Dowding, aircraft strengths were not his chief concern; the UK aviation industry could, and did, produce four and five hundred new fighter aircraft each month in the summer of 1940. Far more important was the question of available pilots and air gunners, few of whom could be replaced rapidly once casualties escalated.

The calibre of Dowding's fighter crews at the outset of the Battle of Britain was high, though apart from the minority which had been blooded in combat over France and Dunkirk, the bulk of Fighter Command's pilots had yet to match their courage and skills against any enemy. In the main they were pre-war trained junior officers and senior NCOs, with an increasing number of recently trained wartime men spread fairly evenly among the squadrons. Other non-regulars were the refugee European pilots – Poles, Czechs, Belgians, French, *et al* – mostly veterans of previous aerial combat with the Luftwaffe in defence of their native countries who were now impatient to continue their personal vendettas with Nazidom. With rare exceptions, all were young, eager, confident in their own abilities, even impatient to test their mettle. Life on a fighter squadron then was reduced to its simplest basic needs – its purpose uncomplicated, with all unnecessary routine matters subverted to that sole purpose – to fight as and whenever called upon to do so. The younger, inexperienced pilots – a majority at that time – might still have retained an adolescent 'glamour' image of their role, but such an image was to be swiftly dispelled in the coming weeks as they witnessed close friends blasted to oblivion or spinning to earth in a ball of flaming wreckage, or juggled with useless, shell-riven controls as a seeming horde of black-crossed Messerschmitts bore in attempting to deliver a *coup de grâce*. Sheer naked fear rode with them in their shattered cockpits on such occasions – and boys became men virtually overnight.

The first three weeks of the Battle, from 10 to 31 July, set the pace for even greater action to come. In those weeks the RAF flew a total of some 12,000 individual fighter sorties during which 270 Luftwaffe aircraft were shot down for the loss of 145 RAF fighters. The aircraft losses could be replaced by merely one week's industrial production, but the inherent loss of 51 pilots killed and 18 others wounded or injured was not so readily replaced. Dowding was forced to scour other RAF Commands, even the Fleet Air Arm, for fresh pilots, most of these receiving the hastiest conversion training in a fighter, then being pitchforked straight into the ranks of a first-line squadron and almost immediate action.

Throughout August, September, and October 1940 the Battle swiftly rose to a peak of savage, desperate effort both by the RAF and the Luftwaffe, then gradually eased and waned as November heralded the incoming shorter hours of daylight, and the Luftwaffe began to concentrate its strength in nightly forays against British cities and the civil population. The turning point of the Battle had come on 15 September, when the RAF finally convinced the German hierarchy that the Luftwaffe's day offensive had failed, and the prepared invasion of England was postponed indefinitely. Though air combat continued thereafter at a fierce pace, the crucial issue had been decided.

The price of that triumph by the RAF's Few was grievous. From 10 July to 31 October alone – the official span dates for the aerial struggle – RAF Fighter Command had 481 pilots killed or missing, while a further 422 had received wounds, burns, or other serious injuries. RAF aircraft losses had totalled 1,140 destroyed or written-off charge due to battle damage, while the Luftwaffe had lost at least 1,733 aircraft and had 650 more damaged. Almost one in three of the overall total of RAF fighter men to have served with Fighter Command during the Battle had been lost or incapacitated; while a further 800 or so were destined to die in the remaining war years. The victory had not been won by any particular group of brilliant fighter aces – it was the outcome of the accumulative, dogged devotion to duty of the unpublicised, 'ordinary' majority of young fighter pilots.

As the pace of the Battle of Britain declined, and the Luftwaffe turned to the protection of darkness to pursue its assaults on Britain, Fighter Command steadily built up its muscle, and by the close of 1940 could muster 71 first-line squadrons – a total of 1,467 fighters fit for immediate operations – and, moreover, had a plentiful supply of pilots to fly in them. It was the time when the Command acquired not only a new leader, with Air Marshal Sholto Douglas succeeding Hugh Dowding as AOC-in-C in November 1940, but also a fresh policy. Until then the Command's prime function had been pure defence of the UK in all facets, but it was now to add a fresh tactic of 'leaning forward' into France – in other words, an *offensive* policy to carry the war *to* the enemy.

Initial probing sorties of this type had indeed been flown throughout the Battle of Britain, with a total of 1,321 individual sorties between 1 July and 31 October, but in December 1940 the first sorties of the 'new' policy were flown as the harbingers of an ever-mounting aerial offensive which would continue until the end of the war. In 1941 this offensive took three main forms i.e. 'Rhubarb', 'Circus', and 'Roadstead'. Of these, Rhubarbs comprised pure fighter roving sorties over enemy-occupied Europe, seeking (mainly) ground targets for destruction; while Circus operations were more complex, involving relatively large fighter escorts to medium bomber sorties, whereby the bombers were intended as 'bait' to suck up the Luftwaffe into a battle of simple attrition. Roadsteads were straightforward offensive anti-shipping sorties, involving both Fighter and Bomber Commands.

The eventual results of these types of offensive operations varied widely, but – contrary to contemporary claims – were unsuccessful in achieving their objectives. Circus sorties proved wasteful in effort and casualties; an example being the tally for just six weeks in June-July 1941 when, in the course of 46 such sorties the RAF lost 123 fighter pilots 'missing'. In balance, the fighters had *claimed* a total of 322 enemy aircraft destroyed – a figure greater than the total Luftwaffe fighter strength based then in the West! Indeed, RAF fighter pilots' claims for the whole period from 14 June 1941 until the end of that year amounted to 731 German aircraft (mainly fighters) destroyed, whereas *actual* Luftwaffe losses totalled 103 destroyed by RAF day sorties, 11 others lost in operations over England, and a further 51 written off due to non-related causes. RAF losses totted up to 416 fighter pilots killed, missing, or known to be prisoners of war – a tally overtly favouring the Luftwaffe by a factor of roughly four to one. Though made in all good faith, such exaggerated claims by RAF fighter pilots remained a constant factor of the fighters' war until the close of hostilities, but it should be emphasised that the same applied to fighter pilots in *all* air forces involved; in itself a significant comment on the subject of aces and their accredited scores ...

If Circus operations proved costly, then relatively speaking the Roadstead sorties were even more tragic in the context of RAF casualties. Such anti-shipping sorties involved light and medium bombers – principally the Blenheim squadrons of No 2 Group –

in wave-height attacks against heavily protected targets, with fighter escorts usually preceding them in the hope of smothering opposition to the bombers' strikes. Inevitably, fighter casualties were high, but the toll of the Blenheim crews was frightening, with monthly casualty rates not uncommonly reaching 30 per cent or more. By October 1941 such losses caused No 2 Group to be withdrawn from Roadstead operations, though Fighter and Coastal Commands continued their efforts thereafter. Only the Rhubarb operations gave the fighter pilots the element of individual action so necessary for their trained role, being unhampered by the need to shepherd slower, less manoeuvrable bombers. Ironically, though the least effective of the three forms of operations, Rhubarbs, cost Fighter Command the loss of many veteran flight and squadron commanders, either killed or incarcerated in prisoner of war camps during the earlier months of 1941; men like Douglas Bader, Bob Tuck, Eric Lock, Mungo-Park, and other stalwarts of the Battle of Britain. Such experienced leaders were not readily replaceable, particularly men like 'Tin-Legs' Bader who had been one of the first men appointed to a new tactical status, Wing Leader; an appointment as the fighting leader and controller of multi-squadron fighter formations which were the latest development in RAF fighter operations.

Such massed fighter cohorts became the order of the day from mid-1941, yet once combat was joined with any Luftwaffe *Jagdgeschwader* the ensuing action inevitably reverted to a tumbling maelstrom of individual duels and jinking tail-chases with every man dependent solely on his own skills, courage, and determination. Fighter-versus-fighter combat was swift and savage necessitating constant vigilance, lightning, instinctive reactions, and the will to conquer – or at least survive; too fast for the brain to rationalise every situation and offer solution. Such clashes seldom lasted more than a few minutes, after which the sky appeared suddenly empty – a facet of aerial combat which came as a shock to the inexperienced.

The extremes in contrast of a fighter pilot's life then provided both peaks and troughs of tension and stress, mental and physical, which could sap even the strongest eventually. Once a pilot knew that he was 'on' an operation, the inner tension steadily mounted, however experienced he might be; no man is impervious to fear when his life is the stake. Once strapped into his cockpit, the pre-flight routine helped to take his mind off the unknown awaiting him, but once airborne and slotted into the pre-briefed formation, the anxiety slowly reurned, and every nerve was strung taut, every sense honed to infinite awareness. On first sighting of an enemy the heart thumped, the stomach felt empty, then things happened too fast for introspection. The ensuing few minutes became a kill-or-be-killed situation, with the primeval instinct of self-preservation – survival – uppermost in most men's consciousness.

The aftermath was a ground-hugging, wave-cutting flight for home, eyes watching the fuel state, checking for damage, slowly winding down mentally, only now conscious of the sweat rivulets soaking his shirt to his skin, running down his arms, forehead. Yet maybe an hour later, he'd be relaxing on the Mess or dispersal grass, sipping hot sweet tea, the summer sun drying him and warming his mask-creased face; the so-recent action now only coming into clearer focus, with details and incidents unnoticed at that moment. All around him were the sights, sounds, and scents of an utterly peaceful rural landscape – utterly divorced from the life-or-death struggle he had just survived; the war seemed so very far away, though he knew that within an hour or two he might well be returning to the fray.

To add to his tension was the absence of men with whom he had only the night before been carousing in the local inn, laughing, joking – friends whom he had seen last disappearing into the French countryside below in an aircraft shrouded in orange flames and trailing a thick plume of greasy oil-smoke, or simply obliterated in a mid-air explosion as a Messerschmitt's cannon shells found their mark. With such recall came the devastating realisation that *he* was not immortal – *he* might be the next to 'disappear' ...

The years 1941-42 saw Fighter Command expand greatly, both in terms of frontline strength but, equally important, in its background training facilities. To train a fighter pilot then took a minimum of 40 weeks on various courses which, added to the normal non-training facets of leave, sickness, *et al*, meant that from scratch it could be twelve to eighteen months at least before any pilot joined his first operational squadron. Even there – by 1942 – he would need further on-the-job inculcation by the squadron before he could be considered reasonably able to earn his pay on actual operations. The emphasis by 1942 was upon teamwork in the air; the day of the loner was past, and aerial combat was now a complex, three-dimensional science whereby each pilot was a segment of an integrated, controlled, fighting formation, albeit retaining the individualism so necessary once actual combat ensued.

First-line strength in the Command reached a total of at least 80 squadrons by April 1941, of which, however, only 30 were flying Hurricanes or Spitfires; the remainder were equipped mainly with obsolescent aircraft designs, still awaiting replacements of more modern types. The period 1941-42 was also one of wide diversification in the types of operations given to the fighter pilots to fulfil.

Apart from the Rhubarb, Circus, and Roadstead sorties, Fighter Command also provided fighter protection above the coastal waters around Britain for the merchant supply shipping providing the country's vital imported resources; a form of defensive operation which involved a total of 7,876 sorties in the month of April 1941 alone. Another minor diversion was the despatch of two Hurricane squadrons to Vaenga airfield, near Murmansk in the autumn of 1941 ostensibly to introduce the Hurricane to Russian fighter pilots.

Yet another facet of the Command's operational responsibilities was the whole question of night defences over the United Kingdom. From meagre beginnings in mid-1940, the Command had struggled manfully to combat the Luftwaffe's night bombing *blitz* throughout the winter 1940-41, with scant success. Suitable types of aircraft were not available, while those 'nightfighters' tasked with the defence – converted Blenheims in the main – were attempting to prove the early forms of AI (Airborne Interception) radar, again with small tangible success to show for the crews' untiring efforts.

By early 1941, however, those efforts began to bear fruit, with each month showing a successive escalation in the number of German bombers intercepted and destroyed over Britain. With improved AI sets, the introduction of AI-equipped Beaufighter aircraft, and no less the pioneering crews' accumulated experience, 22 Luftwaffe victims were claimed in March, while this tally rose to a score of 96 enemy aircraft shot down in the month of May.

Other facets of the night war included the beginning of nightfighter intruder sorties into German-occupied Europe, with lone crews harassing German bomber airfields. By July 1941 the UK night defences included 16 squadrons of nightfighters, but by then Hitler had launched his invasion of Russia with a consequent near-cessation of the Luftwaffe's nightly attacks on Britain. This eased Fighter Command's immediate pressure, but the night defences continued to be strengthened and improved, both in the field of UK defence and, especially, the nocturnal preying of the night intruders against Luftwaffe bases in western Europe.

While the RAF fighter offensive continued throughout 1942, probably the Command's severest test since 1940 came in August, when on the 19th an Allied 'invasion' force sailed across the Channel to attack Dieppe; in effect a test exercise and rehearsal for the ultimate invasion of Europe. Air superiority over the beach-head was the prime necessity for any such venture and, accordingly, Fighter Command assembled a total of 56 squadrons under direct control of No 11 Group, with some 14 other squadrons of light bombers and recce aircraft in support. This air umbrella, by a succession of carefully timed overlaps, remained above the earthbound forces from dawn until mid-afternoon, then protected the invasion force back to England. Throughout those hours the skies over Dieppe were filled with signs and sounds of virtually unceasing air fighting as the relatively meagre Luftwaffe force available attempted to interfere.

Flying a total of almost 3,000 sorties – roughly two-thirds of these by fighters – the RAF lost 106 aircraft that day, but *claimed* to have destroyed at least 91 German aircraft, apart from probably destroying or at least severely damaging some 200 others. In fact, as postwar evidence reveals, the Luftwaffe, with less than 200 fighters available in the area, lost just 48 aircraft destroyed and 24 more seriously damaged. Next morning the German fighter force based in France could only muster 70 serviceable machines, thus – hypothetically speaking – had the RAF continued its air offensive for just one more day at the same pace as that of 19 August it would almost certainly have achieved in merely 48 hours what it had been attempting to do for the past eighteen months of Circus and Rhubarb operations i.e. reduce Luftwaffe fighter strength in Western Europe to effective nullification. While the Dieppe ground operation had been a near-disaster, the air plan had at least illustrated the ability – and need – for the RAF to provide adequate air superiority above any such operation; an ability it was to demonstrate vividly in the following years of the war.

By late 1942 Fighter Command, in common with the rest of the RAF's operational Commands and, indeed, the Luftwaffe, had introduced a number of fresh aircraft designs and improved existing standard types. While still relying principally upon the Spitfire and Hurricane, albeit much improved in performance and armament, Fighter Command also operated Hawker Typhoons, Beaufighters, and De Havilland's 'Wooden Wonder', the sleek Mosquito. The Luftwaffe remained chained to its Bf 109 as its standard fighter, but had supplemented this with the Focke Wulf Fw 190, the latter being a match for even the Spitfire IX. The Command's nightfighter force had also been much improved and expanded and by the start of 1943 included twelve squadrons of Beaufighters, many equipped with the very latest AI 'centimetric' radar sets, alongside six fully operational units flying radar-equipped Mosquitos, with four other squadrons in the process of receiving new Mosquitos; overall a night defence force of more than 400 aircraft.

In that winter of 1942-43 the Luftwaffe re-opened its night bombing assault on Britain, in particular London and other south-east England objectives; a somewhat mixed offensive with Dorniers, Junkers and Heinkels making normal bombing attacks, but interspersed with fast 'hit-and-run' sneak sorties by bomb-laden Focke Wulf Fw 190s. Motivated by Hitler's personal desire to retaliate against the contemporary mounting RAF bombing of German cities, this Luftwaffe bombing campaign produced relatively poor results and at high cost in aircraft losses to the much-improved UK air defences. Moreover, Fighter Command Mosquito intruders were by then making an impact on German bomber bases, leaving Luftwaffe crews vulnerable to attack from take-off to landing.

Though sporadic, these Luftwaffe bombing sorties continued throughout 1943, but on 7 December Hitler, still obsessed with this form of 'retaliation', ordered his air force supremo, Göring, to prepare a massive blow specifically against London. This operation – code-named Steinbock (Ibex) – envisaged a force of at least 500 bombers, including the first operational use of the four-engined Heinkel 177.

On the night of 21 January 1944 Steinbock commenced, when 227 bombers took off to attack London. By dawn on 22 January the cost of that night's foray was counted – 25 bombers lost over England (18 of these to RAF nightfighters), while a further 18 were lost or crashed for reasons unconnected with RAF actions. Nevertheless, this 'Baby Blitz', as Steinbock became dubbed by the British, was to continue until May 1944, by which time the bombing had killed 1,556 and seriously injured nearly 3,000 other British inhabitants, but the Luftwaffe had lost more than 300 aircraft and their crews – virtually two-thirds of the original force assembled for Steinbock. Clearly, attacks on Britain were now far too costly.

Even as the RAF night-fighters were denying British skies to the Luftwaffe, elaborate planning had already begun for the Allies' invasion of France – the long-awaited 'Second Front'. As had been fully demonstrated during the Battle of Britain, Dieppe, and various similar incursions in the Mediterranean theatre of war, the prime prerequisite for any such operation was aerial superiority over and around the intended invasion zones. Fighter Command, which had been created, shaped, and now well-established for defence of the United Kingdom, could hardly forsake its role of shield and buckler; nor was it practicable to simply extend its operational sphere to cover France, the Low Countries, and – eventually – Germany. The only solution was to create a fresh equivalent force, independently controlled and as far as possible self-sustaining, which could literally accompany the invading armies into and across Europe.

The new force was built up in stages, with the first starting from 1 June 1943 when No 2 Group, Bomber Command was temporarily transferred under the aegis of Fighter Command; while two weeks later Army Co-operation Command was disbanded. On 13 November 1943, with the appointment of ACM Sir Trafford Leigh Mallory as its first 'boss' the Allied Expeditionary Air Force (AEAF) came into being, comprised of the USAAF's 9th Air Force, the Second Tactical Air Force (2nd TAF), and the Air Defence of Great Britain (ADGB). On the same date Fighter Command *per se* ceased to exist, being replaced in its functions as the UK air defence force by the ADGB, now commanded by AM Sir Roderic Hill. Hill's new command was hardly a sinecure, comprised now of ten day and eleven night fighter squadrons, though until the AEAF actually moved to Europe, Hill had access to twelve other fighter squadrons if necessary. The 2nd TAF had 'robbed' the former Fighter Command of 32 fighter squadrons, apart from various units of the defunct Army Co-operation organisation. Until the AEAF actually left England, Hill was also responsible for security of the gigantic mass of Allied might then being brought together in southern England in preparation for the projected invasion; a responsibility made even heavier by the ADGB's lack of quantitative strength.

The ADGB was finally absolved of its outside responsibilities on 6 June 1944 when Operation Overlord – the initial invasion of Normandy – got under way, but only seven days later the ADGB was brought to full alert when, in the early hours of 13 June four V1 robot flying-bombs crashed in Kent and Sussex; the first wave of Hitler's first revenge weapons launched at England. Forty-eight hours later a total of 244 'buzz-bombs' left their ramps bound for England, of which only 144 actually reached English shores, and 33 of these were destroyed by UK defences. Roderic Hill immediately swung his contingency operational plans – 'Diver' – into action. The first month of Diver, until 14 June, saw the Germans launch 4,361 V1s, of which 3,000 actually crossed over southern England. A total of 1,241 of these were destroyed by UK defences, 924 of these by ADGB fighters. Engaging the robot V1 was not the simple task it first appeared to be. Though the V1 flew an unwavering course at fairly low altitude, its speed could vary from 320 to 420 mph, it was small with only 26 feet of 'fuselage' and 17½ feet wing span. Closing to pointblank range to ensure accuracy with cannon-fire was fraught with danger for any fighter pilot; the V1's explosive content (1,870 lb of Trialen) could shatter anything within the same area of sky when detonated. Just one unit's record against the V1s might exemplify the hazards. No 486 Squadron RNZAF's Tempest pilots achieved a high tally of V1s intercepted and destroyed, but at a cost of three pilots killed, 10 others seriously injured, and 17 Tempests wrecked or damaged beyond repair. In the event, the V1 onslaught was to last from 13 June 1944 until 29 March 1945, during which time UK anti-aircraft gunners claimed 1,878, the ADGB fighters destroyed 1,846, and a further 231 fell victims to the floating barrage balloon apron.

Even while the ADGB attempted to cope with the unceasing avalanche of V1s penetrating English skies, an even greater menace threatened; the A4 (more commonly titled V2) intercontinental missile, the first of which type of revenge weapon plunged from the stratosphere to explode into Chiswick on 8 September 1944. The V2, weighing 12.7 tons, measured 46 feet in length, had a body diameter of five feet five inches, and packed a punch of 1,650 lb of high explosive. Capable of rising to at least 50 miles height, the V2 then plunged near-vertically to earth (and its target) at a speed in excess of 2,000 mph – a weapon palpably impossible to intercept by any contemporary form of defence. From 8 September 1944 until the ultimate V2 launch on 27 March 1945, a total of 1,403 were aimed at British objectives, of which 1,115 found a mark on English soil. Acknowledging the impossibility of any form of normal interception, Roderic Hill sent his fighters, laden with bombs, to attack V2 bases, while trying to persuade Bomber Command to employ its heavies against the rockets' lairs – in the event achieving little success with either ploy. While thus engaged in combating this dual menace to Britain, the ADGB was retitled as Fighter Command again with effect from 15 October 1944, with Roderic Hill remaining as its AOC-in-C.

While primarily concerned with combating the V1 and V2 assaults, Fighter Command continued to be on the *qui vive* for any 'conventional' attacks against Britain by aircraft of the Luftwaffe. These latter continued in much reduced strength and lengthy intervals during the winter nights of 1944-45, and finally ceased in March 1945. On 4 March, in the pre-dawn small-hours, more than 100 German long-range nightfighters infiltrated the 500-plus strong RAF heavy bomber streams returning from attacks on Kamen and Ladbergen, and in East Anglia, Lincolnshire and East Yorkshire a total of 27 bomber bases were strafed by the Luftwaffe intruders, which claimed 22 bombers shot down and at least 8 others severely damaged. In balance, just six German intruders were brought down by the UK defences. Two weeks later, on 17 March, a small force of 18 Junkers 88 intruders roamed over eastern England seeking prey, but had chosen a night when Bomber Command had not despatched any heavy bomber sorties, and the Junkers' sole victim was an unarmed training aircraft engaged in nightflying practice. It was the Luftwaffe's ultimate appearance over the United Kingdom.

If Fighter Command's defensive role in the UK found few Luftwaffe opponents in the final year of the war, its companion force, 2nd TAF, was in constant action both prior to and, especially from 6 June 1944 – 'D-Day'. The massive Allied air strength eventually assembled to accompany and cover the invasion forces was reflected in the Order of Battle for 2nd TAF alone on the eve of D-Day. This comprised 101 squadrons and two Flights, including four Fleet Air Arm Seafire units and three ADGB Spitfire squadrons temporarily under 2nd TAF control. Of this total, 29 squadrons were flying bomber, PRU, air spotting for naval guns, or other duties; the remainder were pure fighter units. In addition fifteen more ADGB fighter squadrons were tasked with direct support of the invasion's initial stages, apart from the full operational strength of the USAAF's 9th Air Force and elements of Bomber and Coastal Commands, the US 8th Air Force, and No 38 Group RAF's Airborne and Transport squadrons *et al*. Facing this aerial armada the Luftwaffe units based along the Western Front had little more than 300 serviceable aircraft; less than half of these being fighters. This relative handful of German air defenders faced an overall Allied air strength of nearly 9,000 aircraft, more than half of which were fighters.

By 10 June the first emergency landing strips in France had begun receiving Spitfire squadrons for operations over the beach-head area, and by 20 June eight Spitfire, three Typhoon, and three Auster squadrons were operating from French landing strips. Thereafter the build-up of fighter strength actually based in France escalated rapidly providing on-the-spot tactical aid to the ground forces, reaching totals of 19 British and 12 American squadrons by the end of June; by which time the Luftwaffe had managed to reinforce its local air defences to a total of slightly more than 500 operational aircraft in direct opposition. By 1 July pilots of 2nd TAF alone had claimed 219 day and 70 night combat victories. In the interim six squadrons of 2nd TAF had been withdrawn from the French campaign to help the UK-based ADGB to combat the V1 flying bomb menace.

Despite these withdrawals, 2nd TAF maintained its day and night offensive, and by mid-July nearly 80 advanced air strips had been established on French soil and been brought into immediate operational use. In the main, 2nd TAF's fighters by day were employed in tactical ground support sorties – a veritable flying artillery, controlled and guided by air liaison RAF officers attached to forward infantry formations – while a proportion of the Spitfire and Mustang squadrons roamed further inland, seeking out all forms of enemy transportation to strafe and destroy. On one such sortie on 17 July Squadron Leader J.J.Le Roux, a South African, leading his No 602 Squadron's Spitfires, strafed a German staff car near Ste Foy de Montgomerie. The car overturned and its occupant, Generalfeldmarschall Erwin Rommel, the German commander of the *Westfront*, suffered a fractured skull.

Such forms of tactical air support were to remain the tenor of 2nd TAF's fighter operations until the end of the European conflict in May 1945, but pure aerial combat was by no means a minor proportion of the fighters' efforts. On 16 December 1944, for example, Hitler's long planned counter-offensive in the west was launched through the forest-infested Ardennes when some 24 divisions – roughly 200,000 German troops – smashed through the Anglo-American lines, intending to recapture Antwerp and thus divide the Allied armies. For the first eight days weather conditions prevented any aerial support for either side, but on Christmas Eve the Luftwaffe finally flew in some strength; only to be immediately engaged by 2nd TAF and during the next three days losing heavily in casualties to RAF and USAAF fighters. By 27 December the German land forces had begun to regroup, then retreat. The fierce pace of Luftwaffe aerial opposition remained undiminished until the final weeks of war, despite the myriad deficiencies in fuel, equipment, facilities, and available crews. The highest proportion of German fighter effort during the final six months was in pure defence of the Reich from the overwhelming day and night Allied bombing offensives, resulting in mass clashes on many occasions. On 30 April 1945, for example, 2nd TAF fighters claimed 37 German fighters without loss; yet only weeks before, on 7 April, Messerschmitt 262 jet fighters of *Jagdgeschwader* 7 had shot down 28 American fighter escorts to a USAAF bombing force. That same day, however, the Luftwaffe lost no less than 183 fighters to roving American Mustangs and Thunderbolts. Ultimately, on 7 May 1945, a German agreement to unconditional surrender was signed at Rheims, and the following day was designated VE (Victory in Europe) Day; Europe was officially at peace.

Fighter Command's war had been a protracted, bloody struggle against an equally determined opponent throughout 1939-45; an unrelenting conflict which had cost the Command 3,690 pilots or other air crew members killed, a further 1,215 seriously injured or maimed, and 601 prisoners of war. As a *proportion* of the Command's first-line strength at any given period, this scale of sacrifice represented roughly 250-260 *complete* squadrons – a figure at least twice the entire Command's fighting strength even at its peak. For the individual pilot it had been a personal testing of courage and determination *each* time he had taken off to do battle; a summoning from unsuspected depths of a will to win, to kill – to survive. Youngsters still in their 'teens, coming in so many cases almost direct from a school desk, had thrust upon their shoulders the mantle of manhood and maturity almost overnight, as they engaged in their first-ever life-or-death clashes with opponents equally determined to destroy them. Of those who survived the conflict, no few were scarred physically and/or mentally, having been subjected to both the nadir and the 'very acme and pitch' of human experience while still in their formative years. Witnesses to violent and savage forms of death, often on a daily basis, those who survived that ordeal were not always able to re-adjust readily to a mundane and peaceful civilian world with its seeming trivialities and overt selfishness; only the healing process of time and distance would rationalise the utter contrasts, softening the emotional extremes and blurring the imagery of scenes forever imprinted on their minds. The azure skies had been their battleground where death had come swiftly, unheralded – only the quickest survived.

One question perhaps remains – did the fighter pilots' massive efforts and sacrifices contribute significantly to the Allied defeat of the Axis Powers? It is a basic truth that only bombers *could* have any eventual strategic impact and influence on the outcome – thus the bomber was the *prime* weapon of any aerial offensive. But bombers alone could never achieve the necessary air superiority in aerial warfare vital for their ultimate purpose – the fighters could, and did, provide the freedom of the sky for the bombers to pursue their role, as witnessed in the final years of World War Two. Whether in defence or offence, the fighters' role was pivotal; in the final analysis they controlled the air, and to that degree decided the issue in the skies, both tactically and strategically. The bomber was the bludgeon which finally toppled the Axis castle of dreams, but the fighters were the jewelled rapiers which cleared, then protected the air space for their brothers-in-arms.

CHAPTER TWO

Geoffrey Allard

Nestling closely in the ring of the Chiltern Hills in Buckinghamshire is the RAF's No 1 School of Technical Training, Halton. Commencing its Service connections as a tented army dispersal camp in 1916, the area was eventually offered to the War Office by its owner Alfred de Rothschild, and became a Royal Flying Corps training centre for men and 'boys' in 1917-18. In the post-Armistice planning for a peace-time RAF, the contemporary Chief of Air Staff, Hugh Trenchard, selected Halton to be the future fount for technical ground tradesmen for RAF regular service; creating an Aircraft Apprentice scheme whereby boys of good education and physical health would be trained from an acceptance age of fifteen and a half to seventeen years for three years, then complete a twelve year engagement from age eighteen.

This scheme began in 1920, initally at Cranwell whilst accommodation *et al* was completed at Halton, then became a permanent resident at Halton. Since those early days almost 50,000 highly skilled men have been nurtured by the Trenchard scheme and their contribution to the RAF has been of vital significance; ranging from the humblest airmen to the present (1983) Chief of the Air Staff. As the first graduates from Halton entered 'man's service' they were regarded both with suspicion and a modicum of jealousy by the older regular airmen, and were dubbed with derision 'Trenchard's Brats'; yet in the peculiar British manner of turning an insult into a proud title (e.g. Old Contemptibles and Desert Rats) the term 'Brat' quickly became a mark of honour among ex-Apprentices.

Heading the very long list of awards and honours bestowed upon ex-Brats over the years is the name of Sergeant Thomas Gray, who died over Maastricht in May 1940 and was awarded a posthumous Victoria Cross. At the same time as Gray paid the supreme sacrifice, another ex-Halton Brat was creating a minor legend for courage only a few miles away, fighting the Luftwaffe

(Left) Flt Lt Geoffrey — 'Sammy' — Allard, DFC, DFM, early 1941. (Right) Plt Off W H 'Ace' Hodgson, DFC, who died with Allard in the crash on 13 March 1941.

'Sammy' Allard and his 85 Squadron Hurricane, early 1941.

Wg Cdr Alan Deere, DSO,
(lt) with fellow Kiwi, Wg Cc
Colin Gray, DSO, DFC aft
Buckingham Palace invest
1943.

Spitfire XIV, RM787, the
personal aircraft of Colin G
when OC Flying at Lympne
1944, and sporting his initia
'code markings'.

Sqn Ldr R P Stevens, DSC
DFC, the lone Hurricane r
fighter 'ace'. A painting by
Kennington in 1940.

from the cockpit of a Hawker Hurricane. His name was Geoffrey Allard – 'Sammy' to his intimate friends.

Born in York on 20 August 1912, Allard joined the RAF as an Aircraft Apprentice of the 19th Entry, Halton, on 3 September 1929, and spent his three years there training as a metal rigger, finally passing out from his *alma mater* on 19 August 1932 with the top grading of Leading Aircraftman (LAC). A tallish, slim boy, with a shock of sandy-coloured hair, Allard's main recreation was sport, particularly on the hockey field where, according to one of his contemporaries, 'Sammy regarded the opposing team as his mortal enemies, but as soon as the match was over nothing was too much trouble for him in the way of hospitality'.

For his first four years out of Halton Allard continued serving as a rigger, but his prime ambition was to fly – a goal by no means easy to attain for a ranker at that period. In 1936, however, he was accepted for training as a pilot and went first to the Bristol Flying School at Filton for his elementary instruction course, followed by advanced training at No 9 Flying Training School (FTS), Thornaby and his senior term at RAF Hullavington. Graduating as a Sergeant pilot on 23 October 1937, Allard was graded as 'above average pilot' and posted to No 85 Squadron at Debden, to fly Gloster Gladiators; a unit which was yet to be officially reformed under the contemporary Fighter Command expansion programme. No 85 Squadron legally came into being again* on 1 June 1938 from a nucleus supplied by A Flight of No 87 Squadron, but remained at Flight strength only for its first few months. On 4 September 1938 the squadron received its first Hawker Hurricane and was quickly expanded to full squadron establishment with its new monoplane fighters. Allard quickly showed himself to be an exceptional pilot – a 'natural' – equally at home at the controls of the biplane Gladiator or monoplane Hurricane, and was regarded as one of the squadron's foremost exponents of aerobatics. Moreover he was popular with all ranks, without consciously seeking any such status, having a quality of character which earned an unsought respect.

The imminence of war with Germany became apparent to 85 Squadron in the summer of 1939 when, on 27 June, the unit was officially allocated as part of the Air Component of the British

* 85 Squadron, RAF/RAF had been disbanded originally on 3 July 1919.

Expeditionary Force (BEF) earmarked to be the first British forces to go to France if/when war was declared. Eight weeks later, from midnight of 23 August, the squadron was ordered to mobilise to full war status, which state was achieved by 1 September. Two days later war was declared, and 85 Squadron's advance party of ground crews left for France early on 4 September, to be followed by the unit's total sixteen Hurricanes, led by Squadron Leader David Atcherley, on 9 September, which landed initially at Boos, but within the following few weeks moved base further north-east to Lille/Seclin with a detachment at Le Touquet. At this period Allard, still a Sergeant, was flying with A Flight, and along with the other pilots of 85 Squadron, spent most of his airborne time on patrols to protect Allied shipping in the Channel. Aerial clashes with the Luftwaffe were virtually non-existent at that time, though on 21 November Flight Lieutenant R.H.A.Lee caught a Heinkel He 111 near Boulogne and shot it down into the sea – 85 Squadron's first combat victory of World War Two, which earned a DFC for 'Dicky' Lee.

During its first eight months in France, in common with most RAF units, 85 Squadron lived a gipsy existence with several moves of base airfields, but with virtually no live action to break the boredom of the Phoney War. At 0410 hours on 10 May 1940 that boredom was abruptly shattered for 85 Squadron when the drone of numerous German aircraft overhead, combined with the sounds of light and heavy anti-aircraft fire, brought the squadron to full alert. Within minutes two sections of Hurricanes were airborne, returning within forty minutes to refuel and re-arm, their pilots claiming four victories. From then until dusk the Hurricanes continued to fly and fight, pausing between sorties only for the time it took to replenish fuel and ammunition, and at the end of the day 85's pilots had claimed a total of seventeen enemy aircraft, for the loss of three Hurricanes and one pilot severely wounded.

It was a fierce pace of action maintained over the following ten days, despite daily bombing attacks on the squadron's airfield. Each pilot flew four or five offensive sorties each day, and sheer physical exhaustion soon became the prime enemy. In the forefront of this unceasing action, Sammy Allard emerged as the squadron's leading 'killer', accounting for at least ten enemy aircraft between 10 May and 16 May, apart from helping in the destruction of others. By the latter date, however, the inevitable penalty of such prolonged physical and mental stress was taking its toll. That day Allard flew four sorties; the second of these entailing take-off in the midst of a Luftwaffe bombing attack on the airfield, while on the third Allard actually fell asleep while over German-occupied territory. Returning from the fourth and last patrol, Allard's Hurricane touched down neatly and rumbled to a halt, but its pilot remained in his cockpit. When one of the ground crew 'Erks' jumped onto the aircraft's wing root and slid back the cockpit canopy, he was greeted with a deep snore – Allard's exhausted body had finally rebelled and he was fast asleep. He was still unconscious when they lifted him out and put him to bed, but remained that way for the next thirty hours. Accordingly, next day he was one of four pilots airlifted back to England for hospitalisation.

Three days later 85 Squadron's remaining crews were withdrawn to England to recuperate and be brought up to fighting establishment again. In just eleven days of non-stop fighting the squadron had claimed 89 enemy aircraft destroyed but lost two pilots known killed, nine others missing, and a further six wounded, while only three Hurricanes were then fit to fly back across the Channel.

Official recognition of the unit's prowess came at the end of May when the *London Gazette* announced the awards of two DSOs and five DFCs to 85 Squadron pilots, plus a DFM for Sammy Allard, followed next day by Allard's promotion to Flight Sergeant.

On 23 May Squadron Leader Peter Townsend DFC arrived to take command of 85 Squadron, then based at Debden. The unit was for the moment non-operational while fresh pilots and aircraft were posted in, and it fell to the veterans from France – Allard, Lee, Hemingway, Marshall, Lewis, Pat Woods-Scawen, and 'Benny' Goodman – to train and inculcate the newcomers in operational means and methods; a daunting task where some of the incoming sprogs had less than ten hours' experience in flying a Hurricane. During June and July 1940, with detachments at Martlesham and Castle Camps, 85's pilots commenced protection patrols for the Channel shipping convoys and began meeting the Luftwaffe again. Allard, still with A Flight, re-opened his personal tally of German victims by destroying an He 111 six miles south-east of Folkestone in the mid-morning of 8 July, followed by another Heinkel probably destroyed off Harwich in the dawn of 9 July. On 28 July Allard was actually presented with his DFM award at a brief ceremony at Debden, and two days later 'celebrated' this by sharing with Flight Lieutenant Hamilton in the destruction of a Messerschmitt Bf 110, and damaging a second.

A further shared victory came on 6 August when, with Sergeants Evans and Ellis, Allard helped shoot down a Dornier bomber. On 17 August Sammy Allard was commissioned as a Pilot Officer, and two days later was in one of the eighteen Hurricanes led by Peter Townsend from Debden to Croydon to exchange places with No 111 Squadron. Their new base brought them into the heart of the aerial fighting zone, with a return to a pace of combat parallel to the unit's experiences over France a few months before; an intensity of action which would see fourteen of those eighteen pilots shot down (two of them twice) in the ensuing fortnight.

For its first five days at Croydon 85 Squadron saw no action due to weather conditions, but this respite proved to be the lull before the storm. On 24 August the morning started with a German bombing attack, then, just before 8 a.m., twelve Hurricanes were scrambled to patrol Dover and intercept an incoming Luftwaffe force. In the subsequent clash Allard singled out a Bf 109 and shot it into the sea off Ramsgate. Two days later a dozen Hurricanes tackled a force of fifteen Dorniers and some thirty Bf 109s near Eastchurch. Led by Townsend, the squadron ignored the Messerschmitt escort and attacked the bombers from head-on, with Allard accounting for two Dorniers destroyed and a third probably destroyed.

On 28 August Townsend led ten of his men to intercept 'Raid 15' near Tenterden and met a gaggle of twenty Bf 109s and a Bf 110 near Dungeness. Approaching out of the sun, the Hurricanes quickly split the German formation apart, and Allard closed to twenty yards of one Bf 109, set it afire and watched it plunge vertically into the Channel near Folkestone harbour. Switching his sights to a second Bf 109, Allard opened fire at 250 yards' range as the Messerschmitt dived to within twenty feet of the sea and headed for France. As a result of Allard's marksmanship the 109's engine began spuming black smoke and it finally dived into the Channel some five miles north of St Inglevert. The overall combat cost the Luftwaffe six Bf 109s destroyed and the Bf 110 damaged, while 85's casualties were nil; a clash actually witnessed by the Prime Minister, Winston Churchill, while he was visiting south-east coastal defences.

Friday, 30 August, saw the air fighting reaching a peak of action for the next 48 hours. Mid-morning saw eleven of the squadron take off to intercept a variety of raider formations approaching south-east England, and at 16,000 feet over Bethenden they ran into a batch of some 50 Heinkel He 111s, with 100-plus fighter escorts higher up. Coming out of the sun in waves of three, the Hurricanes took the Heinkels from the front, scattering the bombers in all directions by the fury of their attack. Allard sank his bullets into one Heinkel which immediately spun away spewing flames and crashed, then lined up his sight on a second Heinkel from above and to beam. This bomber erupted in flames, dived straight down, and eventually ploughed into a field some thirty miles south-west of Croydon. These were just two of eight German aircraft destroyed in the general mêlée, apart from two 'probables' and three others damaged – all for the loss of one Hurricane whose pilot escaped injury.

Shortly after mid-day on 31 August Croydon airfield was accurately bombed as 85 Squadron scrambled. Climbing as fast as possible, the Hurricanes eventually encountered a mass of 50-plus Germans over Tunbridge Wells and immediately attacked. Peter Townsend, after sending two Bf 109s spinning down, was about to fire at a third 109 when his cockpit received a flurry of cannon shells from a Bf 110 which ruptured his petrol tank and wounded him in the left foot. With little control over his falling Hurricane, Townsend took to his parachute at 1,400 feet and landed near Hawkhurst, where he was taken to hospital. The same day brought Allard three victims – two Dorniers sent down out of control and shedding pieces of metal, with the second having an engine in flames, then on the last patrol of the day a Bf 109 which Sammy shot down near Folkestone.

On 1 September Allard led the remaining squadron from Croydon to the Hawkinge area where they tackled a formation of Bf 109s, with Sammy chasing one Messerschmitt well out to sea before it was finally shot into the sea ten miles from Cap Gris Nez.

In the early afternoon Allard was again airborne, attempting to reach a Luftwaffe force estimated 150-200 strong some 5,000 feet higher than the Hurricanes and running a gauntlet of continuous attacks by German fighters as they climbed. Selecting a Dorner which had strayed out of the main gaggle, Allard carried out three successive attacks and both the bomber's engines began belching smoke and oil, then the port engine burst into flames. The Dornier's rear gunner then baled out but its pilot managed a rough forced landing near the railway line at Lydd. At that moment the oil pressure in Allard's Hurricane dropped and Sammy forcelanded at Lympne with a dead engine. Even as Allard waited for his aircraft to be repaired the Luftwaffe struck again, bombing and strafing Lympne, damaging Allard's aircraft again and killing one of the airmen working on it.

On 2 September the squadron took stock. Without their CO, few serviceable aircraft, many casualties, and the remaining crews, air and ground, reaching exhaustion point, it desperately needed a rest, however brief. In the month of August alone it had claimed 44 enemy aircraft destroyed, 15 more probably destroyed, and at least 15 more seriously damaged – but the cost had been too high. Of the unit tally, Sammy Allard had been personally responsible for nearly 25 per cent. On 3 September the squadron moved back to Castle Camps, then two days later was moved north to Church Fenton well out of the battle zone to rest and re-equip. Awards for gallantry now flowed in. Allard was promoted to Flight Lieutenant and given command of A Flight on 8 September, and then awarded a Bar to his DFM on the 13th, followed by a DFC three days later. Ironically, on 22 September Sammy had a narrow brush with death when atrocious weather conditions forced him to crash-land after a routine training flight. On 20 October 1940 the squadron received notification of a new future role – night fighting – and three days later moved en bloc to Kirton-in-Lindsey, near Scunthorpe to begin specialised training. Two weeks later, on 6 November, Sammy Allard took his A Flight south, back to the squadron's spiritual home, Debden, and there brought his pilots up to operational fitness.

At that time the squadron was still flying Hurricanes, a design with far too many disadvantages for the night role as Peter Townsend was quick to point out to higher authority on his resumption of command, though it fell to Townsend to register the squadron's first night kill while flying a Hurricane on the night of 25 February 1941 – a Dornier which had helpfully kept its navigation lights on. Recognising the validity of his criticisms, higher authority arranged for a few Boulton Paul Defiant two-seat fighters to supplement 85's stalwart Hurricanes as an interim measure, pending complete re-equipment of the squadron with twin-engined Douglas Havoc night fighters fitted with AI Mk IV radar; the first example of which arrived on the squadron on 15 February 1941.

As more Havocs became available Allard threw all his considerable energies into getting his Flight up to operational standard, and utilised his pilots to ferry the fresh aircraft from Maintenance Units *et al* to Debden. In the afternoon of 13 March 1941, Allard decided to take two of his men, the New Zealander Pilot Officer W.H.Hodgson DFC and Sergeant F.R.Walker-Smith, in Havoc BJ500 to Ford to collect some new Havocs for his Flight. Arriving at the Havoc's dispersal Allard found one of the riggers struggling to screw down a reluctant nose panel, took a screwdriver from the erk and fastened the panel, then climbed in to prepare for take-off with his passengers. As the Havoc began to lift off Debden's runway the panel worked loose, detached itself, was blown back over the fuselage and jammed the aircraft's rudder.

The Havoc jerked sideways, recovered, then rolled on its back and plummeted nose-first into the bottom of Mill Field Ley, near Tye Green, just south of Wimbish, exploding into a fireball on contact. Within minutes the Havoc and its three occupants were obliterated by the flames. Geoffrey Allard and his companions, who had survived a hundred aerial combats, had found death in a quiet English pasture far from the turmoil of battle.

They buried 'Sammy' and his friends in Saffron Walden Borough Cemetery, and 85 Squadron mourned a man who had established himself not only as the squadron's highest-scoring ace of the whole 1939-45 war, but a fighting leader whose courage, example, and prowess were rarely matched.

CHAPTER THREE

Colin Gray

The enormous and vital contribution by former British Empire countries to Britain's war effort in 1939-45 is seldom given proper credit in most post-bellum histories of that conflict. A case in point is New Zealand, particularly in the context of the RAF. During the 1914-18 war New Zealanders had established a superb reputation for their fighting courage in the Royal Flying Corps and Royal Naval Air Service; men like Keith Park, later to play a prime role in the Battles of Britain and Malta, Keith 'Grid' Caldwell, Roderick Carr, and a hundred others who set high examples which later generations of young 'Kiwis' were to inherit and embellish.

During the 'peace' years 1919-39, New Zealand created its own national air force which was granted the Royal prefix in early 1934, but in size and quality of equipment the RNZAF was virtually insignificant; by March 1936 it could muster merely 20 officers and 107 non-commissioned airmen, 'backed' by a Territorial Air Force numbering 74 officers. Thus, the only hope for young New Zealanders wanting to fly as a career was to travel to England and try their luck with the RAF. It meant for most working their passage to the Mother Country by any ship needing deck-hands or other menial labourers, and fending for themselves once arrived in England. Even then there was no guarantee of being accepted by RAF selection boards. Such hazards failed to deter many hundreds of young New Zealanders during those years, many of whom were later to have distinguished RAF careers both in war and peace, and by the outbreak of war in 1939 more than 500 'Kiwis' were serving in the ranks of the RAF.

In 1936, at the request of the British government, began a scheme for selection in New Zealand of candidates for service in the RAF as pilots, and suitable volunteers were sent to England for training, the first such group arriving in the UK in July 1937. This scheme was supplemented shortly after by another which had such men trained initially in New Zealand, then sent to England as 'trained cadets' to complete their instruction.* Between 1937 and 1940 a total of 374 men were 'supplied' to the RAF under both schemes. Among the very first to volunteer under the aegis of the initial scheme were twin brothers from Papanui, Christchurch, Kenneth and Colin Gray, both of whom were later to carve out outstanding war careers. By the end of the war Kenneth Gray was dead, but his twin, Colin emerged from the conflict as New Zealand's most decorated and highest-scoring fighter pilot.

Kenneth Neil Gray and Colin Falkland Gray were born in Papanui on 9 November 1914, and in June 1936 both boys applied for acceptance as would-be pilots of the RAF. Ken Gray was duly accepted and sailed to England in 1937, and gained his RAF wings in mid-1938. Colin Gray, due to his medical history of pleurisy, osteomyelitis, and conjunctivitis, was rejected initially, but stubbornly persevered with his attempts to join the RAF and was finally successful in being accepted in 1938. Along with eighteen other young hopefuls, Colin sailed from his native country on 16 December 1938 in RMS *Rangitata*, arrived in London on 18 January 1939, and reported to No 1 EFTS, Hatfield on 23 January to commence *ab initio* pilot training on Tiger Moths. Commissioned as an Acting Pilot Officer on 1 April 1939, Colin progressed steadily through his advanced training at No 11 FTS, Shawbury, flying Harts, Hinds and Audaxes, then went to No 11 (F) Group Pool at St Athans where he was finally given the chance to fly monoplanes, Harvards and Hurricanes, before joining his first squadron, No 54 based at Hornchurch, to fly Spitfires.

Colin Gray's arrival on the squadron on 20 November 1939 unintentionally created something of a stir. As he levelled his

* Such pilots were enlisted in the RAF with a Short Service Commission (SSC), and the UK paid the NZ Government a sum of £1,550 for each pilot trained in New Zealand.

Spitfire out to land he failed to notice a sandbagged air raid shelter on the airfield perimeter, promptly wiped off his undercarriage on this, then belly-landed amid much dust and grinding metal noise. Unfortunately for Colin this performance was being watched by no less a person than the AOC-in-C Fighter Command, Sir Hugh Dowding, accompanied by the Hornchurch Station Commander, and their respective retinues of lesser minions. Sporting a pair of beautifully burgeoning black eyes, Colin Gray was later hauled before said Station Commander who proceeded to tear an almighty strip off the young Kiwi, then threatened to have him posted away to drogue-towing duties at a remote training unit. However, 54's commander, Squadron Leader H.M.Pearson, managed to mollify the senior officer and persuade him to keep Gray on 54 Squadron. For the following six months, apart from occasional fruitless alerts, 54 Squadron made little contact with the Luftwaffe; a situation which changed abruptly shortly after the German invasion of the Low Countries from 10 May 1940. On 16 May Gray flew his first true operational sorties over Calais, Ostend and Dunkirk, but on 24 May came his first combat claim, when 54 Squadron tackled 50-60 Heinkels escorted by Bf 109s and 110s just inland from Calais. As he closed with a Bf 109, Gray's cine-camera film showed his bullets splashing all over the German fighter and he was credited with a 'Damaged' later.

Next day during a furious mêlée with a horde of Bf 109s, Gray so damaged one Messerschmitt that its pilot baled out,* but was then attacked by a second Bf 109, receiving cannon shells in his Spitfire's fuselage and port aileron, bullets in its engine, and had its pitot head shot away. Jinking as best he could out of danger Gray returned to Hornchurch where, with useless flaps and brakes, he operated his undercarriage by its emergency control and managed a safe landing. On 29 May the squadron was moved north to Catterick for a brief spell of recuperation, then returned to Hornchurch on 5 June to resume operations over the Channel. With the Dunkirk evacuation ending aerial combat lessened relatively for the remainder of June as far as 54 Squadron was

---

* As the German baled out Sergeant Norwell of 54 Squadron also fired at the Bf 109, resulting in Gray only being credited with a 'shared' victory.

concerned, but July brought intensified action again. On 3 July Gray shared the destruction of a Dornier bomber, and on the 13th shot a Bf 109 from III/JG51 into the Channel during an early evening sortie from the forward airfield at Manston. On 24 July Gray and his fellow Spitfire pilots dived on a gaggle of German bombers and fighters attempting to attack a shipping convoy off Margate. In the fight which followed Gray sent one Bf 109 down wildly out of control, then bounced a second Bf 109 which he shot down in flames some eight miles east of Margate, its pilot taking to his parachute and falling in the Channel shortly before mid-day.

August 1940 brought the pace of aerial combat over southern England to fierce peaks as the Luftwaffe stepped up its attempts to eradicate Fighter Command, with 54 Squadron in the thick of the daily fighting. On Monday, 12 August the squadron's forward base at Manston was accurately bombed by twenty bomb-carrying Bf 109s and 110s of Hauptmann Walter Rubendorff's Test Gruppe 210, but 54's Spitfires were in action throughout the day. Tackling two dozen Bf 109s at 25,000 feet over Dover, Colin Gray sent one Messerschmitt down in flames, then sank several bursts into a second Bf 109 which promptly dived towards the French coast, its engine streaming glycol from its port radiator. Gray followed it across the Channel waters until the 109 eventually crashed on a beach at Cap Gris Nez. Three days later Gray was again 'mixing it' with a gaggle of Bf 109s over the Dover-Dungeness area in the early evening, shooting one down from 25,000 feet and despatching a second straight into the Channel with 'quite a splash' (*sic*). Next day he shared in the destruction of a Bf 110.

Awarded a DFC for his prowess to date, its citation credited Colin Gray with four 109s destroyed, four more probably destroyed, plus shares in a Dornier and another 109. On Sunday, 18 August, Gray was one of five squadron pilots who trapped a lone Bf 110 over the Thames Estuary and proceeded to send it down riddled with bullets and with both engines afire; while on Gray's third sortie that day he probably destroyed two Bf 110s over Harwich and definitely destroyed a third which tumbled down from 15,000 feet to crash in the centre of Clacton-on-Sea.

As with every other unit of Fighter Command in the front line, each day had become an unceasing repetition of fly, fight, refuel, re-arm, and return to the battle from first light until a late dusk. On the ground the ground crews worked around the clock, patching, repairing, replenishing the battle-scarred Spitfires, snatching such mundane things as meals and sleep only when time permitted a brief break in the unending toil. For the weary pilots, life now revolved around the cockpits of their aircraft, with only brief respite between sorties for a snatched sandwich and cup of tea at their dispersals until darkness brought the relief of a stand-down and much-needed, if usually disturbed, rest for overtaxed minds and bodies. Adding to the strain was the loss of so many friends as each day increased the casualty toll; losses which not only cut into each man's soul but brought the possibility of death so much closer on each flight. The mental resiliency of youth provided some barrier to pessimism but even the fittest had their limits, beyond which the strain and exhaustion would inevitably claim their price. Yet such was the high pitch of action that introspection was rare among the fighter pilots; to live for the moment was sufficient and tomorrow was another day to be tackled when it dawned.

On 24 August Gray closed with a Bf 110 at some 29,000 feet above the Channel in the late morning, closed to killing range, and sent it spinning down in flames, seeing one crew member take to his parachute at 1,000 feet above the sea. Next day, while on patrol from Rochford, Gray's section was jumped by Bf 109s as it descended through cloud near Manston. Gray fastened on the tail of one 109 and this fell apart under his fire. The 109's debris fell to earth a few miles from Manston but its pilot, Oberleutnant Heinrich Held of I/JG54, took to his parachute, only to plunge to his death as his 'chute erupted in flames.

The morning of 31 August saw Hornchurch bombed accurately just as a section of 54 Squadron's Spitfires were taking off, but by afternoon the squadron was attacking a force of German bombers and their Bf 109 escorts over Maidstone. Gray hit one 109 with several concentrated bursts, its engine streamed a plume of escaping coolant, and the Messerschmitt finally forcelanded twelve miles south-east of Folkestone, near Lydd

Ranges. Its pilot, Oberleutnant Karl Westerhof of 6/JG3, under the impression that he'd been shot down by another Messerschmitt's careless shooting, was infuriated, and banged his life preserver jacket on the ground in temper as he climbed out of his aircraft ...

The first day of September saw Gray and his companions diving into the middle of a large formation of Heinkel bombers over Biggin Hill. Gray's fire sank into one Heinkel which spun away with both engines on fire, but the crossfire from its comrades laced through Gray's Spitfire, severing his elevator controls, and he finally landed at Hornchurch by using his trim tabs. After mid-day, however, Gray was back in action, engaging a Bf 109 south-east of Biggin Hill and shattering its engine, then watching it crash to earth. 2 September brought Gray his busiest day, flying a total of five sorties. On the first of these he sent a Bf 109 down on fire, but seconds later a cannon shell exploded in his Spitfire's right cockpit wall, rupturing air pressure lines and his R/T socket, leaving Gray no alternative but to return to Hornchurch. During an afternoon sortie Gray got his revenge by shooting down a Bf 110, which was last seen falling vertically in flames north of the main Southend road.

Early on 3 September Gray's squadron received a 'flap' scramble. North Weald was being attacked by some thirty Dorniers, heavily escorted by Bf 109s. Taking off fast, 54 Squadron was soon in action, with Gray setting a Bf 110 on fire (thereby 'robbing' his fellow New Zealander, Alan Deere, of an intended victim ...), then tackling a Bf 109, hitting its engine, and seeing it trail escaping coolant most of the way back across the Channel. In Gray's own words, 'He didn't quite make it' ...

Shortly after return from their last sortie on 3 September the surviving pilots of 54 Squadron were withdrawn from the battle, and at 6 p.m. moved north to Catterick for rest and refurbishment. Of the original seventeen pilots with 54 Squadron at the start of the Battle of Britain, Colin Gray was one of only five left to fly, while his personal tally of sixteen enemy aircraft destroyed plus eight others probably destroyed or shared placed him among the highest-scoring of the Few. On 16 December 1940 Colin Gray, with promotion to Flight Lieutenant, was appointed A Flight commander on 54 Squadron, and two months later, on 23 February 1941, the squadron returned to Hornchurch, equipped now with Spitfire IIAs, many of these having been taken over from 41 Squadron.

For the next few months Gray led his Flight on offensive sweeps over enemy-occupied territories in France and the Low Countries, but on 12 June 1941 he was posted as a Flight commander to No 1 Squadron at Redhill, to fly Hurricanes on convoy patrols, bomber escorts, and general offensive sweeps. Four days later he shared in the destruction of a Heinkel 59 floatplane off Folkestone. On 1 July his squadron moved base to Tangmere from where it resumed its offensive over France, but on 22 August Gray attached himself to a 41 Squadron patrol and destroyed a Bf 109F east of Le Havre, watching it crash on the southern boundary of its own airfield. It was Gray's 17th *officially* credited combat victory, and on 20 September 1941 he was awarded a Bar to his DFC.

Further promotion to Squadron Leader brought Colin Gray the command of No 403 Squadron RCAF on 28 September 1941, but this was changed to command of No 616 Squadron at Westhampnett two days later, a unit which he led on Rhubarbs and other forms of offensive sweeps over France until 7 March 1942, when he was rested from operations with a posting as Squadron Leader Tactics to HQ No 9 Group at Preston. For the next six months Gray continued to fly a desk, then in mid-September he was attached to No 485 Squadron for two weeks' operational refresher flying, before taking up command of No 64 Squadron on 1 November 1942 at Fairlop, satellite to his old Hornchurch base, to fly Spitfire IXs, 64 being the first squadron to receive this Mark of Spitfire for operations. His stay with 64 Squadron was brief, however, and Christmas 1942 saw Gray on embarkation leave prior to being posted overseas.

Sailing to Gibraltar, Colin took up his appointment there as OC No 81 Squadron (Spitfire Vcs initially) on 22 January 1943, then led his unit to Maison Blanche airfield, and within 24 hours of arrival was leading his squadron into action against a Luftwaffe bombing raid on Algiers, during which his pilots claimed eleven Junkers Ju88s shot down. Moving base to Tingley airfield, near

Bone in Algeria on 27 January, 81 Squadron now became part of No 322 Wing in support of the British 1st Army. Four days later Gray re-opened his personal tally by shooting down a Bf 109 in an inverted spin into the earth near Cap Rosa, but since one of his pilots had also fired at the Messerschmitt Gray made no official claim, preferring the victory to be credited to his subordinate. Further claims for 'probables' came on 22 February and 2 March – both Bf109s – but on 17 March the squadron moved to 'Paddington', an airstrip close to Souk-el-Arba. From here on 23 March, whilst escorting some B-17 Fortress bombers attacking Bizerta, Gray claimed his first Italian victim, a Macchi 202 which dived into the sea.

Two days later, while engaged in a low-level sweep of the Mateur-Medjes-el-Bab area, Gray spotted a Bf 109 at even lower height strafing Allied infantry positions. Leading a section down, his first shots shattered the 109's engine, forcing it to crashland with its pilot becoming a prisoner of war. Another low-level victory followed on 3 April when Gray attacked a Bf 109G-2. Its pilot baled out but his parachute had no time to fully deploy. Two probables on 18 and 19 April were followed on 20 April by a certain score when he destroyed a Bf 109G-2 at 22,000 feet between Tunis and Mateur, its pilot taking to his parachute. Three days later yet another Bf 109 fell to Gray's accurate shooting and was seen to crash north of Beja.* A further Bf 109G was destroyed by Gray on 28 April during a squadron sweep over Medjes-el-Bab, its pilot taking to his 'brolly' at 9,000 feet.

May 12 saw 81 Squadron move base again, this time to La Sebala, Tunis, and three days later Colin Gray was awarded a DSO for 'inspiring leadership'. A further move of the squadron on 19 May took 81's Spitfires to Utique, Tunisia, then on 4 June Gray was promoted to Wing Commander and appointed in command of No 322 Wing, and the same day led 81 Squadron to Ta Kali, Malta.

On 14 June 1943 Colin Gray was back in action, destroying a Bf 109G-2 south of Comiso, while on 17 June he attacked a

---

* On return to 'Paddington' from this sortie, Colin's wing-man put in a claim for the victory, but ground inspection revealed that Gray's No 2 guns had not even been fired ...

Macchi 202 at 29,000 feet and watched the Italian fighter disintegrate under his cannon-fire. With the invasion of Sicily in full stride, Colin led 322 Wing on a patrol of *Cent* beach on 10 July and shot down a Bf 109 in the process, which exploded and erupted in flames. No 322 Wing soon followed the invasion troops into Sicily, moving to Lentini East airfield on 22 July, and within 72 hours the whole Wing took part in a mass sweep of the Gulf of Milazzo just before noon on 25 July. Coming on to a huge formation of Junkers 52 transport aircraft, the Wing proceeded to carry out a near-massacre of the unwieldy German tri-motors, claiming some 26 as destroyed, of which Colin Gray personally accounted for three. In the event these proved to be Gray's final combat victories of the war, because on 7 September 1943 he officially completed his second tour of fighter operations, and one month later he arrived back in England where a Bar to his DSO was awarded in November.

There followed some nine months of staff appointments, serving successively at HQ No 9 Group, 61 OTU, Rednal as OC Flying, and OC Tactics Wing at the Fighter Leaders School, Milfield, but on 27 July 1944 Gray returned to the sharp end with his appointment as Wing Commander Flying at Detling, followed on 11 August with the same appointment at Lympne. Flying Spitfire XIVs, Gray led a number of anti-V1 sweeps, bomber escorts, and general offensive sorties over Holland and Germany, until 2 February 1945 when he became OC RAF Skebrae, where he completed his third operational tour on 8 May 1945 (VE Day).

Throughout the war Colin Gray had amassed a total of 633 operational flying hours, and was finally *officially* credited with a combat tally of 28 victories, although close scrutiny of his combat record would give him totals of at least 30 destroyed, eight more probably destroyed, and a share in the destruction of five more enemy aircraft. Whichever 'score' is accepted, Colin Gray had emerged as the highest-scoring New Zealand fighter pilot of the 1939-45 war, while his awards of DSO, DFC and two Bars made him one of the most-decorated 'Kiwi' fighter pilots of the conflict. Awarded a permanent commission in the RAF in April 1945, Colin Gray's peacetime career followed a normal pattern of varied flying and staff appointments, with a promotion to Group

(Left) Flt Lt Karel Kuttelwascher, DFC. *(Right)* Kuttelwascher with Sqn Ldr J A F Maclachlan, DSO, DFC at a ceremony for presentation of a Czech War Cross to each man.

Lt-rt: Wg Cdrs Mrazec & J Sejbl; Sqn Ldr K Kuttelwascher & his wife, at a London 'Wings for Victory' luncheon.

43 Sqn, January 1939. *Lt-rt:* Sgt J Hallowes; Fg Off Christie; Sgt F Carey; Fg Offs Kilmartin, Rotheram, C B Hull, Pennington-Leigh, Sullivan, Carswell; Sqn Ldr R Bain; Flt Lt F Rosier; Fg Offs J W C Simpson, Folkes, Cos; Sgt G Berry.

Wg Cdr F R Carey in Burma.

Captain in 1955, until his voluntary retirement from the Service on 30 April 1961, when he returned to his native New Zealand.

Colin Gray's return to his homeland had one poignant aspect; his twin brother Kenneth Neil Gray had not survived the war. Flying Whitley bombers on operations over Germany with No 102 Squadron from the first days of the war, Ken had been awarded a DFC and a Czech War Cross by December 1939, but on 7 May 1940, while flying from Kinloss to Driffield to join Colin Gray for a few days leave, Ken Gray's aircraft flew through bad weather and hit a hill north-west of Dyce, killing the whole crew except the rear gunner. They buried Ken Gray and his crew in Dyce old churchyard; just one of nearly 11,000 New Zealanders to have served with the RAF in 1939-45 – and one of the first of the 3,290 young Kiwis who lost their lives.

CHAPTER FOUR

Karel Kuttelwascher

While the exploits of RAF fighter pilots who fought the Luftwaffe over Europe by day received widespread, more-than-generous publicity during World War Two, the role of those who fought by night was rarely afforded such public acclaim. Necessarily, once RAF night pilots began utilising radar sets in their nocturnal foraging, the need for absolute secrecy about the 'black boxes' precluded mention of much of this form of aerial warfare; yet a number of the RAF's night hunters achieved high success without such sophisticated technical aids, relying simply on skill, courage, and an individual streak of sheer daring which exemplified the very singular nature of their particular tasks. Such characteristics were especially true of the early night intruder pilots. Night intrusion was by no means an innovation of the 1939-45 war; in 1918 No 151 (and later 152) Squadrons of the RAF had been sent to France, equipped with Sopwith Camels, as the first operational RAF night intruder units, with no small success for their efforts during the closing months of the so-termed Great War. Nevertheless, at the outbreak of World War Two the RAF had only recently begun hastily modifying former Blenheim bombers to undertake a night *interception* role, while actual *offensive* fighter operations by night had yet to be properly considered or catered for in the context of specialised aircraft, crews, and/or training, or equipment.

One of the first night fighter pilots to achieve a high tally of combat victories by night, without benefit of radar guidance, was Squadron Leader Richard Playne Stevens who, alone in his Hurricane of (appropriately) No 151 Squadron, claimed at least fourteen German aircraft destroyed in the night skies over Britain throughout 1941. Awarded a DSO, DFC and Bar for his unique (then) achievements, Stevens was next posted to No 253 Squadron as a Flight commander on 12 November 1941 and began night intrusion sorties over German-occupied France and Holland, only to fail to return in Hurricane Z3465 on the night of 15/16 December 1941, having crashed to his death at Hulten, near Gilze. Even as Stevens was earning for himself a permanent niche in the annals of RAF fighter history, a young expatriate Czechoslovakian Sergeant pilot was beginning an almost equally remarkable record for individual prowess. His name was Karel Kuttelwascher.

Born in Nemrecky in 1916, young Kuttelwascher became interested in aviation as a schoolboy and in 1934 he joined the Czech air force and was trained as a pilot. The over-run of his native land by Nazi Germany soon led him to escape to France where he was enlisted in the French Foreign Legion, then transferred to the French air service. When France too fell under German invasion Kuttelwascher managed to get to England and volunteered for service with the RAF, in which he was enrolled as a Sergeant pilot in mid-1940, and on 4 October that year was posted to No 1 Squadron at Tangmere to fly Hurricanes. Here he quickly adapted himself to operational routines and dedicated himself wholly to his job, being almost fanatical about not smoking or drinking in case these impaired his physical fitness. Shy in company and reticent in conversation, the young Czech nevertheless displayed an expertise in pure flying which earned admiration from his fellow pilots, while his utterly cool, calm attitude to all circumstances established him as totally unflappable no matter what the situation; a characteristic which remained paramount throughout his flying career, both in war and peacetime.

The winter months of 1940-41 saw him taking part in his squadron's various operations, but it was not until the spring of 1941 that Kuttelwascher had his first successful clashes with the Luftwaffe. By April that year No 1 Squadron was mainly engaged in offensive sweeps over France, Belgium and Holland, interspersed with acting as escorts for day bombing raids, shipping convoys, *et al*, and had in the previous month begun re-equipping with Hurricane II fighters. On 8 April Kuttelwascher was one of three Czech pilots being led by Flying Officer

Robinson on a patrol of the Dungeness area at 28,000 feet, when a trio of Messerschmitt Bf 109s were spotted over the Channel. The Czechs immediately gave chase as the Bf 109s turned tail for the French coast, and Kuttelwascher closed to within 30 yards of one, opened fire, and watched the Bf 109 literally fall apart, scattering wreckage over a wood near Cap Gris Nez.

On 21 May, based by then at Redhill, 1 Squadron was called on to escort eighteen Blenheims to attack oil installations at Béthune. For this sortie the squadron was detailed as top rear cover for the bombers, while the close escort was provided by Nos 302 (Polish) and 258 (New Zealand) Squadrons. As the formation reached the French coast it began being harassed by a succession of German fighters, one Bf 109 apiece being shot down by Kuttelwascher and fellow Czech Sergeant Kratkoruky. A third Bf 109 was to fall to Kuttelwascher's guns on 27 June, but on 2 July the squadron moved base to Tangmere for a new role*, being now tasked with night defence of Portsmouth and Southampton.

From July 1941 the squadron continued to provide occasional day cover for shipping convoys or air-sea rescue operations in the Channel, but its main efforts were channelled into dusk-to-dawn patrols over the southern ports and intensive training in the latest night interception techniques. In August the unit began receiving four-20 mm cannon-armed Hurricane IICs for the latter role, but by then Luftwaffe activities over Britain had virtually died away and the pilots found few opponents.

On 4 November command of 1 Squadron passed into the capable hands of Squadron Leader J.A.F.Maclachlan DFC, an ex-Malta ace with eight combat victories already credited, and who had an artificial left arm due to wounds received over Malta. His arrival more or less coincided with a decision to allow the squadron to undertake night intruder operations over enemy-occupied territories in northern Europe, and training for such a role was under way by November and continued over the following three months. By then Karel Kuttelwascher had been commissioned as a Pilot Officer, and on 14 February 1942 was

* In fact, 1 Squadron had already flown a number of night interception operations, notably on the night of 10 May 1941 when its pilots claimed eight enemy aircraft destroyed and a ninth damaged.

promoted to Flight Lieutenant in command of the squadron's A Flight.

Finally, on 1 April 1942 the squadron officially commenced night intruder operations as its prime role, and that night Maclachlan and Kuttelwascher took off from Tangmere shortly after 10 p.m. to scour the French airfields inland from Le Havre. Maclachlan returned at 3 a.m. with nothing to report, but the Czech, after orbiting Evreux airfield for some time at 3,000 feet without finding any action, had pressed on to Melun aerodrome where he noticed a Junkers Ju 88 about to take off. As the Ju 88 began its first orbit of the field the Czech closed to 100 yards and raked it with cannon shells, causing its starboard wing to explode, and the Ju 88 dived into the earth. Seeing a second Ju 88 on the runway Kuttelwascher promptly strafed this in one low pass, then flew out of the alerted ground defence's fire and returned to Tangmere.

Atrocious weather conditions prevented further sorties for most of the following two weeks, though Kuttelwascher managed to claim a Dornier as probably destroyed on 3/4 April. On 16/17 April, however, Maclachlan found no targets, but the Czech flew to St Andre-de-l'Eure where he found a pair of Dorniers and destroyed one of these with one concentrated burst of cannon shells.

Ten nights later the two men set off yet again. Maclachlan selected St Andre for his hunting ground and destroyed one Dornier and damaged a second, while Kuttelwascher flew to Boos aerodrome, near Rouen, where he sent a Heinkel 111 down in flames with one four-seconds burst. As he watched his victim falling a burst of tracer flashed past his cockpit – he in turn had been stalked by a Ju 88 nightfighter. Reacting immediately, Kuttelwascher dived away, jettisoned his underwing long range fuel tanks, then chased the Ju 88, firing a series of short bursts which appeared to find their mark, and the Ju 88 climbed away rapidly in a turn and disappeared from sight.

On the last night of April the Maclachlan-Kuttelwascher duo were in action again. 'Mac' found no aircraft to engage but shot up two trains and a tug on the French coast, but Kuttelwascher flew further south to Rennes where he caught a Dornier taking off and promptly destroyed it. On his return flight he diverted slightly to look in at Dinard airfield where he saw a Heinkel 111 take off. As the German's silhouette showed up plainly against the moon he attacked it at 1,000 feet, shattering its starboard wing and saw it plunge into the sea with a huge splash in the moonlight.

Kuttelwascher's extreme coolness under any conditions of stress or hazard was well exemplified on the night of 4 May. That night saw five of the squadron's Hurricanes set out on individual roving intrusion sorties, including Maclachlan and Kuttelwascher. The unit commander, after a fruitless search around Rennes, flew to Dinard where he arrived in time to clobber a Dornier as it prepared to land. He then noticed a Heinkel on 'finals' with its undercarriage already lowered, quickly aligned it in his gunsight, gave it just one brief burst, then watched it dive straight into the undershoot area with one engine flaming.

Meantime, Kuttelwascher, flying his usual Hurricane IIC, BE581, 'JX-E', named 'Night Reaper', had begun stooging around his usual haunts at Evreux and St Andre. Early on three searchlights caught him in their glare but the Czech calmly switched his navigation lights on and off several times and the ground defences, assuming he was 'friendly', immediately doused their lights. Arriving over St Andre the Czech found no less than six Heinkel 111s orbiting the lit-up aerodrome at some 1,500 feet. With characteristic aplomb, he calmly tagged on to the circuiting stream for two minutes then, with the Heinkel in front of him centred and large in his sight, he fired all four cannons. With its starboard engine in flames the bomber crashed north-east of its base field. Less than a minute later the Czech had lined up on the next Heinkel ahead of him, fired one burst, and sent this down flaming to crash. Stealthily creeping up behind his third Heinkel Kuttelwascher gave this a two-second burst from dead astern – the stricken bomber dived and exploded into the ground – three victories within just four minutes of action.

Recognition of Kuttelwascher's successes came on 16 May with the award of a DFC, while the one-armed Maclachlan received a DSO to add to his DFC and Bar. Both men added to their scores on the night of 4 June. Maclachlan infiltrated a bunch of Dorniers orbiting St Andre and destroyed two, apart from two others damaged, before the airfield defences had time to activate. An hour later Kuttelwascher arrived over the same airfield and attacked two circling Heinkels, destroying one. He then tackled some Dorniers as these arrived in the area, damaging one and shooting down a second. As a Parthian shot he then dropped to deck-level and beat up the airfield, at the same time strafing some Germans attempting to put out the flaming wreckage of one victim.

The night's work was noted in high places and next day came several congratulatory signals from such VIPs as the AOC-in-C Bomber Command, 'Bert' Harris, the Secretary of State for Air, Sir Archibald Sinclair, and – of especial pride for Kuttelwascher privately – from Air Vice-Marshal Janousek, head of the Free Czechs in Britain.

On 22 June the 'Night Reaper' added more victims to its mounting tally, claiming one Ju 88 destroyed and another damaged over St Andre, and five days later a Bar to Kuttelwascher's DFC was promulgated. Within 48 hours of this latest award, the Czech had destroyed a Dornier. His ultimate victories were claimed on the night of 2 July. Returning to his favourite target, St Andre, Kuttelwascher destroyed two Dorniers and damaged a third in some six minutes of furious action.

By that date No 1 Squadron had been informed that it was shortly to exchange its Hurricanes for Hawker Typhoons, and for this purpose the unit was to move north to Acklington on 8 July. On the day before his squadron left Karel Kuttelwascher was posted away to No 23 Squadron, based at Ford, to fly De Havilland Mosquito II fighters. In its three months of night-hunting over France No 1 Squadron had claimed 22 enemy aircraft destroyed and a further 13 damaged; of which tally Squadron Leader Maclachlan had claimed five of the destroyed, but Karel Kuttelwascher had accounted for 15 destroyed and five damaged. Added to the three day victories the Czech had claimed previously, it meant that Kuttelwascher was the highest-scoring Czechoslovakian fighter pilot of the war. His move to 23 Squadron came at the close of almost two years of active operational flying, and though he flew Mosquitos with his latest unit he flew no further operational sorties.

In December 1942 No 23 Squadron was despatched to Malta but Kuttelwascher remained in England with a staff appointment and promotion to Squadron Leader. Later he undertook a lecture tour of the USA.

At the end of the war Kuttelwascher naturally wished to return to his homeland, but after some eighteen months living in Czechoslovakia and the advent of a new ruling regime there, he decided to return to England in 1947, where he settled with his Welsh-born wife and their three children. On his return he applied for a position as a pilot with British European Airways (BEA) and was accepted as a First Officer initially. As a much-decorated wartime ace, with some twelve years' experience in flying under his belt, Kuttelwascher's status as a First Officer with BEA might well have created some embarrassment for those airline captains tasked with having him as their subordinate. In fact, the quiet Czech was, in the words of one contemporary BEA skipper: 'Perfectly content to sit in the co-pilot's seat and serve his apprenticeship. He would always do as he was told and never grumbled at all'. The Czech's RAF reputation for coolness and unflappability soon spread through the BEA grapevine as he flew first on various airborne icing trials, then as a Captain on Vikings and Elizabethans. By 1960 he was a Captain with BEA's Viscount Flight, but while on holiday that year he died suddenly.

CHAPTER FIVE

Frank Carey

If accredited combat victories were the sole criterion of a fighter pilot's greatness, then the *official* tally of 28 of Frank Reginald Carey places him high in any listing of Allied fighter aces of the 1939-45 aerial warfare. Add to that score his awards of a DFC and two Bars, AFC, DFM, and an American Silver Star, apart from a postwar CBE, and it is apparent that Carey was a remarkable fighter by any standards. Moreover, most contemporaries of Carey are convinced that his official victory total is a gross underestimate, quoting varying figures from 30 to over 50 as the true figure. Yet Carey's prominence derived not merely from his personal prowess in battle but also, perhaps even more importantly, from his outstanding qualities of leadership; an instinctive ability to lead men against daunting odds and still triumph, inspiring the finest efforts from those who followed his lead and example.

Born in Brixton, London on 7 Mary 1912, Frank Carey received an elementary education at Belvedere School, Haywards Heath, and in September 1927 joined the RAF as an Aircraft Apprentice of the 16th Entry, Halton for training as a metal rigger. On completion of his apprenticeship Carey was posted to the ground servicing staff of No 43 Squadron at Tangmere to help maintain the unit's Armstrong Whitworth Siskin IIIA fighters and, from May 1931, sleek Hawker Fury interceptors. Returning to Halton in 1933 for a year's conversion course to become a Fitter II (Airframe), LAC Carey was next posted to Worthy Down, to service the Vickers Virginias of Nos 7 and 58 Squadrons, but his prime ambition to become a pilot was finally realised when he was accepted for training in 1935 and ultimately graduated as a Sergeant pilot the following year from 6 FTS, Netheravon with a 'Distinguished Pass' rating; an early indication of his flying skill which was to be manifested in the years to come.

Carey's first posting as a pilot, to his personal delight, was back to 43 Squadron, joining its A Flight at Tangmere to fly Hawker Furies. Here Carey's polished handling of his aircraft, usually Fury K3740, soon proved to be the equal of any pilot on the squadron – no mean accomplishment considering these included such men as J.W.C.Simpson, F.Rosier, and fellow ex-Halton Brat, Jim Hallowes. By the end of 1938 Carey had accumulated almost 1,000 flying hours in Furies, but in November-December that year the graceful biplanes began being replaced by Hawker Hurricanes, and on 18 November 1939 No 43 Squadron left its spiritual home at Tangmere to move north to Acklington, near Newcastle, as reinforcement to No 13 Group, Fighter Command for defence of the north-east counties' industries.

For the next few months the squadron was engaged in monotonous coastal patrols, protecting inshore shipping lanes off the east coast, with only rare 'interruptions' for direct action against Luftwaffe intrusions. Carey first fired his guns 'in anger' on 29 January 1940 when, in company with the Rhodesian-born Flight Lieutenant Caesar Hull and Pilot Officer North, he attacked a Heinkel 111 some ten miles south-east of Hartlepool, though this escaped into cloud after the initial exchange of bullets. Next day Carey, flying Hurricane L1728, was No 2 to Caesar Hull (L1744) again, intercepted a Heinkel 111 five miles east of Coquet Island, one of a pair attempting to bomb some fishing vessels. Both Carey and Hull closed from the beam on the nearest Heinkel and their combined attack sent the Heinkel down into the sea, its five-man crew being rescued by the crew of the vessel they had only minutes before been trying to kill.

Four days later, in company with Sergeant Ottewill, Frank Carey came upon a Heinkel bombing some ships fifteen miles east of Tynemouth. In simultaneous beam attacks, Carey's and Ottewill's fire stopped both the Heinkel's engines and it fell into the sea. Further lone German raiders were intercepted successfully by 43 Squadron in February, including a Heinkel 111 on 12 February which Carey 'shared' with Hull in downing, and on 21 February Frank Carey was awarded a DFM.* On 26

* *London Gazette* dated 1 March 1940

February the squadron left Acklington to move further north to Wick, there to help in defence of the Scapa Flow naval anchorage, but after a month of freezing non-action Carey was commissioned as Pilot Officer on 1 April, then left 43 to join No 3 Squadron based at Kenley, another Hurricane unit.

Carey had hardly settled in with his latest unit when the war in France erupted overnight into savage action on 10 May 1940 as German forces launched their *blitzkrieg* advances westwards. No 3 Squadron was immediately despatched in part, along with other units, to France to reinforce the relatively meagre fighter strength of the RAF based in France, and Carey's section flew to Merville on the 10th and was almost immediately in action, with Carey alone attacking one mass formation of Heinkel 111s. In the ensuing clash he destroyed one Heinkel and claimed two others as probably destroyed.

On 12 May he claimed two Junkers Ju 87s; on the 13th two more Ju 87s plus a Dornier for good measure; while on 14 May he tackled a gaggle of Dorniers, riddling one in a close stern attack. As the doomed bomber fell away its courageous rear gunner kept firing, raking Carey's Hurricane and wounding him in the right leg. As he watched the Dornier explode into the ground, Carey realised that the gunner's fire had also hit his engine which began running rough. Managing to crashland safely in a field near Grez-Doiceau, south-east of Brussels, Carey was picked up by some Belgian motorcyclists, taken to the village for elementary first aid for his wound, then hitch-hiked his way to Brussels where he obtained fuller medical attention. Eventually, after several moves to various hospitals, Carey managed to scrounge an air lift back to England where, on reporting to his squadron by telephone, he learned he had already been officially reported as 'Missing, believed killed' ...

While recovering from his wound, Carey received the award of a DFC on 31 May 1940, followed on 14 June by the further award of a Bar to his DFC, and in the same month returned to No 43 Squadron as A Flight commander with promotion to Flight Lieutenant. He had arrived just in time to join his old unit's part in the struggle for survival now termed the Battle of Britain. Wasting no time in returning to action Carey claimed a pair of

Messerschmitt Bf 109s as destroyed on 19 June, though officially the squadron was yet to be declared 'fully operational' following a particularly punishing engagement on 7 June which had cost 43 Squadron four pilots.

On 9 July, while flying as No 2 to the squadron commander, George Lott, Carey and his two companions were attacked by six Bf 110s from V/LG1, and Carey shot down one and claimed a share in destroying a second. Nevertheless, Lott's Hurricane received an accurate burst of cannon shells, one of which exploded on his windscreen, blinding him in one eye and setting the Hurricane on fire. Eventually Lott managed to bale out at some 700 feet some three miles from Tangmere, while his aircraft crashed and was fire-gutted on Fontwell racecourse.

Ten days later, on 19 July, Carey was one of six Hurricane pilots from 43 Squadron patrolling the Bognor-Selsey Bill area when they were jumped by some fifteen Bf 109s. Two Hurricane pilots were wounded and forced to bale out (Flight Lieutenant Simpson and Sergeant Buck), but Carey managed to sink a long burst into one Bf 109 which fell vertically through low cloud at 2,000 feet. Following his target down, Carey emerged from the cloud to see oil and wreckage on the sea.* Climbing back to the combat Carey passed an inverted Hurricane, flying steadily straight and level, but with an empty cockpit. It was Sergeant Buck's aircraft, from which he had baled out into the sea, and whose body was found on the following day.

August 8 saw 43 Squadron achieve probably its greatest triumph to date. At 1540 hours twelve Hurricanes took off to cover a convoy (*Peewit*) west-bound south of the Isle of Wight; three sections of three led by Squadron Leader J.V.C.Badger at about 15,000 feet, with Frank Carey and two companions at higher 'top cover' altitude. To quote Carey: 'A most formidable and orderly array of enemy aircraft arrived to interfere with things ...'. This 'array' comprised formations of Bf 110s stretching from the Isle of Wight to the French coast at high level, then *Staffels* of Bf 109s some 5,000 feet lower also extended at

---

* German records admit only one Bf 109 casualty, Leutnant Graf von Kageneck of III/JG27 who returned to base, though wounded. The wreckage seen by Carey was almost certainly that of Simpson's Hurricane.

intervals to the French coast, and under this dual 'umbrella' a mass of Junkers Ju 87s obviously intent on sinking the convoy. As the lower Hurricane sections proceeded to dive at the Ju 87s, Carey led his two men against the Bf 109s attempting to prevent them reaching the rest of 43 Squadron lower down. After the first clash, Carey lost contact with his wing men, then spotted a squadron of fighters in Vic-formation, thought they were Hurricanes, and flew to join up with them. As he got nearer he realised they were Bf 109s! What followed is best described by Carey himself:

'I was happy to note that I had not been seen by them so I continued until I had got behind one of the outside members of the 109 formation. I had just settled down to fire at this aircraft with some success, as bits started to fly off it, when a very large explosion nearly blew me upside down. An Me 110 had seen what was happening, had come down and was sitting about 30 yards behind me, and his explosive 20 mm shots had blown up all the ammunition in my port wing, leaving a hole big enough for a man to crawl through.'

After managing to right his Hurricane, Carey laboriously began climbing again to get back over the convoy when he was again jumped by some Bf 110s.

'This time they blew one elevator and the rudder off and the aircraft did a half bunt before I collected my senses. I had been hit in the arm on the first occasion and what with that and having only about three-quarters of an aircraft left to control, I thought discretion was the better part of valour and slowly brought the remains back to base. As if I hadn't had enough, the Tangmere ack-ack opened up on me as I entered the circuit – I suppose the silhouette must have looked a bit odd – fortunately they didn't hit me'.

Though Carey could only claim one Bf 109 as damaged, the rest of 43 Squadron had claimed five destroyed, plus a further ten probably destroyed, and indeed the German records admit the losses of eight Ju 87s, three Bf 109s and one Bf 110 as well as four others damaged from this particular engagement.

On 12 August Carey was again in action, shooting down a Ju 88 of III/KG51 near Portsmouth shortly after mid-day; while next day saw him taking on three Ju 88s near Littlehampton on his first sortie of the day and claiming one as destroyed. August 15 provided an 'easy victim' when Carey and his section met a lone Ju 88 of 4/LG1 and proceeded to take the opportunity for '... a spot of shooting practice' (*sic*) for the Hurricanes, each in turn riddling the Junkers and sending it down to crash and burn out just north of Emsworth, killing Oberleutnant Möller (acting Observer) and Gefreiter Anders, and having two other crew men taken prisoner. At precisely 1 p.m. on 16 August the squadron base at Tangmere was heavily bombed and strafed with, among other damage, 43's hangar destroyed by blast and fire. Only fifteen minutes before the squadron had taken off to patrol Selsey Bill at some 11,000 feet, with Carey leading A Flight, and soon saw an awesome formation of 100-plus German aircraft, mostly Ju 87s, heading towards the English coast. An extract from Carey's combat report describes the ensuing action:

I gave 'Tally Ho' on sighting waves of Ju 87s. The leader ordered the squadron to attack one formation of 87s from the front and immediately on closing the leader of the enemy aircraft was hit by Squadron Leader and crew baled out. I pulled my Flight over to the left to attack the right-hand formation as we met them. Almost as soon as I opened fire the enemy aircraft's crew baled out and the machine crashed in the sea, just off Selsey Bill. I turned to continue my attack from the rear as enemy aircraft were completely broken up by the frontal attack and several other waves behind them turned back out to sea immediately, although we had not attacked them. I picked out one Ju 87 and fired two two-seconds' bursts at him and the enemy aircraft burst into flames on the port wing root.

I did not wait to see it crash as I turned to attack another. After one burst at the third enemy aircraft, two large pieces of metal broke off the port wing and the enemy aircraft seemed to stop abruptly and go into a dive, but I did not see the machine crash as two other Ju 87s were turning on to my tail. I eventually picked up a fourth, but after firing two bursts and causing its engine to issue black smoke, the enemy aircraft turned out to sea and I ran out of ammunition. I noticed firing from behind me and turned to see a pair of Bf 109s behind me, one firing and the other apparently guarding its tail. After a few evasive actions enemy aircraft broke off and I returned to land and refuel and re-arm at 1340 hrs.

This engagement cost the Luftwaffe's St.G.2 a total of eleven Ju 87s destroyed apart from others which limped home with bullet-racked airframes and wounded crewmen. Carey was credited officially with two Ju 87s confirmed as destroyed, plus two other Ju 87s probably destroyed.

Frank Carey's final combat of the Battle of Britain came on 18 August, a day which brought 43 Squadron into constant action, without pause between sorties, throughout the day. Carey, flying Hurricane R4109, took off with his A Flight from the bomb-cratered Tangmere airfield in mid-afternoon and shortly after reaching patrol altitude was joined by three more Hurricanes from B Flight. His report read, in part:

I took the nine Hurricanes head-on into a large formation of Ju 87s midway between Chichester and Selsey Bill. After turning round to get behind some of them I found myself in the middle of several Ju 87 formations. I fired at one ahead of me – it stood straight up on its nose with flames coming out of it – when I was hit on the right knee by cross-fire, or a stray burst from a Hurricane. Handing over the squadron to someone else I had to drop out of the fight as my knee was locked and I was not feeling too well. I called Tangmere but they advised me to stay away as they expected more bombing. I did for a time, but eventually had to crash-land at Pulborough.*

Surviving the crash without further serious injury, Frank Carey was taken to the Royal Sussex Hospital at Chichester.

By 8 September No 43 Squadron was almost a pale shadow of its initial character at the beginning of the Battle. With only

* Carey's victim was from I/St.G.77, while Hurricane R4109 was repaired and later saw service with No 1 Squadron RCAF in October 1940.

thirteen pilots left – six of these barely out of OTU training – and so many of its stalwarts were dead; Caesar Hull, Dick Reynell, De Mancha, Buck, Montgomery had made the supreme sacrifice, while several others were hospitalised, recovering from wounds. On that date the squadron was withdrawn from the Battle and moved north to Usworth, changing places with a refurbished 607 Squadron. Here Frank Carey rejoined the squadron in September, but in November 1940 he was reposted to No 52 OTU, Debden as a fighting instructor.

His stay at the OTU was brief, however, and early in 1941 he joined No 245 Squadron (Hurricanes) at Aldergrove, Northern Ireland as a Flight commander. This unit, tasked with the defence of Belfast, was commanded by another ex-43 Squadron veteran, Squadron Leader J.W.C.Simpson, DFC. Shortly after this move Carey was promoted to Squadron Leader and given command of No 135 Squadron, which commenced formation at Baginton on 15 August 1941, then later moved base to Honiley, flying Hurricane IIs. Quickly bringing his squadron up to operational status, Carey then received orders for the transfer of his unit to India for active service in the Far East theatre, and on 6 December 1941 the squadron began its sea voyage to Rangoon via Durban – just 24 hours before Japan struck at Malaya and Pearl Harbour.

Reaching Rangoon in January 1942, 135 Squadron was soon in action against raiding Japanese aircraft and, appropriately, it fell to Carey to open the squadron's tally when on 29 January, flying a Hurricane 'borrowed' from No 17 Squadron, he destroyed a Nakajima Ki27 over Rangoon. It was also an introduction to the fanatical nature of their future opponents. Despite Carey sinking burst after burst into the Ki27, its pilot had continued to control his aircraft until diving it deliberately onto a parked Blenheim on Mingaladon airfield. Examination of the Japanese pilot discovered no less than 27 of Carey's bullets in him; 'More than enough to have made most of us lose interest in the handling of an aircraft', as Carey remarked wryly afterwards. Such accuracy in shooting exemplified one of Frank Carey's outstanding attributes in air combat. As a fellow pilot, Squadron Leader D.H.Clarke, DFC has recorded, 'Frank's air-to-air deflection shooting was incredibly accurate, yet his air-to-ground, like that of most great

73 Squadron pilots posing for the press, France, early 1940. Third from rt is Fg Off Edgar 'Cobber' Kain, DFC.

(Left) Fg Off E J Kain, DFC, June 1940. *(Right)* Miss Joyce Phillips, fiancee of 'Cobber' Kain, presenting a Colour to No. 174 (Manchester) Squadron, Air Training Corps.

(Left) Max Aitken after being presented with a Czech War Cross.

(Centre) 601 Squadron Hurricanes refuelling & re-arming between sorties at Tangmere, 1940. Pilot standing far left is Max Aitken.

(Bottom) Blenheim IVF, Z5722, WM-Z, of 68 Sqn, Max Aitken's personal machine.

aces, was below average.' Carey repeated his success on 23 February by destroying an enemy reconnaissance machine, by which time he had been promoted to Wing Commander at Mingaladon.

On 26 February Carey led his men off on three scrambles during the day, and personally accounted for three Ki43 fighters, but on 6 March 1942 the RAF had to evacuate Mingaladon and Carey became commander at RAF Alipore where, on 24 March a second Bar to his DFC was promulgated, its citation emphasising his ' ... high qualities of leadership and high example of devotion to duty'.

By the end of 1942 Carey's score of Japanese aircraft shot down had risen to at least ten, though with the many retreats and evacuations suffered by the Allies many unit and personal records, including Carey's, were inevitably lost or destroyed, thereby precluding positive confirmation of many other victories attributed to Carey by other contemporary pilots. In January 1943 Carey was serving at Air Headquarters, Bengal but in the following month he was appointed O C Air Fighting Training Unit at Amarda Road where his vast experience was put to excellent use inculcating younger fighter pilots into the tactics, skills, and 'know-how' of fighting the Japanese. At this AFTU 'Chota' (Little One) Carey – so nicknamed because of his small stature – employed methods, often highly unorthodox, to polish his pilots' fighting techniques so successfully that it was said of them later that they helped win victory in Burma ' ... with the voice of Frank Carey whispering in their ears', while one official historian commented that 'his teaching put a fine glaze on a highly-finished article'.

In November 1944, with further promotion to Group Captain, Carey left Burma to take up an appointment as commander of No 73 OTU, Abu Sueir in Egypt where his personal example and expertise were again used in good measure to raise the standards of embryo fighter pilots, while his highly individual methods of maintaining discipline on the unit, if not strictly by the book, added to the already deep respect accorded to him by his subordinates. His contributions to training and tactical methods were recognised in the 1945 New Year's Honours List with the award of an AFC.

In July 1945 Frank Carey returned to England and an

appointment as Group Captain Tactics at the Central Fighter Establishment, was then awarded a permanent commission in the postwar RAF and spent two years at the Staff College, Camberley. Various other appointments followed, both flying and administrative, until 1958 when he was made Air Adviser to the UK High Commissioner in Australia, in which country he finally retired from the RAF on 2 June 1960 to take up a position with the Rolls-Royce Aero Engine Division. On the day after his Service retirement he was awarded a CBE; perhaps a fitting mark of the end of 33 years of RAF service for a man once described by one veteran fighter pilot as, 'Small in height, yet tall in our eyes, Chota Carey was to my mind probably the RAF's greatest fighter pilot of the war.'

CHAPTER SIX

Edgar Kain

On 2 September 1939 – the day before Britain's official declaration of war with Germany – the full complement of No 1 Group, Bomber Command comprising ten squadrons of Fairey Battle light bombers left England to fly to France; a force of 160 aircraft* which constituted the Advanced Air Striking Force of the RAF. As fighter protection for these bombers the AASF was allotted just two fighter units, Nos 1 and 73 Squadrons, both equipped with Hurricane Is, both of which joined the AASF a week later. Elsewhere in France was a separately controlled air formation, the Air Component of the British Expeditionary Force (BEF) composed of nine squadrons of bombers and army co-operation aircraft, plus two Hurricane units, Nos 85 and 87 Squadrons. As these RAF formations settled in to their respective French airfields there was a general air of expectancy that aerial, and indeed land, warfare was likely to erupt quickly, but as the winter closed in along the Western Front, apart from spasmodic clashes, the overall lack of full-scale war soon led to the period being dubbed the Phoney War by the popular press in Britain. This relatively inactive state of affairs was to last in France until Germany launched its massive and swift advances to the west on 10 May 1940.

For the Hurricane pilots the first eight months of the war were, in the main, frustrating. Operational sorties usually meant monotonous coastal patrols or general escort duties to bomber-reconnaissance aircraft, with only rare opportunities for direct engagement with the opposing Luftwaffe. While the Battle crews – often unescorted by fighters – had clashes with enemy aircraft from the early weeks of the conflict, the RAF fighters' first

* One Battle ditched in the English Channel en route, though its crew was retrieved safely.

combat victory was not claimed until 31 October 1939, when Pilot Officer P.W.O.Mould – nicknamed 'Boy' from his Halton Aircraft Apprentice origins – destroyed a Dornier bomber while on patrol with No 1 Squadron.

Just eight days later, however, this feat was duplicated by Flying Officer E.J.Kain of 73 Squadron, who shot down a Dornier from some 27,000 feet, chasing his victim almost to deck-level in his determination to destroy the bomber. It was the first of five accredited victories for Kain *before* the German *blitzkrieg* assaults in May 1940, establishing Kain as the RAF's first fighter ace of the war and, moreover, its only fighter ace of the so-termed 'Phoney War' period *per se*. By June 1940 and the collapse of France, Kain was to become virtually the top-scoring RAF fighter pilot of the whole French campaign.

Born on 27 June 1918 in Hastings, New Zealand, Edgar James Kain – later to be universally nicknamed 'Cobber' for his 'Kiwi' origin – was educated at Croydon School, Wellington and Christchurch College, Christchurch with a teaching career in prospect. His prime ambition, however, was to fly, and on leaving college he joined the Wellington Aero Club and made his first solo flight after only six hours' dual instruction. Deciding to make flying a career, and with little hope of gaining a place in the tiny Royal New Zealand Air Force, Kain paid for a ship passage to England in 1936 and applied to join the RAF. Accepted for training as a pilot, Kain was eventually granted a Short Service Commission (SSC) and commissioned as Acting Pilot Officer on 8 March 1937, then posted to No 5 FTS, Sealand on 20 March to commence his Service flying instruction, completing this at Ternhill.

On gaining his RAF wings Kain's first posting was to No 73 Squadron at Digby on 27 November 1937. His new unit, which had only reformed on 15 March 1937, had begun re-equipment with Gloster Gladiators in June, and in these Kain soon showed his capabilities as an aerobatic virtuoso, being selected as one of two Gladiator pilots to give the British public a dazzling display of fighter aerobatics at the May Empire Air Day in 1938. Two months later No 73 Squadron again re-equipped, exchanging their silver biplanes for the new Hawker Hurricane monoplane fighters, and after mastering such 'new-fangled' items as retractable undercarriages, vast increases in most aspects of performance ranges, and accustoming themselves to having no second wing blotting out their upward views from the cockpit, Kain and his fellow pilots on 73 quickly adapted their skills to the new 'kites'.

Though declared still non-operational at the time of the 1938 Munich Crisis, the squadron was fully fit by early 1939, and within days of war being declared against Germany in September the squadron settled in to its first French base at Rouvres as part of No 67 Wing, AASF, where it was to remain resident until early May 1940. Edgar Kain, recently promoted to Flying Officer on 21 July 1939, was but one of several experienced Hurricane pilots with 73 Squadron at that period, flying alongside such squadron stalwarts as R.E.Lovett, N.'Fanny' Orton, 'Ginger' Paul, 'Dicky' Martin, George Berry, 'Tubbs' Perry and others, all commanded by Squadron Leader Brian 'Red' Knox, a Dubliner whose rein on his young pilots was gentle but firm.

For the first few weeks in France 73's pilots, though itching for combat action, had to be content with patrols over the 'front' escorting bombers or merely seeking an elusive Luftwaffe. Then, on 8 November, came Kain's – and the squadron's – first kill. Bad weather put a clamp on flying for the next two weeks but on 23 November action by both 1 and 73 Squadrons resulted in claims for seven German aircraft destroyed; one of these, another Dornier falling to Kain's guns.

The onset of Europe's coldest winter in decades effectively nullified aerial activity in France until early 1940, and it was not until 3 March that Kain was able to add a further 'notch' to his tally. Leading a section of three Hurricanes as escort to a French Potez 63, and having delivered the Potez back safely, Kain continued to patrol at 20,000 feet, though one Hurricane was forced to leave with engine trouble. With his remaining companion, Sergeant Sewell, Kain was just nearing Thionville when he spotted bursts of Allied anti-aircraft fire some 5,000 feet higher up and, on searching that patch of sky saw seven Heinkel He 111s in loose formation. Climbing immediately to engage

these the two Hurricanes were jumped by six Messerschmitt
Bf 109s whose initial fire crippled Sewell's engine and forced
him out of the fight.

Kain felt his aircraft shudder under the impact of cannon and
machine gun fire, but as one Bf 109 floated into his ring sight the
New Zealander fired and saw it spin away in flames. Sinking the
rest of his ammunition into a second Messerschmitt, which fell
away shedding metal, Kain felt the thud of a cannon shell in his
engine, followed by an eruption of flames and thick smoke.
Pushing the Hurricane's nose down, Kain eventually slid back his
canopy hood and prepared to bale out – only to remember he
had not adjusted his parachute straps before take-off. Dropping
back into the smoke-filled cockpit he realised that the flames had
died out, though oil and smoke continued to fill the cockpit. With
almost no forward vision, Kain managed to reach Metz
aerodrome and put his crippled Hurricane down in a safe
landing then climbed out of his seat and, in his own words, 'fell
flat on my bloody face; passed right out like a cissy-boy'.

By then 'Cobber' Kain had, much to his own alarm and
reluctance, become internationally known in the popular presses.
His appearance – over six feet tall, with black hair and clear blue
eyes – added to his heroic image in the lay mind, while his
naturally ebullient character and quick humour were bonuses for
the news-hungry journalists seeking 'glamour' items of the
'Phoney War' to feed to their UK editors. While on leave in Paris
Kain was often besieged by autograph-hunting French citizens,
and such attentions simply increased Kain's sincere embarrassment with his unsought role as a form of national hero. Back
among his squadron friends, however, such things were not
mentioned, and Kain's slightly irreverent attitude to bookish
Service discipline in trivial (to him) matters soon incurred his
squadron commander's displeasure, and Kain was grounded on
CO's orders for a few days as punishment for one very minor
breach of discipline.

On 26 March, however, though still officially grounded, Kain
heard that there was plentiful air activity over the 'front lines' and
pleaded to be released from his punishment. Knox readily agreed
and Kain took off, accompanied by 'Tubbs' Perry and Sergeant

Pyne. His report of the ensuing action reads as follows:

In the Luxembourg corner I saw a number of enemy aircraft and proceeded to investigate at 2.30 p.m. I gave a message on the R/T to Flying Officer Perry and Sergeant Pyne, 'Enemy aircraft ahead' and proceeded to attack. I turned into the enemy, which had started to climb, and gave a burst at the leader, who pulled up, turned on his back, and spun away in flames. I then noticed five more Me 109s working round behind me, so I turned hard right and took a sight on the near machine. I fired a burst at him; he dived away and I took three deflection shots at another Me 109 which was slowly turning ahead of me. I got behind this aircraft and gave it a burst. He turned on his starboard side and dived right down towards earth. I then took observations about me. The sky seemed to clear, so I looked for my other two machines. I was just turning south when my cockpit was hit by a cannon shell, while another hit my gravity tank.

The explosion on the hood of my cockpit rendered me unconscious, but I came to diving steeply. After a while I managed to pull out of the dive and tried to bend down and turn off the petrol but the flames burnt my face. I headed towards France to gain as much ground as possible, and when the flames got too intense I decided to abandon the aircraft. I got out from the port side and pulled my ripcord at 12,000 feet. I came out of cloud at 10,000 feet. It was all very still, and I thought I was in Heaven! Believing I was now near the frontier, I started slipping the air to get down quickly. I landed at Ritzing, near a wood. I gathered in my parachute and scrambled towards the wood, where I hid it. I then headed in a southerly direction, as I didn't know whether I was in France or not. A French captain challenged me at pistol point and asked my nationality, and we set off for Evendorff. The captain told me I had landed in No Man's Land. I was burnt and my leg was hurting, so I received medical attention, and was sent back to Rouvres in a French staff car.

On arrival back on the squadron Kain's injuries were treated by the unit's medical officer, 'Doc' Outfin, who extracted 21 pieces of shell from Kain's leg.

Within a week Edgar Kain was notified that he had been awarded a DFC, and was granted ten days leave in England to convalesce from his wounds. While on leave he became engaged to a beautiful young repertory actress. He also called in at the Air Ministry and suggested that in the light of all the attention being paid to him by the media that, to save further embarrassment to his squadron, he be posted to another unit in France, but this was gently refused.

Returning to his squadron on 11 April, Kain was allotted a fresh Hurricane, 'P', which he promptly had named 'Paddy III' – his third 'Paddy' – and was quickly back in action, claiming a Bf 110 as damaged on 23 April. The squadron now had a new commander, Squadron Leader J.W.C.More, who was still in command on 10 May when the Phoney War finally ended and a fury of action for the squadron commenced.

On that first day of the German *blitzkrieg* 73 squadron was obliged to leave its forward airfield at Rouvres to move to Rheims, but not before it had given the Luftwaffe a taste of its mettle, with Kain destroying a Dornier. Flying into Rheims at the tail-end of a Luftwaffe bombing raid, 73 Squadron was back in action within an hour, with Flight Lieutenant R.E.Lovett leading six Hurricanes into a horde of German bombers. Hit by a hail of crossfire from the German air gunners, Lovett's aircraft was shot down in flames, with its pilot unable to bale out due to badly burned hands, but Lovett still managed a forced landing.*

On 11 May the pace of combat continued at high pitch, with Kain accounting for a Dornier and a Bf 109, followed by a Henschel 126 on 12 May and another Bf 109 on 14 May. On 15 May the New Zealander attacked a formation of Dorniers from head-on, and was astonished to see the crew of one Dornier promptly bale out even before he started firing – a rare bloodless victory.

May 19 brought even more intense action for 73 Squadron, and during the day Kain destroyed a Junkers Ju 88, a Dornier,

* Flight Lieutenant R.E.Lovett, DFC returned to 73 Squadron in July 1940 but was killed in action on 7 September 1940.

and a Bf 110. On the 25th he shot down a Dornier near Rouen, but had his Hurricane's undercarriage damaged and subsequently force-landed. Next day a Henschel 126 was shot down in flames, while on 27 May 'Cobber' Kain scored his final victory, a Dornier which crashed near Meaux.

By then Kain and the B Flight commander, Ian Scoular, were the only two remaining of 73's original pilots on coming to France; the remainder being either dead, wounded, or replaced by new men from England. By then too Kain was rapidly approaching his physical and mental limits due solely to battle fatigue, having been in non-stop action for more than two weeks with no respite, and friends of the New Zealander have commented on Kain's 'twitchy' state; the penalty being paid by mind and body for his unrelenting efforts.

Accordingly, he was ordered back to England, and on Friday, 7 June, on the crude airfield at Blois, he had his personal kit loaded into the spare seat of a Miles Magister 'hack' monoplane, said his goodbyes to the other pilots, climbed into the Maggie and started its engine. Seeing his Hurricane standing empty nearby, however, Kain climbed out again, leaving the Magister's engine ticking over, and jumped into his Hurricane for 'one last beat-up, boys'. Climbing rapidly, Kain turned the Hurricane back towards the airfield, then roared across it low, executing two slow rolls. Spectators watched breathlessly as they saw the Hurricane commence a third consecutive slow roll – it did not complete the manoeuvre. A wing-tip touched the grass and the Hurricane cartwheeled to destruction, throwing Edgar Kain clear some 50 feet away and causing him fatal head injuries.

The news of 'Cobber' Kain's death created a shock for his many friends in the RAF, and the many thousands of others to whom he had been a hero; while his mother, at that moment en route by ship to England to attend her son's wedding, was left with the sad duty of receiving Kain's DFC award from King George VI at a subsequent investiture at Buckingham Palace. A few weeks after Kain's tragic accident his fiancée, Joyce Phillips, kept a promise made by Kain by presenting a Colour to No 174 (Manchester) Squadron of the Air Training Corps.

CHAPTER SEVEN

Max Aitken

To the general public of the 1930s the Auxiliary Air Force (AAF) was often regarded as nothing better than an infernal nuisance, a gathering of wealthy young men whose week-end flying capers merely disturbed the traditional peace and quiet of the British Sunday; aristocratic tomfoolery which appeared to have little justification other than sheer indulgence and the gratification of selfish pleasures by a handful of rich men's sons. It was a view of the AAF often reflected in certain Air Ministry and RAF 'upper circles' by some senior die-hards who looked askance at the highly irreverent regard for rules and regulations overtly displayed by the 'aerated amateurs' at almost every opportunity.

Such superficial judgments were to be sharply revised at the start of the 1939-45 war when the Auxiliaries immediately proved that there had been a serious purpose behind their play, and that AAF crews were the equal of any regular RAF compatriots; exemplified especially during the 1940 Battle of Britain when AAF fighter pilots alone accounted for almost one-third of RAF combat victories throughout that epic struggle.

One of those 'pampered pimpernels' was John William Maxwell Aitken – plain 'Max' to his intimates – whose wartime career placed him in the forefront of the RAF's outstanding fighter pilots and fighting leaders. Born in Montreal, Canada on 15 February 1910, young Aitken was the son of a baron, was brought to England as a boy, and educated at Westminster and Pembroke College, Cambridge. Having been born with a traditional silver sugar-spoon in his mouth, Aitken might well have been content to live out a pampered existence as a monied playboy socialite, but he had also inherited the drive and restless energy of his father. Collecting a blue for soccer and a scratch golf handicap while at Cambridge, Aitken then entered civil aviation as a pilot, flying passengers and freight over Europe and the USA, establishing and breaking several flying records in the process. He next entered his father's world of journalism, but retained his affinity with flying by joining No 601 Squadron AAF in 1935, where (initially) he flew Hawker Harts as stop-gap two-seat fighters.

Termed by outsiders as the Millionaires Mob, but calling themselves The Legion, 601 Squadron's officers at that period were indeed a batch of wealthy youngsters who, in common with the other AAF squadrons, delighted in flouting the rigid bureaucracy of the regular Service. Even their nominally RAF uniforms reflected the Auxiliary spirit; they wore blue ties rather than the funereal official black variety, and lined their tunics with bright red silk, with socks to match. Competition with RAF and all other AAF units was fierce and, in company with such 601 stalwarts as Roger Bushell,* 'Willy' Rhodes-Moorhouse† and Sir Archibald Hope, to name merely three, Max Aitken took his full share of 601's ventures, both on and off duty.

Perhaps the prime keynote of 601 Squadron was individuality, whereby each pilot pursued his own capabilities and talents to their limits, yet paradoxically each man slotted readily into the cohesive whole of a unit bound together by an unbidden disciplinary code which placed The Legion first and self second in priorities. Almost every pilot owned his own private aircraft, in Aitken's case an Aeronca, G-ADZZ, high-wing monoplane. This particular design was claimed by its makers to be spin-proof – a claim which Aitken after many hours of practice managed to dispel by spinning the Aeronca from 2,000 feet almost to the grass during an air display at Hanworth.

During the closing years of peace 601 Squadron was successively re-equipped with Hawker Demons, Gloster Gauntlets, and from January 1939 with Bristol Blenheim IF 'fighters'; the latter being standard Blenheim I bombers 'converted' by

* Squadron Leader Bushell, later OC 92 Squadron RAF, was shot down on 23 May 1940 over Dunkirk, taken prisoner, and eventually shot by the Germans on recapture after the mass escape of Allied POWs from Stalag-Luft III in 1944.
† Flight Lieutenant W. Rhodes Moorhouse, DFC, son of the first-ever air VC, Lieutenant W.B.Rhodes Moorhouse, RFC, was to be killed in action on 6 September 1940.

adding a four-machine gun 'tray' under the forward bomb bay, firing forward. When war was declared on Sunday 3 September, the squadron was based at Biggin Hill, where it was alerted to intercept a mysterious 'radio signal'. Aitken was one of twelve Blenheim pilots sent off hurriedly to tackle the unknown intruder – which turned out to be the motor of a nearby refrigerator and, adding insult to injured pride, the Blenheims were fired at by a local anti-aircraft battery as they returned to base.

The Legion had its first taste of genuine operations on 28 November 1939, when six Blenheim IFs of 601 Squadron, in company with six more from No 25 Squadron, carried out the first long-range fighter attack against Germany. Setting out from Bircham Newton at 1415 hours, Flight Lieutenant Michael Peacock led the first section of three, followed by Aitken leading two of his B Flight, Willy Rhodes Moorhouse and Tom Hubbard. The objective was the German seaplane base at Borkum, on the island of Sylt. Achieving complete surprise on arrival, the Blenheims proceeded to rake the base from every angle at deck-level, then returned to base safely; the leader, Peacock, later receiving a DFC as recognition of his 'splendid dash and courage' (*sic*).

With a move of base to Tangmere in early 1940, the Legion soon began exchanging their outmoded Blenheim 'fighters' for Hurricanes – the latter having been expedited by Max Aitken who had spoken privately with his father, Lord Beaverbrook, who on 14 May had taken over the helm of the newly created Ministry of Aircraft Production. On 16 May the squadron sent its A Flight across the Channel to join with a Flight from No 3 Squadron as added support for the few RAF fighter units in France desperately attempting to stem the massive German onslaught which had begun on 10 May. Two days later 601's pilots claimed seven victories, including a Ju 87 and a Bf 110 by Aitken. The following day Aitken claimed two more victims destroyed and two others probably destroyed. Withdrawn to England, 601's pilots continued to fly and fight over the retreating Allied armies in France, patrolling the skies above Dunkirk, and though Aitken claimed no victories he, like every other pilot, flew hard and long. A private note in his log book for 29 May reads; 'Flew five hours before lunch. AOC asked, "Are you tired?" ' ...

On 6 June 1940, with promotion to Squadron Leader, Max Aitken became commander of 601 Squadron. Three weeks later, on 26 June, Aitken in company with Tom Hubbard, took off at 11 p.m. to intercept a reported enemy aircraft. Spotting a formation of three Heinkel He 111s caught briefly in a searchlight beam, Aitken closed behind one, gave it a long burst aiming between the two engines' exhausts, and sent it down into the Channel, where it floated in a ring of moonlit foam. The following week saw the *London Gazette* announce the award of a DFC to Max Aitken, its citation crediting him with at least eight combat victories.

On 7 July Aitken shared in the destruction of a Dornier, but on 16 August he handed over command of the Legion to Squadron Leader Hope and became bound to a desk in the Directorate of Operations at the Air Ministry. Despite his journalistic background, sifting paper was not Aitken's idea of making war, and he was soon agitating for more active duties, and in early 1941 returned to the operational sharp end on being appointed in command of No 68 Squadron, based at Coltishall, Norfolk.

Reformed on 7 January 1941, 68 Squadron was a night fighter unit, equipped with Blenheim IVF 'fighters' initially and became operational by April that year. In May the Blenheims began being replaced by Beaufighter 1Fs, and the squadron recorded its first victory on 17 June. Aitken was to remain in command of 68 Squadron for two years, during which time, typically, he constantly joined his crews on night patrols, and between April and July 1942 claimed five victims during the Luftwaffe's forays – three Dorniers and two Junkers Ju 88s – which resulted in the award of a DSO in August, the citation for which credited him with fourteen enemy aircraft destroyed to date. A further award resulted from the fact that many of his squadron crews were refugee Czechoslovakians, and the Free Czech government accordingly presented Aitken with their War Cross at a private ceremony conducted by Dr Benes, which also included two other noted night fighters, Karel Kuttelwascher and the one-armed J.A.F.Maclachlan, both from No 1 Squadron.

At the beginning of 1943 the chief of Fighter Command, Sholto

Douglas, was preparing to hand over his command prior to taking up a fresh appointment as C-in-C, Middle East, and as soon as this news filtered through the Command's grapevine – to quote Douglas –

> Several of my fully operational flying officers of Squadron Leader and Wing Commander rank started exerting pressure all the way from their own various subterranean channels of influence to outright personal requests to be allowed to go out with me to the Middle East ... after as pretty a lot of wire-pulling as I did not at the time want to hear about, Max Aitken, Johnny Kent, Ian Gleed, Barry Heath and John Simpson, all Wing Commanders, and pilots in the Battle of Britain, found their way out to the Middle East.*

In Aitken's case this move was not only a question of personal regard for Douglas's leadership qualities, but an attempt to join a more active theatre of operations; with the virtual cessation of Luftwaffe activity over Britain by early 1943, night fighting had become more a boring routine than a truly operational sphere of frequent action.

On arrival in the Middle East, Aitken was given a desk in the Air Headquarters, Eastern Mediterranean in Cairo, in charge of operational training; a job which was not to his liking but one insisted upon by Douglas himself initially, who refused Aitken's immediate agitations for an operational command. By persistence, however, Aitken's continuing campaign for a return to firstline flying wore down Sholto Douglas's resistance, and he was promoted to Group Captain, in command of No 219 Group, with his HQ in Alexandria. His new Group was responsible for the defence of the North African coastal area from Tripoli to the Nile Delta, especially the cities of Cairo and Alexandria.

Taking up this appointment in July 1943, Aitken immediately organised an offensive strike against German-occupied Crete. On 23 July eleven squadrons of Hurricanes (93 aircraft), led by Beaufighters of 227 Squadron, and followed in by eight

* *Years of Command* by Sholto Douglas / R. Wright: Collins, 1966.

Baltimores of 454 Squadron, attacked various areas on the island. Though little Luftwaffe opposition was met, deadly accurate anti-aircraft fire claimed thirteen Hurricanes and five Baltimores.

Though not an auspicious start to his period of command, Aitken's appetite for direct offensive action was soon to be whetted by more ambitious operations around the Aegean zone and, as ever not content to be merely a desk-jockey, he flew with his squadrons whenever an opportunity occurred. One example of this constant urge for action was a so-termed 'Junkers Party' on 5 March 1944 when Aitken 'borrowed' a Beaufighter from No 46 Squadron and personally destroyed two Ju 52s, claiming a further two as probably destroyed.

Late in 1944 he returned to England, having again made a personal request to Sholto Douglas, by then AOC-in-C, Coastal Command, to find an operational command for him; an appointment which Douglas readily arranged by placing Aitken in command of a newly-forming Strike Wing at Banff. Consisting initially of Beaufighters and rocket-armed Mosquitos, the Banff Wing eventually comprised six Mosquito squadrons – nearly 140 aircraft – and its far-ranging depredations over the North Sea and, especially along the Norwegian coastal areas *et al*, proved highly fruitful, as for example, on 9 April 1945 when three U-boats were sunk by close rocket attacks. On 19 April another U-boat was destroyed at sea, while two days later, while returning from an anti-shipping strike, Mosquitos from the Wing ran into a force of eighteen Junkers torpedo-bombers. In the ensuing mêlée the Wing rapidly despatched nine Junkers, so quickly that the Mosquito leader, Wing Commander Chris Foxley-Norris, complained later that he never even managed to get a German in his sights ...!

On 8 May 1945 the European war officially ended, but Max Aitken satisfied his journalistic tidiness of mind by flying one last sortie – an anti-shipping patrol near Aalborg, Denmark – and thus could rightly claim to have flown on both the first and last days of the war. That year saw the first postwar election in Britain, and Aitken won a seat in Parliament as the Conservative MP for (appropriately) Holborn, which he held until 1950. Having left the RAF at the end of the war, he had become general manager of the *Sunday Express* but did not completely sever his deep interest in flying. In June 1946 No 601 Squadron was reformed at Hendon, initially equipped with Harvards and eventually Spitfire XIVs, and Max Aitken, with 'demotion' to Squadron Leader, became CO of the Legion again.

On 16 December 1947 the 'aerated amateurs' were officially designated the Royal Auxiliary Air Force – a regal tribute to the wartime record of the 'week-end fliers' – but in the following year Aitken reluctantly relinquished his command of 601 Squadron, due to the increasing demands of his Parliamentary and business duties and responsibilities. Later knighted, and succeeding to the chairmanship of Beaverbrook Newspapers, Aitken's adventuring spirit and constant willingness to face new challenges became as evident in 'Civvy Street' as it had been throughout the years of war.

(Left) Wg Cdr E J B Nicolson, VC, DFC, seen here in 1940 holding his VC award.

(Centre) E J B Nicolson in his 72 Sqn Gladiator just prior to the war.

(Bottom) Lt-rt: Naik Singh, VC; Rajah of Faridkot; General Auchinleck; Wg Cdr E J B Nicolson, VC, DFC; Grp Capt G L Cheshire, VC, DSO, DFC. Taken at a Viceregal party at New Delhi, India, late 1944.

(Left) Sqn Ldr A A McKellar, DSO, DFC in pre-war full-dress RAF uniform.

(Centre) Spitfire I of 602 Sqn AAF, 1940.

(Bottom) Pilots of 602 Sqn AAF at Dyce, March 1940. McKellar is 3rd from rt, standing.

CHAPTER EIGHT

James Nicolson

The award of a Victoria Cross to any Serviceman has always been regarded by members of all armed Services as recognition of an act (or acts) of superlative courage, and, unlike so many other awards and decorations which are liberally handed out, especially during wartime, the little bronze cross retains total respect from even the most cynical of uniformed men. Of the nineteen VCs awarded to airmen during 1914-19, nine went to pilots who could properly be regarded as fighter pilots; yet of the 32 air VCs bestowed during 1939-46 only one went to a fighter pilot, Eric James Brindley Nicolson, and the act which brought Nicolson the supreme award occurred on his first-ever operational combat engagement. Such honour at the very beginning of a pilot's operational career might well have had unfortunate effect on that man's subsequent attitudes and behaviour, but Nicolson's initial reaction was disbelief, then a continuing determination to 'earn it' in the following years, bringing him further recognition for his determination and prowess, and ultimately death while still flying on operations.

Born in Hampstead on 29 April 1917, Eric James Brindley Nicolson was educated in Tonbridge, Kent, and on leaving school began in business as an experimental engineer in Shoreham. In 1936, however, he decided on the RAF as his future career and commenced pilot instruction at the White Waltham civil flying school on 12 October 1936. Enlisted officially in the RAF on 21 December that year,* he completed his Service training at the Ternhill FTS, and on 7 August 1937 was posted to No 72 Squadron at Church Fenton to fly Gloster Gladiator fighters.

---

* For reasons known only to himself, Nicolson chose to 'drop' the Christian name Eric on enlistment in the RAF, though this name appears on his birth certificate and in his school records.

Once settled in to his first unit, Nicolson quickly proved himself to be a natural pilot, handling Gladiators with ease and skill and revelling in aerobatics. By nature an extrovert, ebullient, gregarious, and a gifted raconteur, 'Nick' could always be found at the centre of any party. As a pilot he was assessed above-average, and was a first class marksman in air-to-air mock fighting. In essence, Nicolson displayed at all times those characteristics usually attributed to what the RAF termed a 'press-on type'.

In April 1939 the squadron began exchanging its Gladiators for Spitfire Is, and in October that year moved base to Leconfield from where it flew its first operational patrols though saw no combat action. Further shifts of base were made to Drem, Church Fenton, and Acklington between October 1939 and March 1940, but Nicolson had still not seen combat when, on 15 May 1940, he was posted to a newly-formed fighter unit, No 249 Squadron, as an acting Flight commander. Moving to Leconfield five days later, 249 exchanged its Spitfires for Hurricanes in mid-June, and from 3 July was stationed at Church Fenton and declared fully operational. On 14 August 1940 the squadron was sent south to Boscombe Down to join the defence forces for the southern counties, as the Battle of Britain was reaching its peak.

Two days later, on Friday, 16 August, Nicolson took off from Boscombe Down in Hurricane P3576, GN-A, as leader of three Hurricanes comprising Red Section, with orders to patrol the Poole-Ringwood-Salisbury air space. His two companions were Pilot Officer M.A.King and Squadron Leader E.B.King; the latter was only attached to 249 Squadron for combat experience prior to taking up command of his own squadron. Thus, for all three pilots the next hour would be their baptism of fire in aerial combat.

Climbing into a cloudless sky the Hurricanes reached their patrol height of 15,000 feet and headed towards Southampton, where a Luftwaffe raid on the airfield at Gosport had just been reported. Nicolson, nervous and eager at this prospect of actual combat at last, spotted some Junkers Ju 88s some four miles away at a slightly higher level and immediately led his section in pursuit, but when within a mile range saw his intended prey being tackled by a bunch of Spitfires. Abandoning his chase of the Ju 88s, Nicolson continued upwards to some 18,000 feet over Southampton's suburbs, intending to rejoin the main 249 Squadron formation.

Then, without warning, he felt his Hurricane shudder under the impact of a flurry of cannon shells – he and his two followers had been successfully bounced by a loose gaggle of marauding Messerschmitt Bf 109s. Their opening fire was deadly accurate, hitting all three Hurricanes. Behind Nicolson, Pilot Officer King's aircraft erupted in flames and the youngster took to his parachute. As he floated down an over-zealous Army officer on the ground ordered his men to fire at the presumed 'Hun'; King's parachute was shredded by rifle fire, and he plunged to his death. Squadron Leader Eric King's Hurricane was also badly damaged but he managed to spin down, recover, and return to Boscombe Down. On 21 August Eric King assumed command of No 151 Squadron, only to be killed in action on 30 August.

Unaware of the fates of his companions, Nicolson had his own troubles to contend with. Four cannon shells (at least) had scored direct hits around the cockpit area. One had exploded through the cockpit canopy, driving a shard of perspex through Nicolson's left eyelid; a second had ruptured his fuselage petrol tank, setting it afire; a third burst through the fuselage side and tore Nicolson's right trouser leg to shreds; while the fourth had hit the heel of his left shoe, wounding his foot. With blood obscuring vision in his left eye, pain in his left leg, and a veritable furnace of petrol flames erupting directly in front of him, Nicolson's instincts made him veer his Hurricane into a right-hand diving curve to escape further punishment.

Then, with flames beginning to lick around his instrument panel into his cockpit, Nicolson prepared painfully to take to his parachute, only to see a Messerschmitt Bf 110 appear ahead of him. Nicolson's reflector gunsight was still switched on from his initial pursuit of the Junkers bombers, and on seeing this German Nicolson 'saw red' (*sic*). Pressing his gun firing button, he saw his tracers splashing along the Bf 110's slim fuselage. The German jinked wildly from left to right, but Nicolson, oblivious to all else for the moment, was totally determined to destroy this enemy.

As he continued firing and following each evasive action by the Bf 110, Nicolson glanced down at his left hand holding the throttle lever and saw the flesh literally peeling away in the heat, through strangely he felt no pain from it as yet. The flames were by now of blowtorch intensity, beating back from the instrument panel into his face, and he realised he could not stay much longer. Giving the German one final blasting from all eight wing guns, Nicolson pushed himself up from his seat, only to bang his head on the broken cockpit framework, still closed above him.

Wrenching back the hood cover, he tried again to get out of his blazing cockpit, forgetting that he was still strapped to his bucket seat. Unbuckling one restraint strap and snapping the other burnt strap, he finally managed to evacuate the cockpit inferno and tumbled into space. Somersaulting down from some 12,000 feet, he was partly revived by the rushing air, realised that he was diving head first to earth, and with difficulty managed to pull the ripcord of his parachute pack. As the silk canopy deployed to its full mushroom shape above his head, Nicolson saw a Messerschmitt flying directly at him. Fearing that the German might try machine-gunning him, Nicolson let his body go completely limp, feigning death, and the Messerschmitt roared past him, turned, came back, then left him.

As the German disappeared from view, Nicolson took stock of his condition. Now, for the first time, he realised he had been wounded in a foot, and could see blood oozing from his shoe. Both of his hands were badly burned; the left already contracted by the heat into a curved claw of exposed finger bones, while the right hand had strips of charred flesh hanging loosely. Over his face his leather face mask was still strapped in position, but above the nose piece his eyelids and brow were burned, and he was still blind in his left eye from a near-severed eyelid. His uniform hung in tatters, with one trouser leg torn away and the other merely shredded rags. Only now did conscious pain all over his body begin, his leg and hands particularly beginning to ache and jar his nervous system.

Remaining fully conscious of his surroundings, Nicolson managed to guide his parachute to take him inland, clear of the English Channel – a descent into the sea would have meant certain drowning in his parlous condition – then contrived to avoid a high tension cable; only to realise his ordeal by fire was not yet over when a group of trigger-happy volunteer 'soldiers' below opened fire at him, with one blast of 12-bore shot wounding him in a buttock.

Coming to earth in an open field, Nicolson remained immobile on the cool grass, unable to release himself from his parachute. From his original take-off from Boscombe Down at 1.5 p.m. his combat 'initiation' had lasted exactly 47 minutes to the moment when he finally baled out of his blazing Hurricane. Rushed immediately to a hospital in Southampton, Nicolson's life hung on a razor's edge for several days and nights; indeed, the first doctor to examine him gave Nicolson only 24 hours to live at most. Far away north, Nick's wife Muriel, only weeks away from the birth of their son, was unable to travel to be by his side.

The battle to live was solely a matter of Nicolson's will-power and the surgeons' skills. His strength of will eventually triumphed, and three weeks later Nicolson had recovered sufficiently to be removed to the RAF Hospital at Halton, the centre then for specialised treatment of burns, and by November 1940 he was a convalescent patient of the Palace Hotel 'hospital' in Torquay. His foot wound had by then healed, as had much of his facial burns and injuries, but his left hand was still virtually unusable, while his right hand had only begun to retrieve a fraction of its normal tractability of movement and control.

On 15 November 1940 the award of a Victoria Cross to Nicolson was promulgated, though Nicolson's personal notification of his award came in a telegram from King George VI, addressed to him at Torquay. Nicolson's immediate reaction was one of bewildered disbelief, and on showing the telegram privately to a close friend and fellow patient, F. 'Hiram' Smith, DFC, his first words were; 'Now I'll have to *earn* it ...'. Ten days after the announcement Nicolson received the cross from the King at Buckingham Palace.

Though still far from medically fit for full flying duties, Nicolson was soon agitating higher authorities for a flying post, preferably an operational job, and on 24 February 1941 he joined the instructional staff of No 54 OTU. His burned hands were slow to heal – he was to suffer bouts of pain from these until his death – but on 22 September 1941 he finally achieved his ambition to return to operations when he was promoted to command No 1459 Flight at Hibaldstow; a night fighter experimental unit flying Douglas Havoc 'Turbinlite' fighters, which was eventually retitled as No 538 Squadron. Remaining with this unit for some six months, Nicolson was then notified of an overseas posting, and on 17 March 1942 he became a staff officer at HQ No 293 Wing, Alipore in India; moving to another desk job at AHQ, Bengal in mid-December.

Continuing to plead for an active operational post, he got his wish on 4 August 1943, on which date he succeeded Wing Commander Harry Daish as commanding officer of No 27 Squadron, based at Agartala, Burma. No 27, known from its inception in 1915 as the 'Flying Elephants' – the motif of its official unit badge – had been the first unit to receive and operate Bristol Beaufighters in the Far East theatre of the war, and had also recently introduced the all-wood De Havilland Mosquito fighter-bomber to the jungle campaign. Tasked primarily with what were later to be termed 'interdiction' operations – attacking logistic ground targets – the 'Elephants' had already achieved a high reputation for its operational results, particularly in its tree-height sorties destroying Japanese road, rail and river transports.

Within days of arriving on the squadron, Nicolson began operational sorties on his unit's Beaufighters, usually with Flight Lieutenant Franklin as his navigator, and was soon adding his quota to the squadron's prodigious record of enemy transports destroyed or damaged. Though Japanese aircraft were rarely met by the 'Elephants' crews, such sorties at jungle height produced myriad hazards, where the loss of even one second's total concentration by pilots could invite instant disaster. Anti-aircraft fire, usually from 20 mm cannons, was normally deadly accurate and claimed several victims from the roving Beaufighters, while other dangers included a Japanese habit of stringing wires across rivers from trees to trees, obstacles virtually impossible for pilots to spot before too late for evasive moves.

Though enemy transports remained the squadron's prime

objectives at that period, the ubiquitous Beaufighters often attacked other 'opportunity' targets such as oil installations, supply dumps, Japanese troops on the move, and aerodrome strafes; an example of the latter was Myitkyina, the largest Japanese air base in the north, where one Beaufighter came upon a Japanese ceremonial parade drawn up in neat ranks in the open, about to honour their Emperor's birthday. Within seconds the Beau's 20 mm cannons had reduced the scene to a bloody shambles, with one shell severing the main flag-mast and draping its Rising Sun ensign over the bodies of its Colour Guard.

Christmas Day 1943 was celebrated by the 'Flying Elephants' with the first premeditated offensive sorties by the unit's DH Mosquitos, when Nicolson (with Franklin) in HX822 and Flying Officer Thompson/Sergeant Chippendale in HS811 left at 6.45 a.m. for a railway strafe, returning later with claims for several 'damaged' to record. The squadron continued to fly a mixture of Beaufighter and Mosquito operations, but on 9 March 1944 Nicolson flew the unit's ultimate Mosquito sortie, and thereafter the squadron remained an all-Beaufighter squadron; its few Mosquitos being handed over (mainly) to a photo-reconnaissance unit.

By that date 27 Squadron had moved to Parashuram, some 50 miles south of their former base, while on 25 March it received orders to move again, this time to Cholavaram, near Madras, where it came under the aegis of No 225 Group, and its role became anti-shipping strikes, alongside No 47 Squadron's Beaufighters. It meant learning to operate over sea instead of land, and for the first two months the air crews were mainly engaged in practice flying for their new role. Then, on 6 June 1944, Nicolson left the squadron, being posted to 3rd Tactical Air Force HQ as its Wing Commander Training. In August 1944 came the award of a DFC to Nicolson, its citation emphasising his; 'Fine example on many most hazardous sorties'.

He was to remain at an HQ staff desk for the remainder of his service, but the constant urge to return to operations led him to persuade his immediate superior to allow him 'one more trip'. On 2 May 1945, accordingly, he climbed aboard a Liberator bomber, KH210, of No 355 Squadron at Salbani, Bengal, officially listed as an 'observer'. Leaving Salbani minutes before 1 p.m. the Liberator had reached a point about 130 miles south of Calcutta en route to its objective when one engine suddenly burst into flames, and the bomber eventually crashed in the ocean. It was to be 16 hours before a Catalina flying boat located the scene of the crash, but found only two senior NCO survivors from the Liberator's crew complement. Wing Commander E.J.B.Nicolson, VC,DFC – RAF Fighter Command's sole VC of the 1939-45 war – had perished along with the rest of the crew.

Nearly 40 years later, on 27 April 1983, Nicolson's VC and other war medals were bought by the Battle of Britain Museum, Hendon, for a record figure of £110,000 when these were put up for auction by Nicolson's son, James.

CHAPTER NINE

Archibald McKellar

The date was 9 September 1940. The Battle of Britain had reached a crucial stage in daily attrition both for the Luftwaffe and, especially, RAF Fighter Command. The latter was barely recovering from many weeks of exhausting action and punitive losses in men and machines, and was only now slowly building its strength again as it continued to engage the seemingly endless armada of German raiders in southern England's skies each day. To the German air crews, however, any slenderness in RAF fighter opposition was by no means apparent on this date. Having collected an impressive quantity of fighter escorts off Calais-Boulogne, the German bombers set course for their prime objective, London, but long before reaching their target they ran into fierce opposition from an overall total of nine squadrons from the RAF's No 11 Group alone; defenders whose ferocity in engagement quickly scattered the orderly German formations.

One such intercepting unit was No 605 Squadron of the AAF, whose Hurricanes tackled one large gaggle of Heinkel He 111s. Leaving one section as top cover to thwart any interference from the German fighters, Blue Section began a diving, head-on attack from out of the sun, urged on by its leader's thickly Glasgow-accented voice saying, 'Right, lads. Each man pick his own target.'

Setting the example, the leader set his sight on the leading Heinkel of a Vic-three section and at 700 yards gave it a broadside from all of his eight wing guns. The German's wings spurted flames as it reeled under the impact. A second later the Hurricane leader switched his fire towards the left-hand Heinkel of the trio, but at that instant his original victim exploded and the third Heinkel erupted in flames, turned on its back, and fell away. Then the second Heinkel lost a wing and spun down in a crazy parabola. The Hurricane's fire had destroyed three Heinkels in just one savage attack. Later the same day the same Hurricane pilot claimed a Bf 109 to bring the day's tally to four; just one more example of this particular pilot's multiple-victory days during the high summer of 1940.

His full name was Archibald Ashmore McKellar, though he was inevitably called 'Archie' by his fellow pilots. A 'pocket Hercules' – his immensely strong, compact body stood only about five feet and three inches in height – McKellar was a Scot, born in Paisley in 1912. Educated at Shawlands Academy, young McKellar's immediate ambition on completing his schooling was to follow in his father's footsteps and become a plasterer, but his father's insistence that his son should instead choose a 'professional career' meant that the boy first took up employment in a stockbroker's office. Nevertheless, his determination soon wore down his father's opposition and Archie was indentured as an apprentice plasterer for five years in his father's firm; a period during which the youngster received no special privileges or treatment even though he was the boss's son.

Though small in stature, Archie was something of a fitness fanatic, constantly taking physical exercise, building up great strength in body, and excelling in virtually every sport available to him. Though he enjoyed good food and wine, and smoked a pipe or occasional cigar, McKellar kept himself in peak athletic condition throughout his all-too brief life, and even at the height of constant action during the Battle of Britain was always clean-shaven and immaculately dressed at all times.

Even as a boy McKellar nursed a second ambition – to fly. During the final year of his apprenticeship as a plasterer, he made enquiries privately about enlistment in the local Auxiliary Air Force, discovered that he would be acceptable for a place with No 602 (City of Glasgow) Squadron, AAF, and promptly discussed this with his father – only to meet complete opposition to the idea. Refusing to agree to what he regarded as a dangerous occupation, his father was adamant, resulting in McKellar secretly joining the Scottish Flying Club and paying for flying lessons out of his own pocket. Completing his apprenticeship, Archie remained with his father's firm, eventually becoming general foreman, but continued with his flying and gaining a pilot's certificate. His love for flying, and the skills he displayed, brought him to the notice of the Marquess of Clydesdale (later, Duke of Hamilton), the commander of 602 Squadron AAF, and in 1936 Archie McKellar was commissioned as a Pilot Officer in this unit, being promoted to Flying Officer on 8 May 1938.

Formed in September 1925 as a bomber unit, 602 Squadron's role was changed to Army Co-operation in 1938, then in January 1939 became a fighter squadron at Abbotsinch by exchanging its Hawker Hectors for Gloster Gauntlets. Working up to operational standards on the Gauntlets, the squadron began exchanging these for Spitfires in May 1939, the first AAF unit to receive R.J.Mitchell's brainchild fighter. Coming under the aegis of No 13 Group, Fighter Command from July 1939, the squadron was fully mobilised for war on 28 August that year, and on 6 October moved to its war station at Grangemouth, then in the same month moved again to Drem. By then its commander was Squadron Leader Andrew Farquhar, the former C Flight commander who had become 602's latest CO on 26 October 1937.

It fell to the Auxiliaries of Nos 602 and 603 Squadrons – both based at Drem – to draw first blood against the Luftwaffe in its earliest attempts to attack British territorial targets. The first Luftwaffe venture came on 16 October 1939, when a Junkers Ju 88 of KG30, based at Sylt, was reported over the RN anchorage in the Firth of Forth. Three 602 Squadron Spitfires managed to intercept and attack this Ju 88, though without visible result. Later the same day nine more Ju 88s of I/KG30 arrived over the same area, intent on bombing HMS *Hood* at its anchorage. A combined force of 602's and 603's Spitfires, led by Farquhar, tackled the Junkers and brought down two (one each by each squadron) into the sea; a victory in which McKellar shared. Then, on 28 October, McKellar was primarily responsible in the shooting down of a Heinkel He 111 onto the Lammermuir Hills – the first German aircraft brought down on British soil since 1918.

A few weeks later, on 29 November, McKellar was patrolling near Tranent when he spotted anti-aircraft fire bursts northwards and promptly investigated. Finding a lone He 111 he attacked several times, silencing the Heinkel's rear gun defence and setting its port engine on fire. As the German pilot attempted to land his crippled machine, three more Spitfires attacked it for good measure, but the 'victory' was confirmed as rightfully belonging to McKellar. It was to be his last combat for many months as the winter closed in and aerial activity entered a period of monotonous and unproductive routine patrols for 602 Squadron.

On 21 June 1940, however, McKellar was promoted to Flight Lieutenant for a posting to No 605 Squadron AAF to fill a vacancy for a Flight commander. From the start of his command of this Flight McKellar instituted a strict code of discipline for his subordinates, insisting that all should be correctly dressed and well turned out at all times, extending this particularly to air discipline. Yet despite such measures he became regarded with huge respect and his personal popularity achieved equal heights as he devoted most waking hours to welding his Flight into an efficient, well-disciplined fighting team. While intensely loyal to anyone he considered to be a friend, McKellar's attitude to others was either of utmost friendliness or utter dislike; a man without a devious thought in his head, he tended to see everything and everyone in pure black or dazzling white, with no 'grey shades' between these extremes.

No 605 Squadron, commanded by Squadron Leader W.M.Churchill, DSO,DFC, was still based at Drem, but was equipped with Hurricanes. On 15 August McKellar re-opened his combat tally in spectacular fashion, as he subsequently described his action in a letter to his mother.

On Thursday, at 12 o'clock, I was sent off with my Flight to patrol Newcastle at 20,000 feet. We all arrived safely and remained there until 1.30, when I saw 70 to 80 Nasties in one big formation, followed by a second formation of 20 to 30. They were approaching Newcastle from the south. I whipped into them with my Flight. I got three down, with one more possible, and the rest of the boys got five down and seven possible – possible being when the Hun breaks away from the formation with engines out or flames coming but is not seen to crash. By this time there was a lot more of our fighters, so everyone gave the Nasties the fright of their lives. I was very proud. The Air Vice-Marshal came along and congratulated the Flight on their good show. It really was, as the majority were all new and inexperienced. Two of the boys were shot down, but without damage to one, and only scalp and head wounds to the other, so I reckon it was pretty good going.

A few days later McKellar was awarded a DFC, then, on 7 September, the squadron flew south to join the main battle, becoming based at Croydon and controlled by Kenley. Next morning 605 Squadron was scrambled to join 253 Squadron in tackling a mixed batch of Dorniers, Ju 88s, and Bf 109s near Tunbridge Wells; while in the afternoon, over Aldershot, Archie claimed one of five enemy aircraft destroyed by 605's men, though two Hurricanes were lost. On 9 September came McKellar's 'four-in-a-day' score already related, followed by several more claims in the following week, resulting in a further award of a Bar to his DFC, its citation quoting him as destroying eight enemy aircraft in eight days' fighting. One of these had in fact been a night combat on 16 September, when McKellar took off alone into the night sky and caught a Heinkel raider when it became coned by searchlights.

On 29 September Squadron Leader Churchill left 605 Squadron on appointment to command of the first American-manned 'Eagle' Squadron, No 71, and Archie McKellar was promoted in his place as 605's new commander. On 7 October, while leading his squadron, McKellar met a formation of fifteen Bf 109s, with waves of some 40-50 more not far behind them, over the Sevenoaks area. Getting his men up-sun, Archie ordered them into a line astern 'file', then attacked the leading fifteen Bf 109s:

I attacked the Number One and saw a bomb dropped from this machine. I fired and pieces fell off his wing and dense white smoke or vapour came from him as he went into a violent outside spin. In my mirror I could see another 109 coming to attack me and therefore turned sharply right and found myself just below and behind another 109. I opened fire and saw my De Wilde (*incendiary ammunition*) hitting this machine. It burst into flames and went down inverted east of Biggin Hill. As I again had a 109 on my tail I spiralled down to 15,000 feet and by this time there appeared to be 109s straggling all over the sky. I followed one, pulled my boost control, and made up on him. I gave a burst from dead astern and at once his radiator appeared to be hit as dense white vapour came back at me and my windscreen fogged up. This speedily cleared and I gave another burst and this machine burst into flames and fell into a wood with a quarry near it, west of Maidstone.

Still not content, McKellar next latched on to a fourth 109 which seemed to be dodging in and out of cloud cover, closed to pointblank range, fired, and saw the German pilot bale out. Two hours later McKellar was back in the air and shot down another Bf 109, his fifth possible victim of the day.

McKellar's success in combat was primarily due to his exceptional eyesight and no less his outstanding marksmanship in air-to-air shooting, yet paradoxically, when on the ground practising with a rifle or 12-bore shotgun his shooting was, if anything, well below average; a trait he shared with many other high-scoring fighter pilots. Undoubtedly too his constant obsession with physical fitness meant that his mind and body were always at a peak of alertness, able to react with lightning swiftness to each and every shift of situation when engaged in combat.

Nor was his personal prowess in action his only asset to his squadron, possessing as he did remarkable, yet instinctive leadership qualities which were supplemented by a natural aggressive fighting spirit. Highly strung, vociferous, and blunt in speech, Archie McKellar's direct honesty and outgoing nature singled him out in any company. His dedication to his job as a fighter, and fighter-leader, led him to refuse any leave from his squadron while the battle lasted, and he invariably led from the front on every possible occasion.

His restless aggressive instinct was further exemplified on 20 October when he led 605 into a clash with a force of Bf 109s over Ashford, destroying one with one concentrated burst; while on 27 October yet another Bf 109 fell to his superb deflection shooting; his 20th claimed combat victory with 605 Squadron. Early in the morning of 1 November – the day *after* the official British closing date for the Battle of Britain – Archie McKellar was, as always, awake and ready for action as dawn broke. A report of enemy activity soon after saw him take off at 0740 hours in Hurricane V6878 for a lone patrol – and he was never seen alive again. Eye witnesses later reported that his Hurricane fell from high altitude, then flew a crazy, inverted circuit of a country mansion before finally plunging into its garden. Nearby was found the wreckage of a Bf 109, which many fellow pilots believe was Archie McKellar's final victory. As the 605 Squadron war diarist recorded that evening:

A sad day for the squadron as Squadron Leader McKellar was killed on the morning patrol. His charming personality, generosity, wit and vivacity will be much missed not only by the squadron but by all with whom he came in contact.

Seven days later the *London Gazette* announced the award of a DSO to Archie McKellar, crediting him with at least twenty enemy aircraft shot down.

On 16 January 1941 Sir Archibald Sinclair, Secretary of State for Air, visited Glasgow where, in a speech of reply to his official welcome, he included:

'Not long ago I visited a fighter squadron which was taking part during the dark days in the battle of this island. That squadron had lost its leader in an air fight – and they felt the loss. He had been wounded in combat and had been withdrawn from service. I found in his place, taking the air with daring and resolve, proving himself a leader amongst leaders, a young Scot. His name was McKellar. He had come from the City of Glasgow Squadron to lift up this squadron in its dark hour and to carry it on to fresh victories and achievement by his spirit. It was quite apparent to me that he had the whole squadron with him. He was regarded with the greatest admiration and affection by his officers. I will never forget the impression he made upon me when I saw him.'

For John McKellar, Archie's father, it had been a poignant moment when King George VI handed to him his dead son's DSO,DFC and Bar awards at a Buckingham Palace investiture.

'You must be very proud of him', remarked the King, and John could only nod, remembering the boy whom he had tried to stop becoming a pilot – 'a dangerous occupation, Archie'.

CHAPTER TEN

Keith Truscott

Keith William Truscott – inevitably 'Bluey' to all fellow Australians because of his mop of red-gold hair – was used to being a winner, a leader, from his earliest years. Born at Prahran, an inner suburb of Melbourne, on 17 May 1916, Truscott grew into a stocky, heavy-muscled, natural athlete who revelled in all forms of competitive sport and excelled in most. During his education at Melbourne High School he became captain of the school's cricket XI,* Rules football XVIII, and the school's athletic champion for two years running. He was also a prefect, captain of Forrest House, and matriculated with honours, displaying a natural academic ability not always commonly associated with top sporting figures at the school. Truscott was also the despair of his tutors occasionally because of his cavalier attitude to some facets of 'the rules'; often challenging book-rigid authority in hair-raising escapades.

The combination of all these distinctions placed Truscott well into the limelight, a position he accepted with relish, and which well suited his highly extrovert nature. Yet Truscott's firm convictions as to his many abilities had no basis in mere shallow conceit. He simply accepted his God-given talents and used them to their utmost when the occasion demanded, but almost every night of his life he knelt by his bedside to say his prayers before retiring. On any sports field he became a relentless fighter, constantly urging and inspiring his team to win, and the harder the fight, the more Truscott enjoyed himself.

On leaving school Truscott became an accounts clerk, but continued his many sporting activities, concentrating particularly on Australian Rules football in which he represented Melbourne and quickly became a local hero for his aggressive, yet cheerful

---

* One small member of the XI was Keith Miller, the later Test player.

performances, and soon became nationally known for his prowess. With the outbreak of the European war in 1939, Truscott, like so many of his generation of young Aussies, took stock of his life. His desk job was hardly compatible with his instinctive urge for a more active form of living; it would be no hardship to leave his office, while the call for volunteers from Australian youth to enlist in one of the armed Services was almost irresistible to one of Truscott's temperament. Accordingly, Bluey volunteered to join the RAAF for training as a pilot, and was eventually enlisted on 21 July 1940.

Posted to the Initial Training Course at Somers, near Western Port Bay, Truscott passed through this nominal two-months inculcation period in one month, passing out with distinction, yet met the first obstacle to his hitherto sublime self-confidence when, on being tested in the Link Trainer simulator, he could not control it, being thoroughly confused and unco-ordinated in handling the 'cardboard fighter'.

Passing on to No 3 EFTS for *ab initio* instruction in real aeroplanes, Truscott found to his dismay that his handling of the unit's De Havilland Tiger Moth trainers was little better. While most pupil-pilots were judged able to fly their first solo after six to eight hours' dual instruction, Truscott was still struggling to master his Tiger Moth after sixteen hours' dual. Fortunately for him his instructor, Pilot Officer Roy Goon, was a patient, understanding man, convinced of Truscott's eventual potential, and the day finally came when Bluey was let off the leash and sent off solo, which he managed to accomplish without breaking anything. The first hurdle was behind him.

In November 1940 Truscott and his fellow embryo pilots sailed from Sydney to Canada, arriving here on 20 November, and eventually arriving at Camp Borden, Ontario for their final training. Truscott's flying in the station's Harvards still showed no great promise, but his overt keenness and determination to win undoubtedly influenced the instructional staff because on 11 February 1941, when Truscott and his fellow Aussies paraded to receive their 'wings' 'Bluey' was commissioned as a Pilot Officer, but most of his companions received Sergeant's chevrons. On 6 March the freshly graduated pilots sailed from Canada to

England, and were sent to No 57 OTU, Hawarden. Here they worked up on tired Hurricanes and Miles Masters, and then were converted onto Spitfires.

Despite his ham-handed style of flying to date, Truscott's first tentative flight in a Spitfire seemed to transform his clumsiness into smooth, co-ordinated control. Man and machine seemed destined to be married, and Truscott, for the first time, felt completely at ease and relaxed as he put the graceful fighter through its paces. It was the start of a 'love affair' between the brash Australian and the Spitfire which was never to be diminished in Truscott's heart. At the OTU Truscott's flying technique in a Spitfire blossomed, and he was soon able to perform fluid aerobatics, while at the same time showing an instinctive skill in air-to-air shooting. Then, on 5 May 1941, came his posting to his first operational unit, No 452 Squadron, RAAF.

As the first RAAF unit to be formed in Britain during World War Two, No 452 Squadron was initially formed on 8 April 1941 at Kirton-in-Lindsey, Lincolnshire, with sixteen Spitfire Is. It was first commanded by Squadron Leader Roy Dutton, DFC, a 19-victory RAF veteran of the battles of France and Britain,* while two other RAF veterans, Flight Lieutenants Brendan Finucane† and Graham Douglas‡, were the Flight commanders. By 10 May a total of twenty RAAF pilots had arrived from the OTU, including Keith Truscott, and intensive training began almost immediately to bring the 'Aussie squadron' up to operational fitness as soon as possible. By 22 May the squadron was officially declared operational for purely defensive action, then on 2 June it was declared fully operational. By then its Spitfire Is had been exchanged for Mk IIas.

When first arriving at Kirton-in-Lindsey, Truscott was allocated to share a room in the officers' mess with Brendan Finucane, and it was to be the start of a friendship so close that they might have been blood-brothers. Indeed, 'Paddy' Finucane's previous RAF service ran curiously in parallel with Truscott's in

* Later, Air Commodore R.G.Dutton, CBE,DSO,DFC
† Later, Wing Commander B.E.Finucane, DSO,DFC, and killed on operations on 15 June 1942
‡ Later, Wing Commander A.G.Douglas, DFC

certain respects. He too had been a ham-fisted pilot during his training, taking over fourteen hours of dual instruction in Tiger Moths before being considered competent enough to go solo, and continuing to be rated 'below average' on his FTS.

Eventually, after some two years' frustration, Finucane achieved his original ambition to become a fighter pilot when posted to the fighter OTU at Hawarden in June 1940. After just two weeks' conversion flying on Spitfires, Paddy was posted to No 65 Squadron in July and was operational within five days of arrival. In the following month Finucane claimed five enemy aircraft destroyed or damaged within 48 hours of furious combat, while in early 1941, prior to his posting to 452 he had claimed a further four victories and been recommended for a DFC award.*
From Finucane the red-headed Australian was to learn the basics of aerial combat, saying later, 'I owe a great deal to Paddy Finucane. He coached me in air fighting and taught me everything I needed to know, both before and after we started ops.' He also added on a personal plane, 'Paddy was the best bloke I've ever met outside Australia' – praise indeed from the ebullient Truscott.

For 452 Squadron the first war casualty occurred before it got to grips properly with the Luftwaffe, when on 5 July young Andy Costello from Queensland was killed by a German intruder while landing at night. By then Roy Dutton had been succeeded in command of the squadron by an Australian, Squadron Leader Bob Bungey, who had arrived on the squadron on 10 June. Truscott flew his first operational sortie on 8 July, in Spitfire P8879, but the squadron's first big 'show' came three days later when 452 was detailed to fly first to West Malling, refuel there, then along with seven other fighter squadrons provide escort for a lone Blenheim on Circus 44, itself a diversionary force for Circus 45 which was due to be flown some 40 minutes after the diversion. Some five miles west of Lille, at 3 p.m. came 452's first clash with the Luftwaffe over France, when eight Messerschmitt Bf 109s tried to bounce 452 from behind. Spotted by Finucane's ever-sharp eyes, these were avoided as they made a diving attack,

* Awarded on 25 April 1941

then Finucane turned behind one Bf 109, gave him a 90-rounds burst at 150 yards, and saw the German pilot promptly bale out – 452 Squadron RAAF was truly blooded.

On 21 June 1941 the Australian squadron moved south to Kenley, a pleasant pre-war 'permanent' station on a plateau in Surrey, just south of London, where it joined Nos 602 and 485 Squadrons to form the all-Spitfire Kenley Wing. This move pleased the eager Australians – from now on 'trade' would be lively. On 2 August the Canadian Wing Commander Johnny Kent, DFC,AFC arrived to take up his appointment as the Kenley Wing Leader, and next day the Wing took part in a Circus at St Omer, encountering several gaggles of Bf 109s, two of which were shot down and a third severely damaged. For Truscott the clash gave him an opportunity to try out his deflection shooting on one skidding Messerschmitt, but his fire completely missed his target – his operational 'eyes' had yet to become accustomed to the lightning cut and thrust of close combat. Nevertheless, his keenness to learn soon sharpened up his reflexes and his first combat success came on 9 August. On that date five fighter Wings escorted five Blenheim bombers on Circus 68 to attack a power station at Gosnay, near Béthune, with Kent's Kenley Wing sharing the target support role with Douglas Bader's Tangmere Wing. Ten-tenths cloud obscured Gosnay, so the secondary target, Gravelines, became the objective.

En route to the latter the Spitfires had to fight off various formations of German fighters, totalling about 100 overall. In one clash with eight Bf 109s over St Omer Truscott was jumped by three Bf 109s, one of which overshot him from behind.* Turning quickly onto its tail Truscott gave it a five-seconds' burst and shattered its tail unit, then saw it dive headlong to earth out of control. Crossing out over the coast Truscott ran a gauntlet of flak, which piqued him and made him turn back at some 200 feet to strafe the harbour defences before resuming his flight across the Channel, still being fired at by flak guns for several miles out to sea. During that same sprawling combat Douglas Bader went

---

* Truscott was flying Spitfire II, P7973, which today is in the Australian War Memorial's Aeroplane Hall at Canberra.

down in his crippled Spitfire, baled out, and became a prisoner of war.

Three sorties were flown on 16 August, and on the third of these – Circus 75 to St Omer – Finucane led his 452 Squadron pilots in a diving attack on eight Bf 109s north-east of Boulogne. The ensuing combat was fierce but brief, with the Australian unit claiming seven victims; one of these by Truscott whose combined 20 mm cannon and machine gun fire sent one Bf 109 down to crash in a field. Three days later, on Circus 81 to Gosnay, Truscott claimed his third victory by gouging a chunk out of a Bf 109's wing and seeing it fall vertically with no hope of recovery.

By September Truscott had been promoted to Flying Officer, and his name had begun to be publicised, along with Finucane and certain other 452 Australians, back in Australia, but he did not add to his combat tally until 18 September, on which date, during Circus 99 to Rouen, Bluey, flying Spitfire Vb,AB781, had his hairiest moments to date. A foul-up by one of the Hurricane escort squadrons disjointed the overall protective fighter cover for the Blenheims, and before the mix-up could be sorted out a flock of determined Bf 109s descended on the Circus. Within seconds the Spitfires were split all over the sky, each fighting individually, with little co-ordination. Truscott found himself being chased at close quarters by one Bf 109, kicked his Spitfire sideways, then closed on his pursuer and gave it one burst of cannon. The Messerschmitt wilted under the shells' impact, rolled sideways, then exploded. Continuing his dive to 100 feet, Truscott teamed up with Flight Lieutenant Douglas, heading north-west towards the Channel, and ran into three Bf 109s which attacked the pair of Spitfires from the beam in line astern. Turning in towards the Germans, Truscott lined his sight on the middle Bf 109, hit it squarely with a two-seconds' burst, and saw it belch black smoke as it fell almost to sea-level before managing to scrape over the cliffs and disappear inland. Landing at Manston because he was short of fuel, Truscott had to be helped out of his cockpit due to his nervous reaction setting in after the recent combat – and was then violently sick on the grass.

Two days later Bluey took part in the biggest combined fighter escort sweep yet mounted; a triple Circus operation involving a total of seven fighter Wings – 23 squadrons, some 270 Spitfires – escorting some 18 Blenheims and Hampdens to three different targets simultaneously. The Kenley Wing flew with Circus 100B to Abbeville's rail yards as top cover, with the Biggin Hill Wing below providing close escort for the Hampden bombers. The layered formation penetrated to within five miles of the target before meeting any opposition, then things happened fast, with successive rushes of Bf 109Fs tackling the Spitfires.

Within seconds 452's pilots were engaged in single combats, and Truscott, in Spitfire W3605, chased one Messerschmitt hard but failed to get within firing range. Abandoning the chase, he looked around for the other Spitfires but saw with a shock that he was alone; the nearest Spitfires milling in combat at least three miles away. Climbing back to 20,000 feet and hoping to rejoin the general brawl, he spotted a stray Bf 109 crossing his flight path, apparently unaware of Truscott. Turning on to the German's beam 'Bluey' dived in to within point-blank range, gave it a full deflection burst and saw his shells hitting the 109's fuselage. The German nosed down at full throttle with Truscott keeping pace until the 109 flew straight into the ground with a flaming explosion.

Easing his Spitfire upwards again Truscott found empty skies, so turned westwards to head for the coast. Four Spitfires in neat formation flashed across his bow so he joined them in the rear – enemy skies were not friendly to lone Spitfires – but as they reached the coastline Truscott could see a batch of 109s queuing up in line astern behind him, about to attack. He bellowed a warning to the other Spitfires over his R/T, with no response – the other Spitfires must have been tuned to another R/T channel and continued blissfully on in formation towards home – leaving Truscott to break away on his own and meet the incoming 109s head-on. At 150 yards and closing, Bluey fired at the leading German, tearing chunks of metal off it. The crippled Messerschmitt fell away to an unknown fate. Seconds later Truscott, weaving desperately to avoid the vengeful onslaughts of the other 109s, saw a pair of his tormentors below him, heading out to sea. In a burst of sheer anger Truscott ignored everything else and dived on this pair, plastering the rear 109 with a prolonged burst of cannon. His target slowed, yawed, then dived at full power straight into the sea. Still fighting off attempts by the remaining 109s, Bluey sped out to sea and eventually found haven in some thick haze. Landing at the first airfield he met, near Portsmouth, Truscott telephoned Kenley to report while his Spitfire was refuelled, then flew back to base, where the returning 452 pilots were met by a horde of newsmen eager to create new headlines.

Next day Truscott notched up another victory – destroying a Bf 109 – by which time photographs and semi-sensational news texts about 452 Squadron were reaching Australia, with Truscott and Finucane's names receiving top billing. Bluey now became a national hero 'down under', and on 29 September he was promoted to Flight Lieutenant to take over command of B Flight, taking up his new appointment on 3 October after a few days' leave, while next day came the award of a DFC. His fame had also spread around Britain, resulting in a particular Spitfire, AB994, being allotted to Truscott which had been 'bought' by donations from 'Red-Heads of Britain' and which Truscott had named 'Gingerbread'.

Losing little time in returning to the action, Truscott claimed two Bf 109s as damaged on 12 October; while next day the Kenley Wing were close escort for six Blenheims attacking Arques on Circus 108A. Luftwaffe opposition was stiff, and Truscott destroyed two Bf 109s during a series of combats. From one of these, its pilot baled out, and Truscott deliberately shot at him as he descended by parachute. On their return to Kenley, Truscott's close friend Bardie Wawn told Bluey; 'You're a bastard, shooting at that Jerry in the parachute.' Truscott's reply was: 'He might have gone up tomorrow and shot you down'. A few days previously Bluey had seen a German pilot shooting at a parachuting RAF pilot, and had sworn to do the same to the next Jerry who baled out. In his log book that night Truscott wrote, 'One Hun parachutist shot' – then never mentioned the subject again.

On 21 October Truscott added another Bf 109 destroyed to his mounting score; followed by a pair of 109s shot down on 23 October. Even as his shells were ripping away his second victim's tail unit that day, he felt the jarring of cannon shells ripping into his Spitfire's starboard wing, while other hits had ruptured his petrol tank and reduced his rudder to shreds. Informing his leader, Bungey, of his predicament, Truscott started to evacuate his cockpit but in his haste accidentally pulled his dinghy release and the self-inflating dinghy started filling the cockpit, preventing him leaving. With near superhuman effort Truscott pushed himself out, his parachute cracked open, then he hit the sea and went deep. The water was freezing cold, and his sole support was his Mae West 'waistcoat', but he was retrieved shortly after by an air-sea rescue launch directed to him by Bob Bungey circling high above. November 1941 brought Truscott three more victories – all Bf 109s destroyed, one on the 6th and a pair on 8 November – and then the winter clamped down on most flying.

With Bungey being promoted and posted, Bluey Truscott was promoted to Squadron Leader in command of 452 Squadron on 25 January 1942. On 12 February the whole squadron left for a patrol along the French coast, seeking prey, and led by the irrepressible Irishman Group Captain Victor Beamish. The only enemy aircraft met was a lone Heinkel 115 floatplane, which promptly became the focus of thirteen Spitfires' undivided attentions, with predictable result. On 9 March, however, Bluey found worthier opponents, destroying one Bf 109 and damaging a second; while on 14 March he claimed his last victory with 452 Squadron by shooting down a Focke Wulf Fw 190. That day also brought the announcement of the award of a Bar to his DFC. Three days later Truscott received orders for his posting back to Australia, and on 14 May he arrived back in his native city to a hero's welcome, and also became unwittingly a leading figure in a fierce controversy.

Australian operational air crews then beginning to return from Europe were being ordered to relinquish all acting ranks (and, therefore, pay rates) achieved in Britain *et al.* Truscott naturally fought against any such ill-advised demotions, refusing to take off his hard-earned Squadron Leader's rank rings, and in the event, due partly to a huge public and Service outcry against such bureaucratic nonsense, the 'demotion' orders were officially rescinded. Nevertheless, the relatively few senior posts available on RAAF squadrons then meant that Truscott (and others of similar background and rank) could not be appointed to appropriate commands. So they posted Bluey to No 76 Squadron RAAF as a supernumerary Squadron Leader to fill a Flight commander's vacancy.

No 76 Squadron was a Curtiss P-40 Kittyhawk unit, commanded by a veteran of the Middle East fighter operations, Squadron Leader P. St G.Turnbull, and originally formed on 14 March 1942 in Queensland. The majority of its pilots were inexperienced in operational flying, and were not entirely happy to learn that the much-lauded Bluey Truscott was to join them; a normal Servicemen's aversion to personal publicity, though few (if any) had actually met Truscott as yet. When Bluey did arrive on the squadron, however, his usual infectious sense of humour and all-out enthusiasm quickly modified the suspicions of the other pilots. After his experience in Spitfires though, Truscott was not so enthusiastic about flying Kittyhawks – 'like a bloody carthorse after flying Spits' – but at least he was back on operations, which helped compensate.

Joining 76 in July 1942, Truscott received a telegram from his old fighting partner Paddy Finucane on 15 July, which said; 'I miss your ugly mug. When are you coming back?' A few days later Bluey was told that Finucane was dead – drowned with his Spitfire while trying to fly back from a sortie with a damaged aircraft on the day Truscott had received that telegram. Finucane's death cut deeply into Truscott's soul – he and Finucane had planned to set up in business together in Australia after the war.

On 19 July No 76 Squadron began preparations to move to Milne Bay, New Guinea, and the Kittyhawks were flown in to the new air strip on 25 July. In August and September Truscott and his fellow Kittyhawk pilots were in daily action, repelling attempts by the Japanese to invade Milne Bay, with Truscott earning a Mentioned in Dispatches for his individual efforts. On 27 August the squadron CO, Peter Turnbull, was killed in action and Bluey took over command of 76, finally leading his unit back to Australia in October for a rest and refurbishment. The squadron then became responsible for fighter support and defence in the

North-Western Area, mainly guarding Darwin in the Northern Territory, and on the night of 21 January 1943 Truscott took off into the night sky, intercepted three Japanese Mitsubishi 'Betty' bombers and shot one down.

By 12 February No 76 Squadron had been moved to Exmouth Gulf to guard the American submarine base there. From here he and his men flew various protection escorts for US Navy Catalina flying boats operating from the waters of the Gulf, and on 28 March Bluey and one of his pilots, Ian Louden, were following a Catalina back to Exmouth at the end of one such patrol. As Exmouth came into view, Truscott and Louden began a few fighter 'attack' manoeuvres around the Catalina – a diversion from monotony often practised by the Kittyhawk men on these sorties. Louden dived from astern of the flying boat, then broke away underneath it and curved upwards for his next 'attack', watching Truscott, in Kittyhawk A29-150, begin a similar 'attack'.

The sea below was glassy calm, and the Catalina was letting down in altitude for its approach to landing as Truscott bore in from the rear. He failed to see the Catalina lower its wing-tip floats preparatory to landing, misjudged the nearness of the flat sea surface, and tried to break away *under* the flying boat as Louden had done. His Kittyhawk's propeller hit the sea, the aircraft bounced flatly forward, then erupted in flames and plunged into the water. The time was 5.35 p.m. local time.

Nearby American ships' crews were quick into action, sending down divers, but to no avail, and Truscott's aircraft was not located until 10 a.m. the following day, lying on its back in 36 feet of water with its wings folded back and Bluey Truscott still strapped in the cockpit. His body was recovered and was found to be virtually unmarked, and they flew him home to be interred eventually in the Perth War Cemetery. By an ironic twist of fate, Truscott had died in exactly the same manner as his greatest friend, Paddy Finucane – trapped in a fighter cockpit in the depths of an unforgiving sea.

CHAPTER ELEVEN

Jean Demozay

When, on 21 June 1940, the proud nation of France was humbled by having to sign an armistice with Hitler in an old rail restaurant car in the forest of Compiègne – the very same carriage in which Imperial Germany had surrendered to France and her Allies in 1918 – the French nation became virtually divided between those who accepted defeat and, in many cases, even collaborated with the German occupation forces, and others who were determined to continue the fight against Nazidom in any or every way possible, no matter what the cost. For many French Servicemen Britain remained the only bastion of continuing opposition to Hitler's grandiose dreams of global conquest, and many thousands made their individual ways to England, often in fraught circumstances. There they were quickly merged with Britain's armed Services initially and, eventually, were often formed into all-French fighting units. Just one such Frenchman determined to fight on was Jean Francois Demozay, a man who had always refused to acknowledge defeat in any endeavour, and who pursued a lone crusade throughout his all-too brief life.

A native of Nantes, where he was born on 23 March 1915 as the son of a weaver, Demozay was educated locally at Beaugency and Nantes, and on 15 October 1936 was conscripted for national service in the French Army Transportation Service, only to be discharged on the grounds of ill-health four weeks later. On 12 November 1937 he was again conscripted to the Army Transportation Service, and again was discharged for health reasons on 26 November. The outbreak of war saw him re-enlisted in his old regiment on 9 September 1939, only to be discharged for a third time on the same grounds of frail health, but Demozay refused to remain a civilian whilst his country was at war, and he next volunteered for service in the French Armée de l'Air on 3 February 1940, being accepted as an *Aspirant* (pupil pilot) with No 217 *Bataillon*.*

Meanwhile he had become accepted by the RAF as an interpreter at Rheims HQ, and by October 1939 was attached to No 1 Squadron RAF for this duty. Remaining with this unit for the rest of the 1939-40 French campaign, Demozay managed to wangle a few flying lessons in RAF communication 'hack' aircraft from some pilots prior to the May 1940 German *blitzkrieg*, but his main duties remained interpreter and general 'welfare officer' to 1 Squadron's crews. Nevertheless, in late April 1940 Demozay piloted the squadron's 'hack' Miles Magister to Amiens, carrying Pilot Officer Billy Drake in the spare seat, who was to collect a new Hurricane from the Amiens Maintenance Unit (MU) to ferry back to his squadron. Drake slept throughout the journey and on arrival at Amiens was surprised to see that the Magister had suffered some fabric damage on its wings. Asking Demozay why, the cool reply from the Frenchman was that they had been attacked by some roving Messerschmitts en route and he had flown through the branches of a tree while taking violent evasive action!

From 10 May 1940 No 1 Squadron became embroiled in constant combat action throughout each day, and was forced to change its airfields at a moment's notice as the German juggernaut penetrated deeper into France. By 16 June orders were received that the unit was to withdraw to England, and from Nantes airfield at midnight on 17 June the last RAF party left by road. Next morning the twelve remaining Hurricanes took off at 1145 hours bound for England, leaving behind them the sixteen groundcrew airmen who had volunteered to stay and ensure the aircraft and pilots got away safely, and Jean Demozay. The latter had received an order to report to the French HQ, but had no intention of staying in a defeated France as long as there was any chance of continuing his war against Germany. The sixteen 'erks' were due to be taken by road to La Rochelle, but the chaotic state of the French road system by then offered only a slim chance that

* From available documentation this appears to have been merely a 'paper' posting. Indeed, several accounts of Demozay's early years credit him with being a civil pilot prior to 1939, but no confirmation of this has been discovered.

they would arrive safely or in time to be evacuated to England.

On the airfield, along with much other abandoned equipment, stood a Bristol Bombay twin-engined transport aircraft, its fuel tanks brimful, but with a broken tail wheel. Demozay asked the airmen if they could rig a temporary repair to the tail wheel, which they proceeded to fix while the Frenchman climbed into the unfamiliar aircraft cockpit and studied the strange instruments and controls. Finally, with all sixteen airmen aboard, and a Sergeant engine fitter at his side to operate the throttles, Demozay accomplished a very shaky take-off and headed the lumbering Bombay towards England.

His intended venue was Tangmere aerodrome on the south coast but when the Sergeant pointed out that most of his airmen lived in the East Anglia region, Demozay politely obliged them by landing at Sutton Bridge instead. Here he met Billy Drake, just released from a hospital where he had been treated for wounds received in France, and Drake told him that most of the original 1 Squadron pilots who survived the French campaign were now posted as instructors to No 5 OTU, Aston Down. Borrowing some money from Drake, Demozay promptly set off for the OTU, determined to become a fully fledged fighter pilot with the RAF.

Accepted by the RAF for training, Demozay followed the war-time practice of adopting a *nom de guerre* in order to protect his family and other relatives still in France from German reprisals. Being a Breton by birth, Demozay selected the name of a Breton town for his surname and henceforth became officially referred to as 'Moses Morlaix', a pseudonym which, curiously, he was to continue to be referred to in French official documentation in the immediate post-1945 era.

In his ten weeks at Aston Down, Demozay learned to fly Hurricanes and on 16 October 1940 arrived at Wittering, near Stamford to join the ranks of No 1 Squadron. Here he was given further intensive instruction in flying and fighting the Hurricane, and on 8 November 1940, while on a solo training flight, spotted a Junkers Ju 88 east of Sutton Bridge. Diving immediately, Demozay closed to 200 yards range through a hail of tracer from the Ju 88's rear gunner, then sank his first burst into the 88's starboard engine. The bomber fell away into clouds, and

Demozay was told on landing that his opponent had crashed. A few days later, on yet another training flight Demozay caught a Messerschmitt Bf 109 and destroyed it after a brief clash.

On 15 December 1940, No 1 Squadron was moved south to Northolt for first-line operations, then moved again on 4 January 1941, this time to Kenley to join with No 615 Squadron in forming a new Hurricane Wing for offensive operations over France *et al*, under the leadership of Wing Commander John Peel, DSO,DFC, an ex-Cranwell cadet who had fought with distinction through the Battle of Britain. At that time Demozay was not the only expatriate serving in 1 Squadron, flying alongside several Czech pilots, including Sergeant Karel Kuttelwascher. The Hurricanes were first used for general patrols to protect Allied shipping convoys, and on 24 March 1941 Demozay was leading a section of three Hurricanes on just such an escort patrol when he was attacked several times by single Bf 109s from out of a higher cloud layer. Finally, exasperated by these sniping attacks Demozay climbed up through the cloud, emerging behind and underneath a tight formation of Bf 109s. Still climbing, he lined his sight on the rearmost Messerschmitt, gave it a long, twelve-second burst, and sent it spinning down through cloud to dive into the sea.

In that month No 1 Squadron exchanged its tired Hurricane Is for a mixture of Hurricane IIbs and IIcs – the former with twelve 0.303-inch Brownings and the latter armed with four 20 mm Hispano cannons – both versions having uprated Merlin engines offering greater performance range. After a temporary move of base to Croydon on 8 April the squadron settled in at Redhill from 2 May, commanded now by an ex-Battle of Britain veteran, Squadron Leader Richard Brooker, DFC. Here, in addition to its prime daylight operational role, the squadron continued to send up night patrols attempting to intercept Luftwaffe bombers.

The night of 10/11 May 1941 saw 1 Squadron's nightly efforts crowned with high success. It was a night of full moonlight, with virtually unlimited visibility, and 12 of the unit's Hurricanes were prepared in three sections of four machines for overlapping patrols. The first section took off at 11 p.m. – Brooker, Flight Lieutenant Bill Sizer, Sergeant Plasil, and Jean Demozay –

climbed to 16,000 feet over London, then separated. Brooker found one Heinkel He 111 over the city centre, dived on its tail, and shot it down in flames. Demozay spotted another Heinkel trapped in searchlight beams over the East India docks, closed to within 30 yards of its tail, and opened fire. The Heinkel jerked over onto its back, belched smoke, then went down, exploding into the Lea Marshes. Before the night was out 1 Squadron's pilots had claimed eight German bombers destroyed and a ninth 'damaged'; three of these by a Czech Sergeant Dygryn (*nom de guerre* 'Ligoticky'). For his part Demozay was decorated in person by General de Gaulle with the French Medal of Liberation, and a *Palme* was added to the *Croix de Guerre* already worn on his tunic.

On 25 May Demozay was at the head of three other Hurricanes on a patrol over Canterbury but lost his colleagues in cloud, and decided to carry out a lone hunt off the French coast. Below him he noticed eight Bf 109s escorting a rescue boat, then spotted three Bf 110s. Stalking the latter carefully, he crept up on the rearmost Bf 110, then at 250 yards gave it one shattering burst of cannon shells. The 110 heeled over left, burst into flames, and plunged into the sea near the Goodwin light ship. It was a 'lone wolf' victory typical of Demozay, who always preferred flying and fighting as an individual rather than as merely one member of a team.

Nevertheless, his private inclinations now had to be put aside when, on 18 June 1941, he was posted to No 242 Squadron as a Flight commander. Based at North Weald and commanded by Squadron Leader Willard Whitney-Straight, MC, 242 was another Hurricane unit, but Demozay stayed with the squadron for just ten days, though he justified his membership by destroying a Bf 109 on 22 June, then clobbered another Bf 109 next day. Five days later he reported as a new Flight commander to No 91 Squadron at Hawkinge to fly Spitfire Vbs. Like so many other fighter pilots, Demozay took to the Spitfire like a duck to water, and now began his most successful run of combat victories.

No 91 Squadron, formed on 11 January 1941 by the retitling of the former No 421 'Jim Crow' Flight, was then tasked with a variety of operational tasks, including coastal patrols, anti-shipping recces, Rhubarbs (offensive sorties into France), escorts to

452 Sqn RAAF. Personalities include Sqn Ldr Bungey (from lt), Flt Lt B Finucane (from lt), and Keith Truscott (from rt). June 1941.

'Bluey' Truscott (rt) and 'Bardie' Wawn, 452 Sqn RAAF.

In the dispersal hut. Lt-rt: Brendan Finucane, Keith Truscott, and Plt Off 'Dick' Lewis.

(Left) Jean Demozay in Free French Air Force uniform. *(Right)* Sqn Ldr J Demozay, DSO, DFC in a Spitfire cockpit.

Wg Cdr John Braham *(rt)* with his navigator Flt Lt 'Sticks' Gregory, 1944.

air-sea rescue aircraft and vessels, and occasional bomber escorts on Circus operations. Thus, its pilots, a truly international mixture of men from a dozen different countries, tended to operate as individuals in most instances; a form of fighting which had always appealed to Demozay in particular.

He opened his tally with 91 Squadron by destroying a Henschel Hs 126 on the ground during a strafe of an enemy airfield on 12 July, then four days later attacked a Bf 109 and probably destroyed this. Next day, 17 July, a Luftwaffe mine-laying aircraft was shot into the sea, and on 25 July he destroyed a Bf 109 by shooting away most of the Messerschmitt's tail unit.

Then on 31 July, while patrolling between Cap Gris Nez and Ostend, he tackled two pairs of Bf 109s over Dunkirk. Firing first at the rear-most, his shells tore off its starboard wing before the 109 exploded in mid-air. Lining up the next in the 109 foursome he fired at 150 yards and watched it dive in flames to crash on the shoreline a little west of Dunkirk. The front pair of 109s had yet to react to the loss of their companions and Demozay crept up on these as they headed out to sea, firing one long burst from 300 yards which splashed around the 109's cockpit area, blowing off its canopy, before Demozay overshot and lost sight of the enemy fighters. The following six months saw Demozay destroy at least eight more Bf 109s and probably destroy two others; his last confirmed victory of that period coming on 2 January 1942, by which time he had been awarded a British DFC in November 1941 to add to the growing medal ribbons on his left tunic-breast. Indeed, the number of *Palmes* to his various French decorations had led his fellow pilots to suggest that his name 'Moses' should be changed to 'Oasis' ...

In January 1942 Jean Demozay was taken off operations for a rest period and went to No 11 Group Headquarters for a staff job, but on 25 June that year he returned to the sharp end when he succeeded Squadron Leader Bobbie Oxspring, DFC as commander of his old unit, 91 Squadron, still based at Hawkinge. Selecting Spitfire Vb,W3122,DL-J, as his personal machine, Demozay returned to operations almost immediately, and in July was notified of the award of a Bar to his DFC. His period of command of 91 Squadron lasted until December 1942, by which time he had added three more victories to his combat tally. The first of these resulted from a lone search flight undertaken by Demozay between Cap Gris Nez and Calais for one of his pilots who had failed to return from an early morning sortie. When some ten miles north-west of Gris Nez a Focke Wulf Fw 190 flew by him, while a second Fw 190 was in the process of getting on the Frenchman's tail, firing as he closed the range. Reefing his Spitfire to the left, Demozay fought off both 190s for some minutes before one of the pair bore in from Demozay's beam. Throttling back sharply, Demozay turned in to his attacker, gave him a two-seconds' broadside with all his guns from 100 yards. The Fw 190 banked steeply, stalled viciously, rolled over and dived straight into the sea inverted. Its companion promptly left the scene.

On 31 October Demozay scrambled hurriedly from Hawkinge at 5 p.m. hoping to intercept some hit-and-run Fw 190s reported attacking Canterbury with bombs, and over Dover caught up with four 190s flying in two pairs. Attacking the rear one from astern, he shot it down in flames into the sea. Returning to refuel and re-arm, Demozay took off again within minutes and found another foursome of Fw 190s near Folkestone. As these split into fighting pairs and began climbing to attack him, Demozay gave the leading machine a quick burst, then latched on to the second pair as these headed towards Dover. Ten miles east of Dover Demozay's fire finally sent one Fw 190 straight into the sea. Outpaced by the remaining 190s, Demozay returned to base and landed at 5.45 p.m. Days later he had a narrow escape from death when bounced by some unseen German fighters, but returned unscathed. In December 1942 he was awarded a DSO, promoted to Wing Commander, and posted back to 11 Group HQ, again for staff duties.

In February 1943 Demozay was sent to North Africa to form a flying school for Free French crews, returning to England in April 1944. After a brief liaison visit to Russia, he returned to the operational scene with an appointment on 9 August 1944 as commander of the Free French *Groupe Patrie*, comprising two bomber squadrons, 'Bearn' and 'Picardie', flying Douglas

Bostons in direct support of the FFI (*Forces Françaises de l'Interieur*) guerilla units in France assisting Allied forces after the Normandy landings.

Never content to fly a desk, Demozay usually led his *Groupe*'s missions – which totalled more than 200 overall by October 1944 – and remained in this appointment until the close of the European war. In December 1944 Demozay was awarded the *Légion d'Honneur* and its citation credited him with at least 21 confirmed aerial victories, several more probably destroyed, and five more destroyed on the ground, and stated that in all he had flown more than 400 operational sorties to date.

With the cessation of hostilities Jean Demozay, already ranked as a Lieutenant-Colonel by General de Gaulle, was appointed Air Schools Inspector for the French Air Force, and was also appointed President of the National Association for Flying Sport; his future in French aviation seemed destined to be a distinguished one. On 19 December 1945, however, he was killed when the Siebel Si 204 transport aircraft in which he was returning from a liaison visit to London crashed at Loge-en-Josas, near Buc, just outside Paris.

CHAPTER TWELVE

John Braham

For most youngsters growing up in the 1930s who aimed to fly with the RAF, the ultimate dream was to become a fighter pilot; an ambition which perhaps inevitably included visions of emulating such men as Albert Ball, Jimmy McCudden, 'Mick' Mannock *et al* whose deeds during the (then) recent 1914-18 war had probably nurtured any such goal in the first place. Nevertheless, such a dream almost exclusively envisaged flying by day in a single-seat fighter aircraft, engaging enemy counterparts in single combat to the death. Few, if indeed any, such would-be aces even considered the prospect of becoming a night fighter pilot; understandably, because in those pre-World War Two years the RAF simply did not possess aircraft specifically designed for the night interceptor role. First-line RAF fighters had flown by night it is true, but more as an experimental venture rather than any regular or routine purpose. Only in mid-1939 did the RAF call for a batch of Blenheim IFs – Blenheim I bombers converted to 'fighters' by simply bolting on a four machine-gun pack under each aircraft's bomb bay – to be fitted with the early form of AI (Airborne Interception) radar (then termed RDF for Radio Direction Finding) sets; the first deliveries of which went to No 25 Squadron on 31 July 1939. By 3 September 1939 a total of fifteen AI-fitted Blenheim IFs had been delivered to 25 Squadron, with six more arriving on the unit by the end of the same month.

As merely one of many hundreds of young men who joined the RAF in the late 1930s with the prime idea of becoming a fighter pilot, John Braham, to his personal dismay, found himself allotted to a night fighter unit after graduating from flying training school, and did his utmost to be posted away to a day fighter squadron, without success. Yet, paradoxically, his lengthy operational service on night fighters was to see him emerge from the war as the RAF's most highly decorated fighter pilot, as well as the Service's highest-scoring night fighter pilot. Born in Bath on 6 April 1920, the son of a vicar, John Robert Daniel Braham's original ambition on leaving school in 1936 was to join the Colonial Police force, and with this in mind his first employment was as a junior clerk in the Wigan police offices. A year of shuffling paper as a police clerk proved too boring, and his thoughts turned to joining the Merchant Navy, only to meet strong disapproval from his father. Accordingly – in his own words, 'For the hell of it' – Braham decided in December 1937 to apply for a five-years' Short Service Commission with the RAF.

Accepted provisionally for pilot training, Braham went to the civilian EFTS at Desford for *ab initio* instruction on De Havilland Tiger Moths, making his very first flight on 9 March 1938 in Tiger Moth G-ADPH. His progress was slow, taking fourteen hours' dual instruction before being allowed to fly his first solo, but he completed EFTS successfully, was sent to Uxbridge for kitting up as an Acting Pilot Officer, RAF (On probation), given a fortnight's 'square-bashing' in drill, discipline, and RAF procedures, then posted in late May 1938 to No 11 FTS at Shawbury, near Shrewsbury, where he flew Hawker Harts and Audaxes in the junior term and, having opted to become a fighter pilot, Hawker Fury fighters in his senior phase. Awarded his wings officially on 20 August 1938, Braham spent the following four months flying Furys on aerobatics, formation work, and gunnery practice, and in December that year graduated with a posting to No 29 Squadron, based at Debden.

His first sight of 29 Squadron came as a shock – the unit was flying Hawker Demon biplane 'fighters', two-seaters with a so-termed gun turret in the rear seat, whereas the other resident units at Debden then, Nos 85 and 87 Squadrons, were equipped with the very latest RAF fighters, Hawker Hurricanes. To add to his disappointment, his initial interview with 29's commanding officer, Squadron Leader P.S.Gomez,* informed him that the squadron was about to exchange the obsolete Demons for

---

* Officially, 29's CO was Squadron Leader M.W.S.Robinson when Braham arrived, but Gomez was due to succeed Robinson shortly, and was officially appointed CO on 13 February 1939.

Blenheim IFs. Braham's reaction to this piece of news was to request a transfer to a single-seat fighter unit, but Gomez's somewhat frosty response could have been summed succinctly as 'Like 29, or lump it' ... A much disillusioned Braham, not yet nineteen years old, soon began to settle in to his unit, and spent some three months converting to the Blenheims, during which time he acquired the nickname 'Bob'; selecting his second Christian name as his personal R/T call-sign due to the several other Johns then on the squadron. Then, in August 1939, his morale received a boost, when he learned that 29 Squadron was to re-equip with Hurricanes and with these No 29 Squadron commenced its second war against Germany on 3 September 1939.

Braham's joy at flying Hurricanes was short-lived; in late September 1939 the squadron exchanged these for Blenheim IFs again for its newly-allotted future role as a nightfighter unit. At first the Blenheim crews had no radar sets and had to rely on make-shift tactics, co-operating with searchlight batteries etc, while they attempted to find the Luftwaffe in the night skies. Constant practice and 'routine' patrols became frustrating, with several crew casualties in accidents and only rare contact with German raiders. A shift of base to Digby, with detachments at Wellingore and Coltishall, came in June 1940, but the Luftwaffe continued to be elusive as far as 29 Squadron was concerned, with only an occasional combat claim registered.

Then, on the night of 24 August 1940, Braham made his first 'kill'. Flying a non-radar Blenheim, with Sergeant Wilsden as his rear gunner, he was patrolling at 10,000 feet over the Humber when his Sector Controller vectored him onto a German raider coned in searchlights some miles away. Opening his throttles to full, Braham eventually caught up with the 'bogey', a Dornier, but as his opening burst of fire poured into the Dornier, causing it to spume smoke, he found himself overtaking his target. Slowing to its starboard side, Braham watched his gunner put burst after burst into the German, saw flames erupt, then watched it fall away to port in a dive, still burning as it dived into the ground.

On 2 September 1940 the squadron took delivery of a Bristol Beaufighter (R2072), fitted with the latest AI Mk IV radar, as the harbinger of its imminent change of aircraft, and by November had become an all-Beaufighter unit. Officially declared fully operational on these new aircraft from 17 September, the squadron worked up quickly on the Beau, and new crews, especially radar set-operators, worked hard to master the still-troublesome AI 'magic boxes', though with little success for some weeks. By the end of 1940 Braham had been promoted to Flying Officer, and shortly after was awarded a DFC for 'Determined operations against the enemy under adverse weather conditions', but his second victory did not come until the night of 13 March 1941 when, with the Canadian Sergeant Ross as his 'crew', Braham intercepted a Dornier over the coast near Skegness. Closing to 400 yards, apparently undetected by the Dornier's crew, Braham opened fire – only to have his cannons jam after one second. Ross worked feverishly on rectifying the Hispanos, Braham tried to fire again but nothing happened.

Determined to destroy the Dornier one way or another, Braham decided to ram the German and warned Ross accordingly, but Ross told him to try the cannons once more first. Pressing the firing button, Braham felt his Beaufighter buck as the Hispanos delivered a salvo of 20 mm shells into the bomber, which immediately exploded in a blinding gout of flames directly in front of Braham, then cascaded in a shower of flaming wreckage into the North Sea.

It was at this period that Braham met an eighteen-year-old VAD nurse, Joan, and within weeks the young couple were married by Braham's father at Duxford; an occasion well-marked by 29 Squadron which flew in formation over the Parish Church in salute. However, their honeymoon was rudely interrupted by a telegram recalling Braham for a squadron move of base to West Malling, near Maidstone, on 1 May, and his young bride had to begin to reconcile herself to the fact that her newly-acquired husband placed his duty to the RAF above all else, at least while the war continued, such was his single-minded dedication.

On 8 May Braham, with Ross as his radar-operator, was vectored on to a 'bogey', which turned out to be a pair of Heinkel He 111s. Ross expertly ushered his pilot in from behind the bombers, gradually closing the range to 200 yards astern and slightly below the targets. Easing the Beaufighter's nose up, Braham fired and his primary target dived to port with one engine smoking, with its alert rear gunner sending a stream of tracers towards the Beau. Concentrating on this Heinkel, Braham attacked again with a long deflection burst. The Heinkel burst into flames, nosed down steeply, and was seen to explode into the earth.

During the next few weeks, while still maintaining its night patrols, 29 Squadron had several changes in personnel, including a new commander, Wing Commander E.L.Colbeck-Welch, DFC, who took up his appointment on 13 June. Braham was promoted to Flight Lieutenant and became deputy leader of B Flight, while Guy Gibson, DFC (later, VC) became OC A Flight as a Squadron Leader. The Braham-Ross duo claimed a Junkers Ju 88 destroyed before June was out, but then Ross, awarded a DFM, was sent to a fighter OTU for a 'rest' as an instructor, and Braham now teamed up with Sergeant W.J. 'Sticks' Gregory as his navigator.

Their first success as a team came on 6 July, when Braham intercepted a Ju 88 over the Thames Estuary. His intended victim's crew became aware of the Beaufighter before it was within firing range, and began evasive manoeuvres with its rear gunner firing a hail of tracers towards Braham. Staying with the desperately jinking bomber, Braham gave it three short bursts at close range, the rear gunner ceased firing, and the Ju 88 started burning and dived into the Thames from some 3,000 feet. That same night Guy Gibson destroyed a Heinkel over Sheerness.

By the end of the year Braham was to claim a further three bombers destroyed, a fourth probably destroyed, and another severely damaged. In December that year he received a Bar to his DFC, and was detached briefly to No 141 Squadron at Ayr, Scotland to help this unit convert from Defiant night fighters to Beaufighters, but shortly after his return both he and Gregory were posted as instructors at 51 OTU, Cranfield to train night fighter crews in the latest operational techniques.

Gregory, already awarded a DFM, was commissioned in February 1942, and in June went with Braham for a 'private' visit to their old unit, 29 Squadron, where Braham 'borrowed' a new Beaufighter fitted with AI Mk 7 radar and proceeded to 'test' this new radar by shooting down a Dornier Do 217 into the sea off Sandwich. His return from this patrol, in filthy weather conditions, led to him being diverted to Manston, where he landed too fast and too high, clipped a small building with one wing-tip, and eventually rolled to a stop in a ploughed field.

That same month Braham was promoted to Squadron Leader at the OTU, but shortly after he and Gregory were posted back to 29 Squadron, where Braham became A Flight commander and selected Beaufighter V8284 as his personal 'warhorse'. The Gregory-Braham team were quickly back into the shooting war, spotting a Dornier at 7,000 feet over the Thames approaches and sending it down into the sea on 9 August; and destroying two more and damaging three others before the month was out. The last of these occurred on 28 August, a Ju 88 destroyed, but during a second patrol in the early hours of 29 August he closed with another Ju 88 whose gunner shattered one of the Beaufighter's engines, setting it on fire, forcing Braham eventually to belly-land on a small crash airstrip at Friston, Beachy Head. Inspection of the damage afterwards revealed that one bullet had actually passed through Braham's cockpit seat, missing his back by mere inches.

In October 1942 Braham was awarded a DSO and added a Ju 88 and Dornier 217 to his tally in the same month; then in December he was summoned to No 11 Group Headquarters, Uxbridge where the AOC told him he was to be promoted to Wing Commander and take over command of No 141 Squadron at Ford; a unit which was 'in a rut' (*sic*) and needed its spirits 'bolstering'.

On arrival at Ford Braham realised there was some truth in the AOC's remarks but found that most of the old personnel had now begun to be replaced by fresh crews, whom he determined to inculcate with the will to become 'the best nightfighter squadron in the RAF', as Braham himself expressed it.

Setting the pace by destroying a Dornier at 15,000 feet, Braham decided his squadron really needed a brief non-operational period in which to work up his crews to fighting fitness. His request to the AOC was agreed and 141 Squadron exchanged bases with No 604 Squadron, moving to Predannack, Cornwall on 17 February 1943. Here intensive training began immediately, but Braham found time for several individual sorties alongside nearby Coastal Command strike units, attacking a U-boat and causing it to crash-dive on one occasion, and shattering an enemy torpedo boat which erupted in flames and left its crew struggling in the sea. Shortly after, he received the award of a second Bar to his DFC.

Within a few weeks he considered his squadron combat-ready and volunteered his crews to undertake roving *Ranger* operations over the Brest Peninsula area, seeking rail and road targets to destroy, mixed with daylight patrols of the Bay of Biscay in the hope of catching Luftwaffe aircraft attacking Allied merchant shipping convoys and/or assisting U-boats. Accordingly, the squadron flew its first *Ranger* sorties on the night of 20 March, when three Beaufighters, including Braham, set out to scour the enemy rail systems in the Brest area. Crossing the Channel at 300 feet to avoid German radar, the Beaufighters then climbed to 1,500 feet over the Brittany coast and flew inland. Braham found the Brest-Rennes rail line, followed it, found a speeding train and left it halted, erupting in steam and smoke. It was the start of several weeks of such operations, interspersed with continuing practice for the squadron's prime role as nightfighters.

Braham was then called to Fighter Command HQ at Stanmore where he was told that 141 Squadron had been selected to pioneer a new form of radar operational work, code-named Serrate, involving flying with Bomber Command's main bomber streams and hunting any German nightfighters attempting to infiltrate those streams; the new radar enabling the Beaufighter crews to home in on German fighters' own radar. In the two weeks remaining at Predannack, Braham flew an anti-shipping sortie, during which a faulty 20 mm shell in one of his cannons exploded prematurely, blowing a hole in the Beau and forcing Braham to return to base.

On the last day of April the squadron flew to Wittering, where it spent its first two weeks in modifying its Beaufighter IVs to have the new radar installed, then in May was detached to Drem to practise their future Serrate techniques. Then on 14 June, having returned to Wittering, 141 Squadron flew its first Serrate operation with six aircraft, supplementing a bomber operation against Oberhausen in the Ruhr. Flying to Coltishall, refuelling, and then taking off at 11.30 p.m. the Beaufighters joined the main bomber stream as it winged over the North Sea heading for Germany.

Braham had 'Sticks' Gregory with him and after several unfruitful AI contacts finally picked up a Messerschmitt Bf 110 near Oberhausen. Closing to 400 yards, Braham splashed his cannon shells all over the Bf 110 *Nachtjäger* which immediately burst into bright flames and crashed.

In the following three months Braham added six more to his kill-tally, though on one occasion when he tackled a pair of Ju 88s their return fire set one of the Beaufighter's motors aflame. Diving steeply, Braham managed to extinguish the fire but returned to base on one engine. By July 1943 Braham's insatiable urge to fly operations had begun to affect his faithful team-mate Gregory who was showing distinct signs of battle fatigue, so Braham arranged for Sticks to be rested as Squadron Operational Planning Officer, and in his place wangled a posting in for Flight Lieutenant 'Jacko' Jacobs, DFC, a former team-mate. Gregory eventually became Flight Lieutenant, DSO,DFC,DFM.

On the night of 17 August 1943 Bomber Command laid on a special raid against the German V-weapons research establishment at Peenemünde, and Braham was one of the Serrate pilots who flew with the bombers; destroying two Bf 110s in the course of his sortie.* He was awarded a Bar to his DSO soon after, its citation emphasising his ' ... brilliant leadership of 141 Squadron and exceptional skill and gallantry on operations'. By now Bob Braham, though unknowingly, was rapidly becoming operationally fatigued – 'getting the twitch', as operational crews referred to near-exhaustion from flying on ops longer than was advisable. It showed in many ways – short temper, irritability, and – more dangerously – lack of total concentration when flying occasionally. That higher authority realised Braham's condition is shown by an order posting him from 141 Squadron to the Army Staff College at Camberley, beginning 21 October 1943.

* His victims were Feldwebel Heinz Vinke (54 victories) and Oberfeldwebel Georg Kraft (15 victories)

His last combat sortie with 141 was flown on 29 September when he shot down a Bf 110* and at least damaged a Ju 88 in separate fights over the Zuyder Zee; thus bringing his official score of enemy aircraft destroyed to twenty, apart from many others probably destroyed or damaged.

The Staff College course lasted until 11 February 1944, when Braham was then posted to the Operational Staff of No 2 Group, under the command of the dynamic Air Vice-Marshal Basil Embry. Though mainly absorbed in the pre-planning of the Group's operations, Braham had made it plain that he wished to fly operationally too. Since Embry's constant creed was that senior officers *should* set an example by flying occasional sorties with their subordinates – exemplified by his personal exploits – he readily agreed that Braham would get his 'ops ration', which in Braham's case amounted on average to at least one sortie per week thereafter.

During five such trips in March-April 1944 Braham destroyed seven enemy aircraft, followed by a Ju 88 shot down near Copenhagen on 6 May. Six days later he was flying his Mosquito on an intruder sortie over Denmark and clashed with a Bf 109 and a Focke Wulf Fw 190. Chasing the Fw 190, his Mosquito was hit by its Bf 109 companion, but Braham persisted in attacking the 190 and shot it down to a crash-landing near Aalborg. Turning to deal with the Messerschmitt, his Mosquito was further damaged by flak. Attempting to reach England again, Braham was forced to ditch his aircraft some 70 miles short of the English coast and take to his dinghy, being picked up by the Air-Sea Rescue Service shortly after.

His ordeal was far from over when he returned to shore because his trip had been flown without the express permission of Basil Embry, and next day Braham was on the mat before Embry, who quietly but devastatingly reduced Braham to near-tears with his dressing-down – then said to Braham, 'The matter is now forgotten. Have a beer with me at lunch-time' ...

Grounded from then until D-Day – as were most operational staff crews – Braham next flew on the evening of 6 June, with Air

* Hauptmann August Geiger (53 victories) of NJG.1

Commodore David Atcherley as his navigator, despite Atcherley having one arm encased in a plaster cast! The sortie resulted in a German vehicle column being thoroughly strafed and bombed. Braham flew two more sorties in the next fortnight, one a night-strafe and the other a daylight intruder patrol over Denmark.

On 25 June Braham 'borrowed' a Mosquito, LR373, from Wing Commander 'Daddy' Dale, OC No 21 Squadron, flew to West Raynham to top up with fuel, then set out for a long-range intruder sortie to the Barth area on the Baltic coast. Accompanying him as navigator was an Australian, Don Walsh, and Braham was in a particularly good humour, having a few days before been awarded a second Bar to his DSO. The sortie became a succession of seemingly minor mishaps and errors of judgment on Braham's part. Their presence near the Danish coast was radioed to the land defences by several ships passed en route; German radar began searching the ether for them; then two German fighters, Fw 190s, were vectored on to their tail. These soon closed with the Mosquito and Braham had his hands full in close combat manoeuvring.

The Fw 190s split up and made co-ordinated attacks, until finally one 190's fire crippled Braham's Mosquito and he had to crash-land on a sand-strip separating the Ringköbing Fiord from the North Sea. With his port engine and wing in flames, and his cockpit canopy shattered by bullets, Braham put the Mosquito down on the sand at 150 mph, bounced wildly, then slithered to a halt on the sea edge.

Evacuating the burning wreck rapidly, both men were quickly captured by German troops from a nearby radar site. Taken to the main interrogation centre on the outskirts of Frankfurt, Braham met the Fw 190 pilot who had shot him down, Leutnant Robert Spreckels of JG.1, holder of the Knight's Cross of the Iron Cross, for whom Braham was his 45th *Luftsieg*. Eventually sent to the notorious Stalag Luft 3 at Sagan, Braham endured ten months of captivity until finally being liberated by Allied troops on 2 May 1945.

Given a permanent commission in the RAF at the end of the war, Braham was unable to settle to peacetime routine Service life and resigned his commission in March 1946, only to re-enlist soon after and continue to serve in the RAF until May 1952, when he transferred to the RCAF and with his family emigrated to Canada. In early 1961 he met again Robert Spreckels, by then a successful business man in shipping in Hamburg, and their reunion forged a life-long friendship. With 29 combat victories credited to him, a triple DSO, triple DFC, and (later) AFC, John 'Bob' Braham, the boy who had wanted to be a fighter pilot by day, had achieved higher success and honours by night than almost any RAF fighter pilot of the 1939-45 war.

CHAPTER THIRTEEN

James Hallowes

It is seldom appreciated that of the air crew personnel officially entitled to wear the Battle of Britain Clasp – the so-termed Few – almost exactly 44 per cent were non-commissioned men; the great majority of these holding the lowest senior non-commissioned officer (SNCO) rank of Sergeant. By the prevailing pre-1939 RAF practice, all pilots on graduation from flying training were awarded their wings brevet and at the same time became either Pilot Officers or (at least) Sergeant. Those selected for immediate commissioning (albeit 'On Probation') were chosen in the main on the basis of class, educational background, sporting activities, and the 'right accent'; with pure leadership qualities not always being given the highest priority in consideration by contemporary selection boards *et al.*

It is, perhaps, an ironic comment on such methods of assessing officer material that no small proportion of those SNCO pilots were to become, within two or three years, outstanding fighting leaders spearheading RAF Fighter Command's escalating aerial offensive over enemy-occupied territories. Such men as Frank Carey, Don Kingaby, 'Ginger' Lacey, Joseph Frantisek, George Unwin, Ronald Hamlyn, 'Sammy' Allard, Charlton 'Wag' Haw, and dozens of others forged huge reputations for courage and instinctive leadership qualities during the first year of the war, and nearly all had become Squadron Leaders or Wing Commanders by 1942-43, still flying operationally and destined to rise even higher in rank and responsibilities.

Conditions of service at hangar floor level for Sergeant pilots in the pre-1939 years were no sinecure. With rare exception such men were highly qualified technical tradesmen, mainly ex-Aircraft Apprentices with several years' service in the lower ranks of their respective trades. Remustering to become pilots did not absolve them from the day to day routines and responsibilities of being a SNCO, a rank and status regarded with far greater respect and dignity than it was to become in the post-bellum RAF.

Such was made crystal clear to one newly-promoted, freshly graduated Sergeant pilot on his arrival on his first unit, No 43 Squadron, in August 1936, Sergeant Herbert James Lempriere Hallowes. Reporting to the Flight Sergeant in charge of his future Flight, Hallowes was told in no uncertain terms, 'You're not here merely to fly those Furys and then sit back and take things easy; there are other jobs to do – or else! Every week the aircraft are to be cleaned and polished, pilots are expected to get into overalls and scrub down with soft soap and water. Then polish all the aluminium cowlings. And *if* you chaps get your backs into it I'll even let the fitters and riggers give you a hand.'* Yet, as 'Jim' Hallowes was to learn quickly, ' ... on the ground and in the air, on the sports field or playing fields, *esprit de corps* was drummed into all ranks. It was a great honour to be a member of such a squadron ... always it was '43' above *all*'.* In the following four years of his membership of 43 Squadron, Hallowes was to add honours to the already proud record of that distinguished company of men.

Born in Lambeth on 17 April 1912, Jim Hallowes joined the RAF as an Aircraft Apprentice at Halton in January 1929, and on passing out from Halton in 1932 spent the next three years as a ground maintenance airman before being accepted for pilot training and graduating in 1936 with the rank of Sergeant. When he arrived on 43 Squadron the unit was based at Tangmere flying Hawker Fury I biplane fighters, commanded temporarily by Flight Lieutenant R.I.G.Macdougall, who was succeeded in February 1937 by Squadron Leader R.E.Bain (later, Group Captain, Retd). The accent on flying then was discipline, exemplified in perfected formations and polished manoeuvring in air drills which were to stand 43's pilots in good stead a few years later when engaged in combat with the Luftwaffe.

The squadron was still flying Fury fighters when the Munich

* *43 Squadron* by J.Beedle; Beaumont Aviation, 1966.

A Mosquito's bite . . . . four 20mm Hispano cannons & four 0.303-inch Browning machine guns in 'full voice'.

43 Sqn group. *Lt-rt:* Sgts Arbuthnot, Plenderleith, Hallowes; Fg Off J Simpson; Sqn Ldr P Townsend; Plt Off Upton. Taken at Wick, 1940.

Wg Cdr J H L Hallowes, DFC, DFM.

Hornchurch Wing, Spring 1942. Jim Hallowes is seated 5th from left, while other personalities include Grp Capt Harry Broadhurst *(seated, 8th from lt)* and Wg Cdr Duncan-Smith *(9th from lt)*.

Crisis of September 1938 brought Europe teetering on the brink of war, but on 29 November that year two Hawker Hurricanes (L1725 and L1727) were delivered to the squadron as the start of re-equipment, and before Christmas the squadron was up to its full establishment of sixteen Hurricanes, and the last six Furys were despatched to Kemble Maintenance Unit on 2 February 1939. The following months became one long, intensive flying training programme for 43's crews as they mastered the heavier, faster, and far-better armed metal monoplanes, including participation in the final peacetime 'war' exercises of August 1939. Already mobilised since 5 August, the squadron was brought to full Readiness state at 11.15 hours on 3 September – Britain was now legally at war with Hitler's Nazi Germany.

For the first few days of war 43's crews stood by their Hurricanes at dispersals throughout the hours of daylight, but the first opportunity for the pilots to fire their guns came on 8 September – destroying a rogue barrage balloon which had snapped its cable. Gale-force winds over the next two weeks saw 43's men engaged in more balloon-busting, including Hallowes whose accuracy in shooting showed him using less ammunition to destroy a 'gas-bag' than any of his fellow pilots.

On 18 November the squadron left its traditional home at Tangmere to fly north to Acklington, to reinforce No 13 Group in defence of the industrial North and Midlands. By then command of 43 Squadron had passed into the hands of Squadron Leader George Lott, another ex-Aircraft Apprentice, who had succeeded Bain in October 1939.* Here, in arctic winter conditions, and with fairly primitive living circumstances, the squadron flew monotonously boring coastal patrols over merchant shipping convoys, fishing fleets, minesweepers, and other vessels plying the near waters of the North Sea, and saw no German aircraft until the end of January 1940, when on the 29th a Heinkel He 111 was intercepted but escaped in low cloud. Next day, however, a Heinkel was caught five miles east of Coquet Island and shot into the sea. On 3 February Jim Hallowes was flying with two other Hurricanes of 'Black Flight' in Hurricane

* Later, Air Vice-Marshal, CB,CBE,DSO,DFC.

L1847,FT-J, when the trio trapped a Heinkel just east of Whitby and had sent it down to crash near Sneaton Castle Farm, Whitby.

On 9 February Hallowes again saw combat, joining with two other Hurricanes in attacking a pair of He 111s near Coquet Island. Following his section leader, Peter Townsend, he sank a full deflection burst into one Heinkel, seeing pieces of metal flying off it before it jettisoned its bomb load and flew unsteadily into low cloud.* Nearly two weeks later, on 26 February, the squadron moved even further north to Wick, ostensibly to protect the naval anchorage at Scapa Flow, though atrocious weather conditions reduced possible sorties to a bare minimum for several weeks.

On 8 April, however, action erupted briefly when a force of German bombers threatened to raid Scapa Flow. Hallowes, flying Hurricane L1742, was returning from patrol when he noticed anti-aircraft fire bursting at 8,000 feet west of Pentland Firth and spotted two Heinkel He 111s. Closing to 400 yards of one of these he opened fire, but after one second's firing his guns stopped – a fractured pneumatic line – and both Germans dived into a rain cloud. Landing back at Wick, Hallowes was astonished to find one of these Heinkels follow him in to land alongside. Hallowes' fire had killed two gunners in the Heinkel's crew and its pilot had decided not to try to return to base across an uninviting North Sea. Hallowes was then told to report to the Wick Station Commander, who was apparently infuriated at Jim shooting down a 'friendly Hudson' ...! Hallowes politely invited him to meet the 'Hudson's' crew ...

The beginning of the German assault on France on 10 May 1940 left 43 Squadron's pilots frustrated with inactivity at Wick until finally being ordered south, back to Tangmere, on 31 May. At 1100 hours the following day, 43 Squadron sent off its second patrol of the morning to patrol the Calais-Dunkirk line. Before this patrol was over nine Hurricanes from 43 had tackled a total of some 80 or more Luftwaffe fighters and accounted for nine destroyed and six others either probably destroyed or damaged

* Though captured enemy evidence a year later confirmed that this aircraft crashed 150 miles short of its base airfield, Hallowes was never officially credited with a victory.

heavily, for the loss of two Hurricanes, one pilot killed and a second pilot wounded.

The highest individual 'bag' went to Jim Hallowes, flying Hurricane N2585. Seeing a Bf 109 about to attack a Hurricane, Hallowes closed to 150 yards and opened fire. The 109 burst into flames and fell into the sea. Shortly after, while at about 10,000 feet, he turned in behind two Bf 109s which had dropped out of the clouds, chased them down to 7,000 feet firing at 30-45 degrees deflection, and saw one roll onto its back, catch fire and shed a mainplane before tumbling down to crash. Minutes later Hallowes had an inconclusive clash with a passing Bf 109, but next saw four Bf 110 two-seat fighters diving through cloud. Picking the rearmost he delivered two short bursts from below and behind, slicing off the 110's complete tail unit, leaving it to fall into the sea. His final opponent of the patrol was a Bf 109 which fled inland as Hallowes attacked. Hallowes kept up his chase for some fifteen miles, firing brief bursts and seeing his target shedding metal pieces before his ammunition became exhausted. He watched it dive steeply towards the ground but then left to return and land at Manston.

The story of 7 June, however, was one of near-disaster. During the day's fighting, the squadron suffered the loss of eight out of ten Hurricanes, with two pilots killed and the rest injured or 'missing'. Hallowes, flying with Squadron Leader Lott and eight other Hurricanes, was bounced by some Bf 109s which crippled four Hurricanes on their first pass. All four fell away burning, including Hallowes who began to evacuate his smoke-filled cockpit but then saw one Bf 109 in front of him. Dropping back into his bucket seat, Hallowes fired a long burst into the German, then resumed baling out, landing heavily and dislocating an ankle. His victim crashed nearby, and Hallowes was taken to No 4 Base Hospital at La Bause for attention to his ankle.

In the event he and five of the other missing pilots returned to the squadron, but it was not until 21 June that George Lott could report his squadron to HQ as fully fit for all operations. Hallowes' action on 7 June was described in the *London Gazette* citation dated 6 September 1940 which awarded him a DFM. Having rejoined his unit Hallowes had another dicey moment on

20 July when his Hurricane's engine seized up, resulting in a crashlanding alongside the river Arun at Amberley, fortunately without injury to himself.

In August 1940 the 'Fighting Cocks' – No 43 Squadron's traditional soubriquet – underwent its severest testing to date, with high successes and relatively serious losses. On 8 August, in the late afternoon, the squadron was protecting a convoy off the Isle of Wight when they met a formidable array of Bf 109s, Bf 110s, and Junkers Ju 87s stepped at intervals of altitude and seemingly stretching back to France. The ensuing maelstrom of action saw 43's pilots claim five enemy aircraft destroyed and ten others 'unconfirmed' as destroyed of which Hallowes personally destroyed two Bf 109s.

Four or five 109s detached themselves from the main formation as we engaged, and a 110 came in taking a deflection shot at myself. I turned sharply to avoid his fire and found myself about 300 yards astern and slightly to starboard of an Me 109. I gave a short burst of approximately two seconds and was gratified to see the 109 burst into flames and go into a vertical dive, the pilot baling out at about 15,000 feet … I was then fired at by a Hurricane which came in from the beam but his shots appeared to pass about 100 yards behind me. I gave another short burst at two Me 109s in fairly close formation; these two parted and turned back towards France, one diving steeply … after this I climbed to rejoin what I took to be a formation of three of our machines at about 26,000 to 28,000 feet. These aircraft were circling round, more or less in the sun, in line astern formation. On joining the circle I caught up with No 3 quite easily and noticing the tail struts under the tailplane and two radiators, realised I was in an enemy formation. The top camouflage was similar to our own, and I do not think the pilot of the Me 109 saw me as I was able to take plenty of time sighting before opening fire. After a short burst at about 200 yards range the aircraft burst into flames and went into a vertical dive. The pilot escaped by parachute at about 20,000 feet.

I had pulled up the nose of my machine too steeply as I

fired, causing the aircraft to stall and spin. The leader of the formation must have seen his No 3 go down in flames because he and his No 2 came at me as I stalled. Being well out to sea and knowing well that the 109s had the legs of the Hurricane, I kept in the spin and did everything I could to spoil the aim of the Jerries. Finally I corrected the spin and went into a falling leaf, and I think I persuaded them that I had been hit and was out of control as they left me and went south. I pulled out at about 5,000 feet and returned to Tangmere.*

Five days later Hallowes, in Hurricane P3386, was over the Southampton area shortly after 4 p.m. when he attacked a Ju 88 from head-on – 'a frightening experience as our closing speed was so great' – Having time only for a two-seconds' burst, he then followed the Ju 88 as it dived and saw it crash in flames in a small wood at Thorness Bay on the Isle of Wight. Being alone now he climbed to 9,000 feet, sighted a Dornier flying south-east, and shortened the range to 300 yards before opening fire. The Dornier snapped into a dive over Ventnor with Hallowes in close pursuit firing each time the German tried to straighten out.

Eventually the Dornier's fuselage emitted flames and plumed a trail of thick black smoke, turned north-east and glided down. In his cockpit Hallowes could smell burning as it filled with smoke but this cleared when he opened his canopy – later found to be an incendiary bullet which had detonated in the breech of one gun – and he climbed back to 9000 feet. Here he noticed an apparently damaged Ju 88 flying slowly south, closed to 300 yards and gave it a short burst from astern, chewing metal out of its tail. The Ju 88 dived raggedly into cloud and disappeared from Hallowes' view.

Every day now brought 43 Squadron into action, while on 16 August Tangmere airfield was heavily attacked at 1 p.m. The unit's twelve Hurricanes were airborne at the time, intercepting a force of about 100 Junkers Ju 87s stepped up in waves from 12,000 to 15,000 feet, all apparently heading for Tangmere too. Tackling this armada from the front the dozen Hurricanes split the Ju 87 horde apart, claiming no less than seventeen destroyed

* *43 Squadron* by J.Beedle; Beaumont Aviation, 1966.

or probably shot down in mere minutes of furious action. Hallowes' contribution to that tally amounted to three Ju 87s destroyed; the first exploding in mid-air, the others shot into the sea.

Next day Hallowes caught up with a Dornier at high altitude and attacked as it commenced a steep dive. Following it down, still firing, Hallowes' Hurricane steadily built up speed until at 12,000 feet it began shuddering with vibration as the wings fluttered alarmingly. With his ASI (Air Speed Indicator) already 'off the clock', and a control column rigidly immovable, he finally regained control via the elevator trimming wheel and regained level flight at about 5000 feet. Examination of the Hurricane back at base showed the wing root fittings bent and the wings with undesigned additional sweepback; a condition which resulted from, in the opinion of the Hawker technical inspectors later, a speed 'in excess of 620 m.p.h. ...'

Sunday, 18 August, brought 43 Squadron into virtually continuous combat from dawn to dusk. For Jim Hallowes it was to be another day of multiple success. In mid-afternoon 43 and 601 Squadrons – a total of 18 Hurricanes – intercepted a force of 28 Ju 87s of *Geschwader* 77's 1st *Gruppe* attempting to bomb RAF Thorney Island, with an escort of Bf 109s from II/JG27, just as they crossed the English coast. Flying Hurricane P3386, Hallowes described events as follows:

I caught up with one formation of five Ju 87s in line astern, opened fire at about 300 yards, two people baled out of No 5 aircraft and a further two from No 4 machine, both aircraft going into a vertical dive about three to four miles east of Thorney Island. I then carried out a quarter attack on a third Ju 87 without any apparent result. Observing another Ju 87 at about 200 feet which had released its bombs on Thorney Island, I came up into a position astern and gave it three short bursts; I was closing too fast and had to break away to the right, coming in again for a beam attack on the same machine which broke in two, just in front of the tail fin, and fell into the Solent halfway between the mainland and the Isle of Wight. I then spotted a Hurricane which was closing astern of a Ju 87

with an Me 109 coming up in turn behind the Hurricane. The
Hurricane turned left and I was in a good position for a beam
, attack on the 109. I could clearly see my bullets entering the
fuselage from the nose to the tailplane and could see the holes
as the 109 flashed past me about 100 yards ahead, going south.
I heard the order to return to base and being almost out of
ammunition I returned, landed and re-armed. I claimed the
109 as damaged, but at a later date heard that an unclaimed
109 had crashed on the Isle of Wight that day with a row of
bullet holes along the fuselage and assumed it was the one I
fired at.*

The next few days saw something of a lull as far as 43 Squadron
was concerned, though patrols continued to be flown each day.
On 26 August a dozen Hurricanes took off at 4 p.m. led by
Squadron Leader J.V.C.Badger, including Hallowes in aircraft
V6542. Vectored against a reported incoming raid against
Portsmouth, the Hurricanes met about 100 bombers with
some 50 escort fighters from *Luftflotte* 3.

Selecting a batch of Heinkel He 111s in the rough centre of
this awesome array 43 Squadron bore in head-on, with
Hallowes fastening on to one Heinkel as it broke formation
over Havant. His fire put one of the Heinkel's engines out of
action and, apparently, ruptured its hydraulic system because
the bomber's undercarriage flopped down. Staying with the
Heinkel, Hallowes continued his attacks as the bomber flew
across Tangmere and Ford through an inaccurate barrage of
fire from each airfield's ground defences – which were as much
a menace to Hallowes as to his victim – and, when out of
ammunition, made dummy attacks hoping to make the
German crew surrender, but the crippled Heinkel finally
crashed beside the Arun at Littlehampton. The *London Gazette*
dated 6 September 1940 which awarded Hallowes his DFM
cited also a Bar to his DFM, the latter's citation crediting
Hallowes with 21 enemy aircraft destroyed to date.

On 18 September Jim Hallowes was commissioned as a Pilot

* *43 Squadron* by J.Beedle; Beaumont Aviation,1966.

Officer, and in December was posted briefly to No 96 Squadron before returning to 43 Squadron, only to be re-posted, this time to No 65 Squadron at Kirton-in-Lindsey to fly Spitfires. By 1941 Hallowes was serving with 122 Squadron as a Flight commander and in May 1942 added two Fw 190s destroyed and four others at least damaged to his tally between 5 and 17 May during offensive sweeps over France. Promoted to Squadron Leader, he was given command of No 222 Squadron from June to August 1942, then became OC No 165 Squadron based at Eastchurch from August 1942 until March 1943.

Only days after taking up his appointment to 165 Squadron Hallowes, flying Spitfire BL664,SK-A, was leading his new unit on sorties over the Dieppe 'invasion' on 19 August, and personally destroyed one Dornier and damaged a second. His final combat claim for 1942 was an Fw 190 damaged on 8 November, and on 19 January 1943 the *London Gazette* confirmed the award of a DFC to him, describing him as 'an outstanding and relentless fighter ... whose skill and unswerving devotion to duty have set an example in keeping with the highest traditions of the Royal Air Force' a description only too valid for a man who had been flying on operations with virtually no rest since the first days of the war.

In October 1943, still a Squadron Leader, Hallowes was appointed OC No 504 Squadron at Peterhead (later, Horn-church), and remained with this unit until his promotion to Wing Commander in July 1944 and a final rest from operations. Remaining in the RAF after the war, Wing Commander Hallowes eventually retired from the Service on 8 July 1956.

CHAPTER FOURTEEN

Russell Bannock

While many of the better-known RAF fighter pilots of 1939-45 established their reputations initially over France and Britain during the earliest years of the war, a number of men eventually to be recognised as outstanding leaders only came to the operational scene in the final years of the conflict, then rapidly earned a niche in RAF Fighter Command's gallery of 'greats'. One such late-starter was Russell Bannock – 'Russ' – who flew his first-ever operational sortie on 14 June 1944, but ended his personal war eleven months later as one of Canada's leading fighter pilots.

Canadian-born, from Alberta, Bannock learned to fly before the war and on enlisting in the RCAF was retained in Canada as an instructor for much of his service, but he finally arrived in England as a Squadron Leader, took a short conversion course onto Mosquito aircraft, and joined his first unit, No 418 Squadron RCAF, at Holmsley South in June 1944 just as the Allied invasion of Normandy got under way. Known as the 'City of Edmonton' squadron, commanded then by Wing Commander A.Barker, 418 was equipped with Mosquito Mk IIs when Bannock arrived, and its role was primarily day and night intrusion deep into German-occupied Europe. Teaming up with Flying Officer R.R.Bruce as his navigator, Bannock took off on 14 June for his first intruder trip and on arriving over the Luftwaffe airfield at Avord saw a Messerschmitt Bf 110 beginning its take-off run with its navigation lights on. One low pass and a deadly accurate burst of cannon and machine gun fire resulted in the 110 bursting into flames and wrecking itself in a sprawling train of destruction.

By that date the German 'Revenge Weapons' assault on Britain using robot V1 'flying bombs' had begun to increase in volume and regularity both by day and by night, and 418 Squadron commenced its own campaign against these unmanned buzz-bombs. On 19 June Bannock opened his tally of V1s by destroying one as it crossed the English Channel; then on the night of 2/3 July flew to a V1 launching site near Abbeville and destroyed three in twenty minutes as these left their launching ramps. Three nights later, patrolling over the Channel, the Bannock/Bruce team destroyed four more V1s – three over the Channel and a fourth as it crossed the coast near Hastings. Two nights later they scored another double.

On 14 July the squadron moved base to Hurn, from where Bannock and Bruce accounted for two German aircraft on 17 July. Flying deep into Germany, they reached an airfield at Altenburg, south of Leipzig, to 'interrupt' a local searchlight co-operation exercise by chasing one German aircraft for some 75 miles, chewing pieces out of it with their cannons, before returning to the airfield and shooting down a second German in flames. Returning to their anti-V1 patrols, Bannock destroyed two more on 19 July, and scored yet another pair on 23 July. On the 26th and 27th he added another V1 destroyed each night, but operations were briefly interrupted on 29 July when 418 Squadron changed base again, going to Middle Wallop.

It remained at Middle Wallop for just four weeks, moving yet again on 28 August to Hunsdon, but in the interim Bannock had destroyed three more V1s – two on 4 August and the third on 12 August. Once settled in at Hunsdon, the squadron virtually returned to its prime role of intrusion operations, and Bannock flew many sorties at low level over the Continent seeking out road and rail transports and destroying or at least damaging dozens of both types of target.

Within 24 hours of moving to Hunsdon, however, Bannock and Bruce were flying on a daylight intruder sortie to the Luftwaffe base at Vaerlose, north-west of Copenhagen, where they were greeted by heavy defensive flak from a string of flak-posts around the airfield. Pushing the nose of his Mosquito down, Bannock streaked across the field, ignoring the flak, and blasted first a Ju 88 on the near perimeter track, then a Bf 110 in its blast bay dispersal, setting both on fire.

On 2 September Bannock was notified that he had been

awarded a DFC, and 'celebrated' this ten days later during a *Flower* sortie in support of Bomber Command. His combat report read:

We crossed the French coast at Coxyde at 2254 hrs and proceeded directly to the target area (Illesheim). After patrolling in the target area from 0044 hrs to 0212 hrs, we set course homewards. While passing just south of Kitzsingen at 0220 hrs we saw this aerodrome lit with double flare-path and east-west V/L. The right-hand bar of the outer and inner horizons were not lit. We commenced to prowl around the airfield at about 400 feet and almost immediately observed an aircraft with navigation lights on coming towards us, doing a steep climbing turn towards the aerodrome. I did a 180-degrees turn to port and followed the aircraft which was climbing steeply over the airfield. I positioned myself at about 125 yards behind and slightly below and fired a 1½-second burst of cannon and machine gun at about five-degrees angle-off to starboard. There were numerous strikes on the starboard side of the fuselage and along the starboard wing. Almost immediately I fired another 1½-second burst of both cannon and machine gun fire from the same position. Numerous strikes were again observed along the starboard wing and fuselage and the starboard engine exploded. The aircraft immediately dropped straight down and as we passed over it I started a turn to the right to observe results. During the turn there was a large flash on the ground below us, but as we completed the turn we could not see any fire on the ground. Since there was not a fire, we are claiming this aircraft as only probably destroyed, but as the starboard engine was seen to explode, and the subsequent flash seen from an explosion on the ground, we are almost certain that it crashed and request that the claim be raised to destroyed.

It is significant in the wording of his report that Russ Bannock continually referred to 'we', thus acknowledging readily the equal share in his successes of his navigator, Bruce. In doing so he shared the views of all other Mosquito intruder pilots that their

'Nav' was not merely a map-shuffling passenger but an essential fighting partner, due for as much recognition as themselves in any plaudits and successes. In Bruce's case his highly successful teamwork with Bannock was to earn him a DFC and Bar eventually.

September 27 brought further successes for Bannock and Bruce when they 'hunted for game' near the Parow airfield. As they arrived they saw six Messerschmitt Bf 108 training aircraft take off. Turning in behind this sextet, Bannock attacked one Bf 108 from dead astern and it disintegrated in mid-air. Then, near the adjacent Kubitzer Bay, he fastened his sight on a second Bf 108, fired, and saw his victim stagger under the impact of his cannon shells. It then turned in towards him, apparently seeking to ram the Mosquito. As it flashed past prior to diving headlong into the sea, the Bf 108 hit the Mosquito's port engine which erupted in flames. Bannock punched the propeller feathering button, then the engine fire extinguisher control, and the fire died out. Dropping to tree-top height, Bannock nursed his Mosquito homewards – a trip of some 600 miles – and by pure skill on his part, and accurate navigation from Bruce, finally reached base some four hours later: a feat of pure airmanship on both men's part which brought Bannock the award of a Bar to his DFC, and the DFC to Bruce.

Promotion to Wing Commander shortly after brought Bannock an appointment as commander of 418 Squadron on 10 October, succeeding Tony Barker at the helm, but his reign was relatively brief. Flying several more intrusion sorties, mainly strafing ground targets, 418 Squadron was officially withdrawn from operations on 20 November and moved next day to Hartford Bridge for a future role in support of the Allied armies in France as part of the 2nd Tactical Air Force (2nd TAF). Bannock, accordingly, relinquished command of 418 on 22 November and was immediately appointed OC No 406 Squadron RCAF at Colerne, which Mosquito unit moved base to the forward airfield at Manston on 27 November to commence intruder operations.

This move meant the parting of the Bannock-Bruce team, and with his new squadron Bannock selected Flight Lieutenant

C.J.Kirkpatrick, DFC as his new partner. Appropriately, this partnership registered 406 Squadron's first victory in its new role. On Christmas Eve Bannock and Kirkpatrick set out for Germany and found Paderborn airfield 'festively' lit up. Circling the field as unobtrusively as possible, Bannock waited patiently until, in the bright moonlight, he saw a Junkers Ju 88 with its undercarriage lowered turn in downwind, obviously preparing to land. Bannock closed to short range and his first burst set the Ju 88's port engine afire before exploding and setting the whole port wing on fire. The Ju 88 spiralled down to crash about three miles north-west of the airfield, spilling flaming wreckage over a wide area of the countryside.

The new year brought further action, and on 5 January Bannock and Kirkpatrick began a hunt in the Schleswig area and found Husum airfield lit up to receive a Heinkel He 111 which the Mosquito crew promptly shot down, the Heinkel spinning into a wooded dispersal area southwest of the airfield. Husum lights were immediately doused, so Bannock flew towards Schleswig where the ground defences challenged them. Switching on his navigation lights in the hope of fooling the ground gunners, Bannock then realised that they were in fact challenging another aircraft in the circuit – which was shot down in flames seconds later, though whether this unfortunate aircraft was German or British there was no way of knowing. Flying further afield to Jagel Bannock found nothing to attack so returned to Husum where he spotted another airfield nearby lit up – probably Eggebeck. Edging towards this field he saw a German aircraft briefly flash its lights on just before touching down, and as it taxied towards its dispersal Bannock strafed it, claiming it later as merely damaged.

The following weeks brought appalling weather conditions which restricted the intruders' activities to shallow penetration sorties, attacking railways and communications, but in April 1945 406 Squadron resumed its long-range operations in greater strength. The night of 4 April proved 'interesting' (*sic*) for Russ Bannock and a new navigator, Flight Lieutenant W.A.Boak, when they were initially despatched to the Fassberg area to stalk Luftwaffe night-fighter bases. En route to their objective they noticed the airfield at Delmenhorst lit up for night flying and decided to investigate. Even as they approached Delmenhorst they spotted a Focke Wulf Fw 190 burning its navigation lights and about to land. Giving it two short bursts, they saw sparks ricocheting off the 190 as their shells impacted, but then all lights were extinguished and they could only claim the 190 as damaged. Ten minutes later, having remained circuiting widely in the same area, they had a contact with another German aircraft, stalking this two or three times across the airfield, but eventually losing contact.

Shortly after, however, a German aircraft flew across the airfield with its navigation lights on. Chasing this latest potential victim, the Mosquito crew noticed that its lights were switched off as they approached, after which it flew straight across the centre of the airfield at some 3/400 feet. Bannock's instincts told him this might be a decoy for a second fighter to use as bait, looked around him and spotted just such a fighter behind and to one side of him. It was a single-engined aircraft and Bannock began a series of tail-chasing circuits with it at heights from 200 to 700 feet, but was still unable to get into a firing position, and his elusive opponent was swallowed up in the darkness.

Continuing their patrol, Bannock and Boak finally received a contact an hour later, followed it down to 400 feet, but then overshot the target aircraft as it was about to settle onto the end of a flarepath. Turning quickly, Bannock gave the machine a long burst and watched it abandon its landing to make another circuit. Four minutes later Bannock saw some faint green and white lights passing below him, 'investigated', and spotted an aircraft sneaking in for a quick landing at tree-top height. Just as its wheels were about to touch down Bannock fired, saw strikes on his target, and then watched it crash and explode on the edge of the flarepath. As he flew around the field Bannock could see the wreckage burning fiercely with ammunition exploding in all directions. He remained on patrol in the area for another thirty minutes, then with fuel states dictating caution, set course for Manston, satisfied with the night's work.

By late April 1945 the squadron's operational commitments had lessened considerably as the end of the European war neared.

23 April saw Bannock and Boak achieve their ultimate successes. In a 'borrowed' Mosquito, Bannock set out from Swannington to fly to Gilze-Rijen, refuelled there, then set off again to intrude to Rechlin and Wittstock. En route they made three separate contacts, chasing one of these for some considerable time, but all three proved to be other Mosquitos on similar missions. At Wittstock a fourth contact was received but this was lost, so Bannock visited Neubrandenburg and Neuruppin in turn, again with no success. Returning to Wittstock they made yet another contact which quickly developed into a determined stern chase. Their target, soon identified as a Ju 88, was taking violent evasive action, but when Bannock fired his first burst strikes were seen on the Ju 88, which went into a vertical dive, with its top, rear gunner opening up with accurate streams of red tracers at the Mosquito. On firing his second burst Bannock saw one German crew member take to his parachute, but his third burst sealed the Ju 88's fate. It burst into flames and crashed in a wood.

No 406 Squadron's final sorties were flown on 9 May 1945, when six of its Mosquito crews from Manston covered the Allied liberation of the Channel Islands. For Russ Bannock his war was over, and on 14 May he handed over the reins of squadron command to Wing Commander R.G.Gray, DFC, and was posted to RCAF headquarters in London as Director Operations.

On 17 August 1945 Bannock was awarded a DSO, its citation crediting him with the destruction of 'at least 11 enemy aircraft and others damaged, and he has also destroyed 19 flying bombs, in addition to causing considerable disruption to the enemy's lines of communication. Under this officer's inspiring leadership his squadron has obtained a fine record of successes.'

In September 1945 Bannock attended the RAF Staff College, but in the following year he returned to his native Canada, was released from the RCAF, and became a Sales Director for De Havilland (Canada) Aircraft.

CHAPTER FIFTEEN

Chesley Peterson

On Thursday, 11 December 1941 – four days after Japan devastated the American naval base at Pearl Harbour and simultaneously invaded Siam and Malaya – Germany and Italy formally declared war against the USA. Until then the USA had remained ostensibly neutral as far as the European conflict was concerned, though US President Franklin D. Roosevelt's interpretation of American 'neutrality' during 1939-41 had been, to say the least, equivocal, pursuing policies of overt support for the British cause. This sympathy with Britain's plight was reflected privately by the many Americans who made their individual ways to Britain with the hope of enlisting in one of its fighting Services, often at great personal risk and expense.

Perhaps typical of those eager volunteers were some 240 men who were eventually to form and serve with three 'all-American' fighter units in the RAF, Nos 71, 121, and 133 Squadrons – the 'Eagle' Squadrons. They came from all walks of American life and society, in varying shapes and sizes, ranging in years from the youngest, Gilmore Daniel, born in November 1925, to near-40 years old Harold Strickland. They reached Britain in myriad ways, some joining the French Foreign Legion and Armée de l'Air, others via the RCAF, while others came by boat or air at private expense despite legal opposition by American authorities. Many padded out their claimed flying experience, exaggerating totals of flying hours in order to short-cut their passage to a fighter squadron, some had to 'adjust' birth certificates to make them sound older than their true ages.

Among those early 'neutral' volunteers determined to get into the war was a lanky, blonde-haired, Mormon farmboy, Chesley Gordon Peterson. Born in 1920 in Santaquin, Utah, the son of a Mormon farmer, Brigham Peterson, young Chesley altered his

dr R Bannock *(lt)* and Fg
Bruce.

ey Peterson *(rt)* with
American 'Eagle', 'Gus'
ond, 71 Squadron, 1941.

ane V7608, XR-J, 71
' Sqn at Kirton-in-
ey, Lincs, early 1941.

(Left) Group Captain P G Jameson, DSO, DFC. *(Right)* Group Captain C B F Kingcome, DSO, DFC.

65 Sqn Spitfires just prior to the outbreak of war, 1939. Pilots were; Roland Tuck (FZ-L); Brian Kingcome (FZ-O); George Proudman (FZ-P); and Gordon Olive (FZ-A).

birth certificate in 1939 by adding two years to make him eligible to join the US Army Air Corps for pilot training. After primary flight instruction at Lindbergh Field, San Diego, he went to Randolph Field, Texas for basic flight training – and was quickly washed out, with his release documents annotated, 'Inherent lack of flying ability'. Determined to remain in aviation somehow, Peterson next took a job with the Douglas Aircraft company at Santa Monica, California where he befriended several other USAAC rejects and promptly helped form a 'Wash-Outs Club' as Vice-President.

While with the Douglas firm Peterson and his fellow 'Wash-Outs' were introduced to a Colonel Charles Sweeny who was privately (and strictly speaking, illegally) recruiting men to fight in some capacity with the Allied forces in Europe. Accepted by Sweeny for eventual enlistment in the RAF, Peterson and a few colleagues took a train to Canada in February 1940 – only to be met by American FBI agents who ordered them back to the USA with threats of gaol if they tried it again. In June 1940, however, Peterson again took a train over the Canadian border, then sailed from Halifax in the *Duchess of Richmond* in early July, arriving in England on 1 August 1940.

Commissioned as a Pilot Officer, RAF, Peterson was sent to No 5 FTS, Sealand for a short training course on RAF aircraft and procedures, then on 7 November 1940 arrived at Church Fenton to join the newly-forming No 71 Squadron, the first 'Eagle' unit. His arrival, with seven other Americans, coincided with the delivery of the first nine Hurricanes allotted to 71, these being flown in by No 85 Squadron. Two weeks later 71 Squadron was transferred to Kirton-in-Lindsey to begin working up to operation fitness; a status which became official from late January 1941. Commanded then by Squadron Leader William E.G.Taylor, an American, with Peterson already tacitly acknowledged as his virtual deputy, 71 Squadron flew its first operational sorties on 5 February – a shipping cover patrol – and within days had lost two pilots in unexplained circumstances. The Eagles' first taste of actual 'combat' with the Luftwaffe did not come until 13 April, when a lone Junkers Ju 88 was chased but eluded its pursuers. That same evening, near Calais, one Eagle,

Jim Alexander, tried to engage a Messerschmitt Bf 109 as it chased a fellow Hurricane pilot, John Flynn, and though Alexander's fire caused the Bf 109 to break away trailing smoke, it also damaged Flynn's aircraft ...! 71's base by then, since 5 April, was Martlesham Heath from where it operated very much as a lone unit, and in May Peterson was promoted to Flight Lieutenant as a Flight commander, while the squadron exchanged its Hurricane Is for Mk IIAs.

In June the squadron was moved again, this time to North Weald as part of the North Weald Wing, and from where Peterson claimed his first combat victory on 6 July by probably destroying a Bf 109. On 20 August 1941, after flying Hurricanes for some nine months, 71 Squadron received its first Spitfires, fourteen Mk IIAs, and on 7 September set out on a pure fighter sweep with the rest of the Wing to blood its Spitfires in action.

Led by their latest CO, Squadron Leader S.T.Meares, an RAF Battle of Britain veteran who had succeeded to command of 71 on 22 August, nine Spitfires of the squadron penetrated the French sky for some 75 miles inland and were about to turn for home when they were warned of a mass of Bf 109s between them and the French coast. As the top cover unit, 71 Squadron bore the brunt of the ensuing clash with an estimated force of about 100 Bf 109s. The Messerschmitts contented themselves with diving attacks by sections of three or four from some 29,000 feet, pecking away at the Spitfires, then climbing back to higher altitude. These tactics soon began to have deadly effect. Gene 'Red' Tobin and Hillard Fenlaw were killed, 'Bill' Nichols was forced to bale out of his burning aircraft and became a prisoner of war, 'Jack' Fessler suffered anoxia and narrowly escaped death in his diving Spitfire while unconscious and only recovering at virtual deck-level to fly home for an emergency landing at Shoreham, while Forrest 'Pappy' Dowling was shot down out of control, recovered, was chased halfway across the Channel by one determined Bf 109, and eventually crashlanded just inland from the Dover cliffs, scattering pieces of Spitfire in a broken trail across some farmland and hitting a stone wall – though apart from shock and bruising, his only injury proved to be a broken collar bone.

In balance, Peterson destroyed one Bf 109 for certain, while other pilots claimed a few as probables. Ten days later 71 Squadron were part of the escort for 24 Blenheim bombers which ran into heavy Luftwaffe opposition and lost two more pilots, one killed and one eventual prisoner, near Dunkirk. From this sortie Peterson could only claim one Bf 109 as damaged, but next day he destroyed a Messerschmitt, followed by another Bf 109 probably destroyed on 27 July.

On 15 November the squadron took off for a training flight in formation manoeuvres, with its commander, Meares, flying at the starboard rear position in order to watch his men, and Peterson leading the three four-aircraft formation as acting leader for this exercise. As the three sections began closing into a tight close-up manoeuvre two Spitfires collided, Meares and the Californian, Ross Scarborough. Meares' aircraft burst into flames and both Spitfires fell to earth, with neither pilot baling out. Next day Chesley Peterson was appointed as commanding officer of 71 Squadron, at the age of 21, and now wore the ribbon of a British DFC below his RAF wings. In December 1941, when the news of Japan's attack on Pearl Harbour was announced, Peterson immediately contacted the US Embassy in London to volunteer himself and his squadron for active duty with the Americans but was merely assured that 'something will be done' to transfer the Eagles to the USAAF eventually.

Days later Peterson received orders from No 11 Group HQ to prepare 71 Squadron for a move north, back to Kirton-in-Lindsey. Furious at the idea of being withdrawn from the action, Peterson went to Group HQ to see Air Marshal Leigh-Mallory to plead for his unit to remain in the south, but only met with a blunt refusal. Incensed, Peterson then went directly over his AOC's head to the AOC-in-C, Fighter Command, Sholto Douglas and put his case forcibly. A few days later 71 Squadron was on the move – not to Kirton-in-Lindsey but to Martlesham Heath; Peterson had won his point.

At Martlesham 71 became a free-lance squadron in Peterson's own description:

Ready to fly with any Wing that was short. Usually a Wing

consisted of three squadrons, and when it had a job of high cover for bombers it really needed to be reinforced with an additional squadron. Some of the really tough battles were fought by the top cover. Whenever the North Weald Wing drew the top cover assignment, we would reinforce them. The same with the Wings at Tangmere, Hornchurch, Biggin Hill or Duxford. For six months we really had a good time. I don't think Leigh-Mallory ever forgave me, but he never mentioned it.*

Part of that 'good time' was a continuance of flying escorts for the many RAF *Circus* operations over France, and Peterson notched up a Focke Wulf Fw 190 as 'damaged' on 25 April 1942, but two days later destroyed two Fw 190s and damaged a third during a particularly fierce series of combats. That day 71's pilots claimed a total of five 190s destroyed besides several probables and damaged, but lost John Flynn killed, while 'Bill' O'Reagan brought a severely damaged Spitfire back from the Dunkirk area in a virtual flat-glide to a safe landing in Kent.

In the first week of May 1942 Peterson led his squadron to a new base, Debden, and on the 19th probably destroyed a Fw 190. On 1 June the entire Debden Wing, including 71 Squadron, provided escort for eight Hurricanes bombing Bruges, and were attacked by some 50 Fw 190s. Peterson destroyed one 190, then shot pieces out of a second which disappeared spinning into a general mêlée below. That month Peterson got married to the South African-born actress Audrey Boyes, to whom he had been introduced by Wing Commander J.R.Robinson, MP (later, Lord Martonmere); the wedding took place at St Margaret's, Westminster.

Back again with his squadron, Peterson again led his men to a fresh base in mid-August, flying in to Gravesend in preparation for the Allied 'invasion' of Dieppe on 19 August. That day saw Peterson fly three sorties in Spitfire Vb, BM361, claiming a Junkers Ju 88 damaged on his first trip. On his third sortie he shot down a Ju 88 which spun into the sea but not before its rear

* *The Eagle Squadrons* by V.Haugland: David & Charles, 1979

gunner had slammed an accurate burst into Peterson's aircraft. Smoke filled Peterson's cockpit, so he jettisoned the cockpit canopy and took to his parachute.

As he floated down Peterson remembered that he had a revolver stuffed in one flying boot. Since he had never fired this weapon yet, he drew it out of his boot, fired off all six rounds, then threw it ahead of him into the sea. Hitting the water, Peterson extricated himself from his parachute harness, but within minutes was hauled out of the sea by the crew of a British motor torpedo-boat (MTB). On board he sat next to a Canadian RAF pilot also retrieved from a ditching. As the MTB headed back towards England a Fw 190 appeared out of low cloud and strafed the boat with cannon and machine gun, and when Peterson raised his head again it was to see that his companion had been killed, mere inches away from him.

On his return to his squadron Peterson learned that he had been awarded a DSO, and that he was to be rested from operations. With promotion to Lt-Colonel, USAAF, he was sent to the American HQ in London for a staff appointment, then detached to the USA to the Wright-Patterson Centre, Ohio to test American-designed fighter aircraft. Finally, on 29 September 1942 all three American Eagle squadrons were formally transferred from the RAF to the USAAF on a ceremonial parade at Debden. All three were then amalgamated to become the 4th Fighter Group of the USAAF's 8th Air Force, still flying Spitfires but eventually exchanging these for P-47 Thunderbolts and later P-51 Mustangs.

Peterson rejoined his Eagles on 20 August 1943 as the Group's commander, with full Colonel rank. Resuming operational flying with the Group, Peterson was to claim one more combat victory in July 1943 while escorting a B-17 Fortress bombing mission, and survived yet another bale-out into the sea, this time at about 1,000 feet which gave his parachute no time to deploy fully. Hitting the sea face-first, Peterson, in his own words, ' ... took a high dive into the briny, got two beautiful "shiners", and drank some of the coldest damned water ever'.

As with his first ditching, Peterson was rescued quickly, this time by a Supermarine Walrus from No 276 Squadron RAF.

Hospitalised for nearly a week, shocked, badly bruised, and temporarily blinded, Peterson soon recovered and returned to duty. Awarded an American Distinguished Service Cross soon after, Peterson relinquished command of the 4th FG on 23 December 1943 on appointment to a staff job at the USAAF's 9th Air Force headquarters.

By the end of the war, Peterson's combat record showed nearly 200 operational sorties, during which he had destroyed nine enemy aircraft confirmed, probably destroyed seven, and damaged at least five others – a fairly distinguished record for a boy once graded as having 'Inherent inability to fly'. Remaining in the American air force, Peterson eventually rose to the rank of Major-General, USAF.

CHAPTER SIXTEEN

Patrick Jameson

Early in 1941 RAF Fighter Command created a new operational appointment, that of Wing Leader. Relating only (initially) to single-seat fighter aircraft units, this command position was for a Wing Commander literally to lead the three, four, or (eventually) up to five fighter squadrons of each Command Sector on operations, not only as the literal spearhead but also the tactical planner and shepherd of his particular flock. Patently, such high responsibilities called for men well experienced already in modern aerial combat, well used to commanding men in battle, and the first two appointed Wing Leaders were Douglas Bader and Adolph 'Sailor' Malan.

While, inevitably, a majority of Wing Leaders throughout the years 1941-45 were established high-scoring aces, pure victory tallies were by no means the criterion for filling such vital posts. The prime needs were coolness in judgment under fire, instinctive tactical know-how, initiative, and – by no means least – personal example which would inspire trust and confidence in all subordinates. It was no job for the individual glory-hunter or men solely concerned with increasing their score; once airborne with his Wing the Leader's prime concern was in placing his formations in the best possible position at all times to fulfil any given task. Once combat was joined with any enemy forces it was his role to keep an overall watch on the ensuing maelstrom as far as humanly possible; guiding, advising, protecting, marshalling his men, yet taking a full personal part in the fighting. One such outstanding leader was Patrick Geraint – 'Jamie' - Jameson.

Born on 10 November 1912 in Wellington, New Zealand, Jameson was the son of R.D.Jameson, a Dublin Irishman who had emigrated to New Zealand to provide his family with a better living. Educated at Hutt Central School and Hutt Valley High School, young Jameson completed his schooling in August 1929 and took employment with an assurance company as a clerk in Wellington. Four years later, having been bitten by the flying bug, he learned to fly privately at the Wellington Aero Club, Rongotai, proving himself to be a 'natural' by making his first solo flight after merely 2½ hours' dual instruction on DH Gipsy Moth biplanes.

Gaining further flying experience over the next two years, Jameson left New Zealand on 7 January 1936 to sail to England in the *Aorangi* at his own expense in the hope of joining the RAF. Accepted initially for pilot training on 9 March 1936, his *ab initio* pilot instruction was carried out at the civil De Havilland School at Hatfield. On completion of that phase he was enlisted as an Acting Pilot Officer (on probation) with effect from 4 May 1936 for a Short Service Commission, and on 16 May was posted to No 8 FTS, Montrose for Service flying training; other men on his particular course including such future fighter notables as Ian Gleed, N.J.Starr, and L.G.Schwab. In October 1936 came his graduation and RAF 'wings', with a 'Distinguished Pass' annotated on his records, followed on Christmas Day by official notification that he was to join No 46 Squadron.

Based then at Kenley, commanded by Squadron Leader P.R. 'Dickie' - Barwell, No 46 Squadron was a fighter unit, flying Gloster Gauntlets, doped overall in silver finish with the red arrow-head unit markings superimposed along the flanks of fuselages. As in all peacetime RAF fighter squadrons, the accent in flying was on formation work and aerobatics, and Jameson's natural affinity with his aircraft led to his inclusion in the unit's aerobatic team which took part in the 1937 RAF Annual Display at Hendon. Remaining with 46 Squadron when it moved base to Digby in November 1937, Jameson converted to Hurricanes in February 1939 as these began replacing the unit's obsolete biplanes, and in April that year received promotion to Flight Lieutenant and given command of 46's 'B' Flight. Still based at Digby when war was declared in September 1939, the squadron immediately commenced coastal patrols over the nearby North Sea shipping lanes, and in the following month received a new commander, Squadron Leader Kenneth Cross.* Its first real

* Later, Air Chief Marshal Sir Kenneth B.B.Cross, KCB,CBE,DSO,DFC.

contact with the Luftwaffe came on 21 October when a patrol encountered about nine Heinkel He 115 floatplanes and promptly shot down three and damaged a fourth. Though a boost to squadron morale, this engagement proved to be an exception to the routine patrols which continued for the following six months.

The prospect of 'live' action finally arrived in April 1940 when 46 Squadron was warned to prepare for a move to France, and Jameson was among a small party of unit officers who flew to Rheims to complete preparations, but only a week later the order was cancelled, and instead 46 Squadron was issued with Arctic clothing and despatched in some haste to Scotland where the Hurricanes were put aboard the aircraft carrier HMS *Glorious*. On 18 May, in company with HMS *Furious* which was carrying No 263 Squadron (Gladiators), and four destroyer escorts, HMS *Glorious* sailed for Norway. On 21 May a signal was received to say that 46 Squadron's intended destination airfield, Skaanland, was unable to receive Hurricanes until at least 26 May, so the naval force, after disembarking 263 Squadron, returned to Scapa Flow, refuelled, then sailed again for Norway on 24 May.

Two days later Squadron Leader Cross led the first batch of 46's Hurricanes off the *Glorious* and flew to Skaanland where two aircraft crashed on landing due to the airfield surface still being unsuitable for heavy fighters. Immediately signalling to Jameson, who by then was leading the remaining Hurricanes to shore, Cross ordered him to divert to Bardufoss, a nearby field more amenable to Hurricane landings. Operations commenced next day without incident, but on 28 May Jameson and a second Hurricane pilot located two four-engined Dornier Do 26 flying boats moored close under a near-perpendicular cliff in Rombaks Fiord. By attacking these from 90-degrees to the cliff face, Jameson and his companion managed to set both flying boats on fire, though the necessary vertical climb to avoid hitting the fiord wall proved 'slightly hairy' (*sic*).

Next morning Jameson was again on patrol seeking the Luftwaffe when he spotted a Vic of three Ju 88s over Ofot Fiord. Closing under the tail of the rearmost Ju 88 to some 200 yards range, Jameson put a burst into its starboard engine which promptly plumed smoke. As he turned in for a second attack the Ju 88 jettisoned its bomb-load. Jameson's second burst hit the Ju 88's already damaged engine which now erupted in flames, spreading the fire to its fuselage, then one crew man baled out, and the burning Junkers demolished itself against a cliff face.

Within a week the British 'presence' in Norway was clearly untenable, despite almost continuous action by the two RAF squadrons, and on 7 June the survivors of 263 Squadron flew back to HMS *Glorious* for return to Britain, but Kenneth Cross received an order to destroy all 46's Hurricanes before embarking personnel to the Royal Navy force standing by off the Norwegian coast. Having no form of arrester gear, the Hurricanes were considered impossible to land safely aboard an aircraft carrier. The thought of deliberately destroying his squadron's aircraft was repugnant to Cross, who prevailed upon Captain d'Oyly Hughes of the *Glorious* to allow him to try to 'fly on' his ten Hurricanes. This request was granted, the Hurricanes had 15 lb sandbags stowed in each tail section, and Jameson led the first three aboard the carrier without mishap, to be followed later by Cross and the remaining Hurricanes; though none of the pilots had ever attempted a landing aboard an aircraft carrier before. Though its stay in Norway had been brief, 46 Squadron had totted up 249 individual sorties, engaged in 26 combats with the Luftwaffe, and claimed at least 11 German aircraft destroyed.

Setting sail to England on 8 June, the *Glorious* was sighted by the German raiders *Scharnhorst* and *Gneisenau* late that evening, and in the early hours of 9 June the guns of the *Scharnhorst* straddled the carrier with deadly accuracy, and also sank its attendant destroyers *Ardent* and *Acasta*. Jameson, who was sleeping in a cabin when the *Glorious* was shelled, awoke to hear the order to abandon ship, dived into the sea and swam to a Carley Float on which he found Kenneth Cross and several seamen. Other ship's crew were soon clambering aboard or clinging to the float until eventually 29 men, including Jameson and Cross, were holding on to the float.

For the next three days and nights the float's passengers declined in numbers as the freezing air and sea took their toll, until when a Norwegian fishing boat hove alongside and retrieved Jameson he was one of only seven men left aboard the float. Their rescuers, a Norwegian crew who had decided to sail to England to continue their war with Germany, had only spotted the float by chance en route. Eventually reaching England all seven survivors were hospitalised for many weeks, but two seamen died, leaving just Jameson and Cross and three seamen of the original complement of 29.

Three months were to pass before Jameson was declared fully fit for flying again, but in the interim he was awarded a DFC on 19 July for his Norwegian venture. His return to operations came at the height of the Battle of Britain, when on 17 September 1940 he succeeded to the command of No 266 Squadron, a Spitfire unit based at Wittering which had been recently heavily involved in the Battle over London, and was now only half-operational in strength, replenishing its personnel and equipment. Jameson soon brought 266 up to full operational fitness but by that time the Battle of Britain by day was petering out and the Luftwaffe had turned mainly to night-bombing British cities and industrial centres.

By the spring of 1941 Jameson's squadron was one of several day fighter units which flew 'Fighter Nights' – night patrols by free-lancing Spitfires *et al* on moonlit nights seeking German bombers above the anti-aircraft guns' maximum fire heights, albeit without benefit of radar or even elementary night-flying aids. On one such night-hunt on 9 April Jameson was patrolling above Coventry at 18,000 feet when he sighted a Heinkel He 111 and quickly attacked. His tracer and incendiary bullets dazzled him as they struck home on the bomber but he made a second attack, setting the Heinkel on fire and sending it down steadily disintegrating as it fell. On 10 May, over London, Jameson claimed another He 111 destroyed.

With promotion to Wing Commander in June 1941, Jameson handed over command of 266 Squadron to Squadron Leader T.B.de la P.Beresford, and became Wing Leader for the Wittering Wing. On 23 June Jameson led his Wing as part of an 18-squadron fighter escort for 24 Blenheim bombers attacking a power station in northern France; his Wing's specific role being top cover for the withdrawal phase by patrolling between Le

Touquet and Hardelot between 15,000 and 20,000 feet.

The operation was uneventful until the Blenheims began their return journey, when a strong force of Messerschmitt Bf 109s descended on the 'retreating' bombers. Two Bf 109s fastened onto Jameson's tail, but as one overshot him he sank a brief burst into its belly and it fell to earth.

The next few weeks kept Jameson busy, organising and (usually) leading the Wittering Wing on sweeps over France, but in September 1941 he took time out from his duties to marry Hilda Webster, a New Zealander from his home town who had travelled to England in the previous May to be with her fiancée. On 15 September he was back in action, destroying a Bf 110, and in the following month was awarded a Bar to his DFC, followed by a 'Mentioned in Despatches' in the 1942 New Year's Honours List. Remaining as commander of the Wittering Wing throughout 1942, Jameson did not add to his personal tally until 19 August, the day of the Allied one-day 'invasion' of Dieppe.

Moving his Wing temporarily to West Malling for this operation, Jameson 'borrowed' a Spitfire, BM232, from No 485 Squadron and led three sorties over the invasion forces that day. On the first of these he spotted a Focke Wulf Fw 190 diving on one of his Spitfires, closed behind it, then shot it in flames into the sea. In December 1942, Jameson's high reputation led to his transfer to become leader of the Norwegian Wing – Nos 331 and 332 Squadrons – based at North Weald, an appropriate appointment in view of his 1940 sojourn in Norway.

During the first four months of 1943 'Jamie' Jameson led his new Wing on almost every occasion it operated, including 21 sorties in a nine-weeks period which saw the Wing claim at least thirteen German fighters destroyed for the loss of just two pilots. Two of these – Fw 190s – fell to Jameson's cannons on 15 February while escorting a B-24 Liberator bombing mission; followed by another Fw 190 damaged on 10 March.

In early February, during one such sweep, Jameson came very close to death in a lone fight against eight Germans. Leading his Wing over the Ypres-St Omer-Gravelines area, he was warned of enemy fighters high above and started climbing to manoeuvre into an attacking position. Having done so, he noticed more enemy fighters higher still so continued to climb, not realising that his two wing-men had dived after the first batch of Fw 190s, each thinking the other was Jameson. Still blissfully unaware he was on his own, he dived on a gaggle of nine Fw 190s below him, following them down to 2,500 feet before breaking off the pursuit and finally realising his solitary state.

Starting to climb towards Gravelines he reached 20,000 feet – only to be jumped by eight Fw 190s. His combat report read in part:

I turned to meet the attack but the Huns formed a sort of circle around me and kept darting in to attack from all directions. I fired one burst and at the end of two seconds both my cannons stopped. I called up the Wing and told them I was being attacked but gave no height and only a very rough position. I had by this time got a little 'het up' and although I did try to tell the Wing my position, I think that I forgot to press the R/T switch.

The Huns continued to attack, sometimes in to 100 yards. I could see two great balls of fire coming from their cannons. I continually turned steeply almost in a stalled condition and every time I saw a Hun firing I clicked on a little top or bottom rudder. Realising that I could not stay there forever, I wound the tail wheel forward and went down almost vertically doing tight aileron turns. The aircraft became unstable at the speed I achieved and on at least four occasions the nose dropped quickly and I hit my head on the cockpit cover with a bang. By the time I got down to the cloud my windscreen and hood were completely frosted over with the exception of a visor about one inch wide around the rear of the hood.

The Huns were still following as I flew into cloud. I then turned north-east and crossed the coast north of Dunkirk, by this time flying on the deck. I steered a course of 280-degrees for what seemed an incredibly long time and at last saw land, cliffs, a lighthouse and high ground behind. These made no sense, but after cudgelling my brains I looked at the sun … it was Cap Gris Nez … my compass was u/s [unserviceable]. Turning and keeping the sun behind my left shoulder, I cut the engine revolutions and boost down and made for home, landing after being airborne for two hours with 15 gallons [of petrol] still in the tanks, the aircraft and myself unscathed.

By the close of March 1943 Jameson had been flying on operations almost continually for three and a half years, and accordingly was rested with a posting to No 11 Group HQ as a planning officer, and in the same month he was awarded a DSO, the citation for which laid heavy emphasis on his 'zealous leadership'. On 1 October 1943 he received a further honour, the award of the Norwegian War Cross with Sword – Norway's highest decoration – for his leadership of the Norwegian Wing; and in November he was promoted to Group Captain Plans, though he still managed to slot in occasional fighter sorties with 11 Group operations. He remained at his planning desk for the pre-invasion period prior to 6 June 1944, but on 25 July returned to operations at the sharp end by succeeding Wing Commander C.F. – 'Bunny' – Currant, DFC as commander of No 122 Wing, 2nd Tactical Air Force, flying Mustangs and, later, Tempests over Europe. From then until the end of hostilities in Europe Jameson participated in most Wing operations, strafing, rocketing, fighting anything marked with a Nazi swastika.

After the war his Wing was disbanded on 7 September 1945 and Jameson became Station Commander of first Schleswigland, then Wunstorf airfields. Remaining in the RAF he was eventually promoted to Air Commodore in April 1956, and finally retired from service on 6 August 1960, returning with his childhood sweetheart, now his wife, to Lower Hutt, New Zealand in December of that year.

CHAPTER SEVENTEEN

Brian Kingcome

While Hugh Trenchard's Aircraft Apprenticeship scheme centred upon RAF Halton was intended as the fount of his Service's future technical spine, his visionary proposals for the post-World War One air force included the equally important intention for RAF Cranwell to be the foundation for the RAF's new officer 'corps'. Here carefully selected embryo officers were to receive two years' concentrated flying and technical instruction, be inculcated into the traditions and very spirit of Trenchard's vision of the future Third Service, then emerge permanently commissioned to build the Service to a status at least equal to its much older Army and Royal Navy brothers in efficiency and strategic importance.

The years 1920-39 were to see Cranwell produce a host of men who, in their highly individual ways, were to fulfil all Trenchard's predictions. Whatever their· particular character, the majority of ex-Cranwell cadets had at least one facet in common – professionalism. Though the prime incentive for most on enlistment had been – indeed, remained – the desire to fly, it was an ambition soon tinged with the realisation that they were not simply being nurtured as pilots but as the professional core of a fighting Service, as leaders of men, as exponents of a form of strategic warfare only vaguely understood for its eventual impact on the future of mankind.

While undergoing the rigours of cadet training such serious implications were not always apparent to the light-hearted youngsters at Cranwell, yet if only unconsciously they gradually absorbed such lessons, developing a distinctive attitude to their job which was to be exemplified in myriad ways when the crucial test of war came. One of so many ex-cadets to demonstrate the true value of his Cranwell training was Charles Brian Fabris

Kingcome, a fighter pilot whose apparent imperturbability in combat was matched by an uncommon vitality in off-duty pleasures. Born on 31 May 1917 and educated at Bedford, Kingcome entered Cranwell as a cadet in the summer of 1936 and eventually graduated and was commissioned on 30 July 1938 with a posting as a fighter pilot to No 65 Squadron at Hornchurch. Flying Gloster Gladiators, 65 Squadron was commanded then by Squadron Leader Desmond Cooke,* and among its pilots was a slim, rakish young Flying Officer whom Kingcome was to befriend, Robert Tuck,† with whom Kingcome shared a somewhat similar attitude to life in general and their professional role in particular. In March 1939 the squadron began exchanging its Gladiator biplanes for Spitfire Is, and was fully operational on these on the outbreak of war, still based at Hornchurch.

No 65 Squadron flew its first war sorties on 5 September 1939 – an uneventful patrol – and in October was moved to Northolt, but was to see no combat until May 1940, by which time it had returned to its peacetime base at Hornchurch. On 17 May 1940, however, it opened its war tally with the destruction of a Ju 88 over Flushing, and was soon embroiled in daily air cover for the Allied armies in France as these retreated to Dunkirk and began to be evacuated to England.

Kingcome first fired his guns in anger on 25 May when he shared in the destruction of a Dornier, but two days later he was posted to No 92 Squadron at Duxford. Having had several days of intensive fighting and heavy losses, including its CO, Squadron Leader Roger Bushell, 92 Squadron was temporarily 'resting' while it replaced its casualties in men and machines, and was now commanded by Bob Tuck who had organised Kingcome's transfer, promoted him to Flight Lieutenant, and given him a Flight to command. The move was virtually a reunion of kindred spirits for Tuck and Kingcome who now became close friends and fighting partners, both on and off duty.

On 2 June No 92 Squadron was ordered to Martlesham Heath to take part in a four-squadrons' sweep of the Calais-Dunkirk air zone – the other units being Nos 32, 266, and 611 Squadrons – led

* Killed in action with 65 Squadron on 8 July 1940
† Later, Wing Commander R.R.S.Tuck, DSO,DFC.

92 Sqn's 1940 tally. *Lt-rt:* Two non-flying officers; Plt Off R Mottram; Sgt R E 'Titch' Havercroft; Flt Lt Brian Kingcome; Sqn Ldr J A Kent (OC); Flt Lt J W 'Pancho' Villa; Plt Off C H 'Fishy' Saunders; Fg Off R H 'Dutch' Holland; Fg Off A R 'Tony' Wright; Sgt Bowen-Morris; Sgt Don Kingaby.

(Left) Flight Sergeant Don Kingaby after a Palace investiture of his 'triple' DFM award.
(Right) Wing Commander D E Kingaby, DSO, DFM.

(Left) Wg Cdr B R O'B Hoare, DSO, D

(Below) Wg Cdr B R O'B Hoare receiv
a silver model of a Mosquito to mark N
605 Sqn's 100th victory, Dorchester
Hotel, 15 April 1944. *Lt-rt:* Fg Off Potte
DFC; Hoare; Grp Capt J A Cecil, AFC,
MP; Air Cmdre Sir Lindsay Everard, M

by Tuck and his men of 92 Squadron. In separate layers spread from 23,000 feet down to 14,000 feet, the squadrons reached the Dunkirk scene, with Tuck leading his own unit down to 9,000 feet to tackle a loose formation of Heinkel He 111s. These were soon joined by more He 111s and their escorting Bf 109s.

Kingcome, leading Red Section, joined the initial dive at the Heinkels but on seeing two other Sections already about to engage them veered to the right to attack three others. Selecting the right-hand Heinkel he riddled both its engines, one of them bursting into flames, the other belched smoke, and the bomber's undercarriage fell down, presumably due to ruptured hydraulics. As it fell into low cloud Kingcome's Spitfire became coated in oil from the Heinkel. Switching to a second Heinkel he probably destroyed it, then used up his remaining ammunition by slashing pieces of metal out of its wings and fuselage.

The squadron diary that night claimed a total of fourteen He 111s and four Bf 109s destroyed, though the score was later amended by officialdom to read eleven He 111s and two Bf 109s confirmed destroyed, with six Heinkels and one 109 probably destroyed.

On 18 June the squadron was transferred from No 11 Group to Pembrey to help guard the Bristol Channel area, a less hectic zone of the aerial war but one which offered occasional clashes with would-be German raiders; two of which, both Ju 88s, Kingcome shared in shooting down on 10 and 24 July respectively. On 9 September, however, the 'Ninety-Second Foot and Mouth' (their own derisive nickname) returned to the hot war with a move to Biggin Hill, changing stations with No 79 Squadron. On arrival at 'The Bump', as Biggin Hill was dubbed locally, 92 Squadron was under the command of Squadron Leader P.J.Sanders, but by now Brian Kingcome, boss of A Flight, was usually the leader in the air.

Within 24 hours of arrival 92 had made its mark, claiming a Heinkel destroyed and two Bf 109s almost certainly shot down; the Heinkel and one Messerschmitt falling to Kingcome's guns. Within days the squadron's pilots had been billeted in Southwood, a manor house some two miles away from the airfield, for their safety; Biggin Hill was still a principal bombing target for the Luftwaffe. Here the pilots quickly settled in:

> Once the owner, Captain McNair, had stored his precious
> furnishings and pictures in safety, the squadron moved in
> complete with jazz band (the batmen had been selected for
> their skills with saxophone, trumpet and trombone) and
> cellarful of liquor. Lit by oil lamps and candles, with casual,
> cigarette-scarred furniture, 92 Squadron's new home carelessly
> achieved the effect of a sophisticated night club, occasionally
> the scene of parties which lasted until dawn warned the
> roisterers that it was time to prepare for another day of battle.*

While Kingcome was virtually the squadron's fighting leader, he
was also very much the moving spirit of the unit on the ground,
the focal point around which most squadron activities revolved,
and fully exemplifying his usual nickname 'Kingpin'. Over the
following weeks the squadron had two official commanding
officers but 'lost' both quickly; Sanders was wounded on 23
September, while his replacement, Squadron Leader A.M.Mac-
lachlan, was hospitalised with severed tendons of a hand when
battering his way out of a jammed cockpit in October.

Accordingly, 92's men simply accepted Kingcome as their boss
in most matters – he at least seemed indestructible. Whether
lounging in the dispersal hut, or crisply guiding his men in battle,
Kingcome never flapped, displaying an apparent air of disdain
mixed with a form of pragmatism which contrasted greatly with
the overt gaiety and energy he demonstrated during the off-duty
parties. His attitude to his job was disarmingly simple; do the
maximum damage to the greatest number of German aircraft
possible.

By the close of the Battle Kingcome's combat record would
show a lot more enemy aircraft claimed as probably destroyed or
damaged than definite, confirmed victories; to Kingcome it was a
matter of indifference whether his claims were confirmed, just as
long as *he* knew he'd 'clobbered' every aircraft he had fired at.
Totting up a score of personal victories was of no interest,

* *RAF Biggin Hill* by G. Wallace; Putnam, 1957.

glory-hunting was just not his style, though he derived as much satisfaction as any other 92 Squadron member in watching the unit's combat log increase almost daily. Kingcome's particular cronies were A.C. 'Tony' Bartley and 'Bob' Holland, but other stalwarts at this time included such fighters as Roy Mottram, Johnny Bryson, Allan Wright, and the non-commissioned 'Titch' Havercroft and Don Kingaby. Some would not survive the war, others were destined for high rank and honours.

At Biggin Hill that September 92 Squadron was in combat daily, with trade plentiful and abundantly 'accessible'. On the 11th Kingcome destroyed a Heinkel, on the 14th damaged a pair of Bf 109s, damaged a Dornier next day, then on the 18th had something of a field day, destroying two Ju 88s, probably destroying an He 111 and at least damaging another Heinkel. His award of a DFC followed with a citation crediting him with six victories. The fighting continued apace, with Kingcome destroying a Bf 109 on 23 September, probably destroying a Bf 109 and damaging a Ju 88 next day, and on 27 September he shared the destruction of a Ju 88, probably destroyed a Dornier, and damaged two more Ju 88s and a second Dornier. October brought little slackening in the pace. On the consecutive days 11th, 12th, and 13th Kingcome's guns accounted for three Bf 109s destroyed and a fourth damaged in toto, but on 15 October he was at the receiving end, being shot down, wounded, and having to bale out of his crippled Spitfire – though Kingcome later gave as his opinion that he'd been the victim of another Spitfire's wild shooting.

He was taken to the naval hospital at Chatham for treatment, but eventually returned to 92 Squadron after the Battle had ceased. His temporary loss meant that 92 Squadron was again leaderless, and on 26 October Squadron Leader John Kent, DFC,AFC, arrived to take up his new command, and on 27 February 1941, the Canadian Kent was in turn succeeded by the Scots Squadron Leader 'Jamie' Rankin.

Kingcome's remaining months with 92 Squadron brought him two more victories – a Bf 109 on 16 June and another on 24 July – but he was then rested for some six months, having been continually operating for almost exactly two years without real respite. Promotion to Squadron Leader brought him command of No 72 Squadron at Gravesend in February 1942, and within days of taking up this appointment he was hastily ordered to take his squadron off to escort six RN Swordfish on 12 February, as part of the various aerial forces despatched to attack the German battleships *Scharnhorst, Gneisenau,* and *Prinz Eugen* as these approached the Dover Straits in their break-out run eastwards from Brest.

In the event, Kingcome's 72 Squadron was the only one of five Spitfire squadrons detailed for the task to rendezvous with the six Swordfish, and had to face greatly superior numbers of German fighters over the Channel. In the fighting which followed Kingcome shot down a Focke Wulf FW 190. By then he had been awarded a Bar to his DFC in late 1941, its citation noting a total of ten confirmed victories, while further promotion to Wing Commander in 1942 gave him command of the Kenley Wing, which he led over France and the Low Countries and gained three more combat victories by probably destroying a FW 190 on April 15, destroying a Bf 109 and probably destroying another fighter in the following month.

Awarded a DSO for 'inspiring leadership', Kingcome was next posted to the Middle East where, with promotion to Group Captain, he commanded No 244 Wing of the Western Desert Air Force; a grouping of fighter squadrons which included his former 92 Squadron. He remained in command of this Wing until October 1944, when he was succeeded by Group Captain Hugh 'Cocky' Dundas, DSO,DFC, and became a senior administration officer (SASO) to a Liberator bomber group flying over the Italian and Balkans areas of operations. Though still a senior staff officer, Kingcome still managed to fly occasionally, on one occasion as a Liberator's waist gunner on a sortie over Yugoslavia. Remaining in the RAF after the war Brian Kingcome eventually retired as a Group Captain on 26 January 1954.

CHAPTER EIGHTEEN

Donald Kingaby

Each year for the past forty years the date 15 September has been celebrated as the official commemoration anniversary of the RAF's victory in 1940 over the Luftwaffe – the British-termed Battle of Britain. On that day RAF fighter pilots' claims for enemy aircraft shot down totalled 185, the greatest single day's tally of the Battle, although postwar evidence confirms the *actual* number as only a third of that figure. If indeed sheer casualties were to be the criterion for selection of a particular day to commemorate, then Sunday, 18 August, proved to be the most destructive for both the RAF and the Luftwaffe; the Germans losing an overall total of 100 aircraft put out of action, while the RAF lost 135 aircraft either in the air or on the ground directly attributable to Luftwaffe activities. Eight of those RAF fighters either destroyed or damaged on the ground were from a formation of eleven Spitfires of No 266 Squadron. Normally based at Wittering, the 266 Squadron Spitfires had been airborne shortly after midday attempting to thwart determined German bomber assaults on various RAF fighter airfields. As they began to return to base to refuel and re-arm, their leader, Flight Lieutenant Dennis Armitage, received an order from his controller to land at the forward base at Manston instead, and accordingly took his men down to the already bomb-cratered landing ground.

Even as 266's Spitfires threaded their way through the bomb craters on Manston, they had been spotted by Oberleutnant Wolfgang Ewald leading sixteen Messerschmitt Bf 109s from JG52 on a general 'hunt' over Kent. Ordering ten Bf 109s from *Staffel* 3 to remain as top cover, Ewald led the remaining six from *Staffel* 2 down, aiming for the bunched up Spitfires as these were beginning to be refuelled. His attack came in at deck-level, catching everyone on the airfield by surprise; the grounded

165

airmen only realising they were under attack as cannon shells and machine gun bullets began tearing furrows in the grass around them. Among the final section of 266's Spitfires to land and taxi towards a refuelling bowser was Sergeant Don Kingaby who recalled: 'They hit us soon after I taxied in. There was no warning, just the roar of their engines. I glanced round and found myself looking along the nose of a Messerschmitt coming straight for me.'

Jumping away from his aircraft, Kingaby flung himself flat, face down, as the earth spouted in front of him. Marking those spouts, he then rolled sideways as the next burst reached towards him, felt a blow on his hand, but was too busy watching the bullet spouts to worry about any injury, and continued rolling from side to side dodging each succeeding hail of fire. When the last Bf 109 had left the scene, Kingaby could see two of his unit's Spitfires burning fiercely, while six others bore the scars of the Bf 109's accurate firing. Looking at his hand he found one finger scarred from a bullet strike. It was the only combat injury Don Kingaby was to suffer throughout nearly five years of air fighting, during which time he was to rise to high rank and become one of Fighter Command's premier pilots.

The son of the Reverend P.F.Kingaby, Donald Ernest Kingaby was born in Holloway, London on 7 January 1920, and was educated at King's School, Ely, near Impington, Cambridgeshire where his father was Vicar. On leaving school Kingaby took a job as a clerk in an insurance office, but in April 1939 he joined the RAF Volunteer Reserve, and was consequently enlisted in the RAFVR from the start of the war, being trained as a pilot and, in June 1940, joining No 266 Squadron at Wittering to fly Spitfires, with the rank of Sergeant.

Of medium build and mild in manner, Kingaby slotted into his unit almost unobtrusively, with no hint of his future prowess, but after several weeks of mainly uneventful patrols, he had his first combat successes on 12 August, 1940, when he damaged two Ju 88s and then shot chunks out of a Bf 110. In action almost daily over the next few weeks, Kingaby failed to register any further claims while with 266, but on 25 September he joined

92 Squadron at Biggin Hill and two days later claimed a Bf 109 as damaged, followed by another Bf 109 on the 30th. Four more victories came in October – two Bf 109s, a Bf 110, and a Dornier – but he hit the headlines in November. Destroying yet another Bf 109 on 1 November, his greatest day came two weeks later on the 15th. On that date the 'unobtrusive' Sergeant shot down four Bf 109s in the course of two sorties.

As he described the day in a later radio broadcast: 'On this particular occasion our squadron was sent out in the morning and intercepted a formation of fifty 109s coming in over the Channel. When our leader gave the order to attack I got on the tail of four 109s at about 17,000 feet and attacked the outside one. After I had given him two bursts of fire he crashed near Gravesend. When I looked round again the sky was full of Messerschmitts scattering in all directions. We chased them back to France and returned to our stations for lunch.

'In the afternoon we were sent up again and told that there were 109s off Selsey Bill. We saw them when we were at 20,000 feet. There were 40 of them about 500 feet above us. As they outnumbered us by more than three to one, I suppose they thought they were onto a good thing. At all events, they started to dive on us. We evaded their first attack and then turned on them. I picked on three. They made off towards France, one straggling a bit behind. I concentrated my fire on him and he went down in flames. The other two Messerschmitts had not seen me come up so I closed up behind the leader and gave him a burst. As I did so the other one on my right came up on my tail. But I held onto the fellow I'd got. He must have been carrying a bomb for, after another burst from my guns, he blew up before the one behind could protect him. There was nothing left in the sky that you could recognise as part of a plane. Just a flash and a puff of smoke and bits of debris hurtling all over the place.'

Kingaby's fourth victim that day was also shot down in the afternoon sortie. Three days later he destroyed another Bf 109, and was awarded a DFM, by which time the popular press was highlighting Kingaby's seeming penchant for shooting down Messerschmitts, calling him 'The 109 Specialist'. And it was a Bf 109 destroyed on 1 December which closed his 1940 tally.

In early 1941 92 Squadron, like most units of Fighter Command, turned from defensive to offensive operations, flying day sweeps over France, usually in support of *Circus* bomber sorties designed to suck up the Luftwaffe's defending fighters into a battle of attrition. On one such sweep on 14 February Kingaby fastened on the tail of one Bf 109 and chased it across the Channel before finally sending it down to crash near Cap Gris Nez. On 16 May he destroyed another 109 and at least damaged a second, while on 23 June he sent a Bf 109 spinning down to crash near Béthune. On 2 July, while returning from a sortie to the Lille area, Kingaby saw a pair of Bf 109s dive across his front, followed seconds later by a second pair. Turning quickly behind the second duo he snapped a burst into each then climbed away in case any others were following. Below him one Bf 109 pilot took to his parachute but both 109s plunged straight into the sea. Next day he claimed another Bf 109 as probably destroyed. In the same month Kingaby was awarded a Bar to his DFM and was promoted to Flight Sergeant. He duly celebrated by probably destroying one Bf 109 and damaging another on 7 August.

The target area on 9 August was Boulogne and Kingaby's formation attacked a swarm of Bf 109s as these rose in defence. Four 109s appeared bent on shooting down Kingaby by closing on his tail, but he climbed towards the sun at full boost and 'lost' them, then spotted a pair of 109s in the Le Touquet zone and proceeded to stalk them. Having closed to 150 yards of one 109 he gave it a two-seconds' burst and saw it roll jerkily onto its back before falling away spuming smoke and glycol. Climbing after its partner Kingaby fastened on its tail and began circling tightly with the 109 until a final burst of cannon sent it down to crash south of Le Touquet.

September 1941 brought relatively few contacts with the Luftwaffe, though fighter sweeps continued to be the order of the day for Fighter Command. On 1 October Kingaby attacked a Bf 109 over Cap Gris Nez and his cannon shells literally ripped the tail section off the Messerschmitt, but two days later Kingaby came close to death during a 'routine' bomber escort sortie in the Ostend area. Even before he met any opposition Kingaby was in trouble, with both his R/T and his reflector gunsight inoperable due to an electrical fault. He might easily have aborted his sortie in these circumstances, but decided to remain with his squadron and complete the operation. He then saw some twenty Bf 109s apparently about to bounce the squadron from behind. Unable to warn the others by radio, Kingaby calmly turned into the oncoming 109s and immediately became embroiled with six 109s in fierce no-quarter fighting.

As the combat progressed Kingaby suddenly saw glycol filling his cockpit – his engine must have been hit. In a bid to regain the English coast he put his Spitfire into a fast dive but was chased by some seven 109s for part of the way. His pursuers gradually turned back to France all except one which seemed determined to nail the Spitfire and slowly closed the range between them. Though convinced that his engine was liable to seize up at any moment, Kingaby felt he had little alternative but to turn and fight his opponent. The two fighters circled, each seeking the other's tail, until Kingaby finally latched on to the 109's rear and followed it as it dived to within 500 feet of the sea before firing a short burst, using a fixed bead sight, and seeing smoke erupt from the 109 before it heeled over into the sea. Landing at Manston Kingaby then discovered that the glycol in his cockpit had come from a faulty windscreen de-icing fitting, not as he'd feared his engine. On 2 November Kingaby was awarded an unprecedented second Bar to his DFM, and on that date officially completed his tour of operations. Two weeks later, on 15 November, he was commissioned as Pilot Officer, then posted as an instructor to an OTU at Grangemouth.

His rest period as an instructor was relatively brief for in March 1942 he was posted to 111 Squadron, but in the following month was transferred to 64 Squadron based at Hornchurch. His return to operations soon saw him adding to his already impressive tally of enemy aircraft despatched, first damaging a Focke Wulf Fw 190 on 2 June, then destroying a Fw 190 on 30 July. By August 1942 Kingaby had been promoted to Flight Lieutenant and on the 19th was flying a Spitfire IX over the Dieppe beach-head when he encountered a Dornier Do 217 and shot it down to crash some eight miles inland from Dieppe.

Claiming another Fw 190 as damaged in the same month,

Kingaby was then transferred to 122 Squadron as a Flight commander, still based at Hornchurch, and by November that year had been further promoted to Squadron Leader and succeeded to command of 122 Squadron. To Kingaby command of a fighting unit meant personal leadership in the air, not chairborne administration, and on 20 January 1943 he led his men off shortly after noon, in company with No 350 Squadron, to patrol the Dover area looking for reported German fighters at 8000 feet. Sighting four Bf 109s, Kingaby chased these and destroyed one. Next day his squadron clashed with some particularly aggressive Fw 190s, but Kingaby destroyed one of these and hit a second which disappeared into cloud shedding metal pieces.

Don Kingaby's leadership of 122 Squadron brought him the award of a DSO on 3 March 1943, the citation for which credited him with more than 300 operational sorties to date, and the destruction of 21 enemy aircraft. Just five days later he added yet another to this total by destroying a Fw 190. As part of the fighter escort for a bombing operation, 122 Squadron was attacked by a mixed gaggle of Messerschmitts and Focke Wulfs. Seeing one Fw 190 attempting to attack one of the bombers Kingaby climbed at full boost under the 190, fired briefly and shot one of its elevators away, then watched it spin down in a crazy parabola before its pilot managed to bale out by parachute.

The following day, however, Kingaby was for once taken by surprise – his wife Helen presented him with a son, several days in advance of its 'scheduled ETA' (Estimated Time of Arrival)! Continuing to lead his squadron Kingaby had several brushes with disaster, owing his survival to sheer skill and experience, but in May 1943 his operational tour was completed and he handed over his command to an ex-Cranwell man, Squadron Leader Peter Wickham, DFC, and, with promotion to Wing Commander, was appointed to a staff desk at Fighter Command Headquarters at Bentley Priory, Stanmore.

Kingaby was destined to remain chairborne at Stanmore for slightly more than a year, but when the Allied invasion of Normany came in June 1944 he (like many other ex-operational men now lingering behind desks) obtained permission to fly several operational sorties over the invasion beaches, and on 30 June he made his final kill of the war by sharing equally in the destruction of a German fighter over Normandy. In July 1944 he left Stanmore on being posted to the gunnery school at Catfoss, while in October he received fresh honours with the awards of an American DFC and a Belgian *Croix de Guerre*. He remained at Catfoss until the end of the European war, and was then given a permanent commission in the peacetime RAF.

His ultimate officially credited fighting tally gave him totals of 22 aircraft destroyed plus a half-share in a 23rd, eight others probably destroyed, and a further 16 damaged. In the post-bellum years Kingaby held several posts, including command of No 72 Squadron from February 1949 to April 1952, while in June 1952 he received an Air Force Cross to add to his many decorations. He retired from the RAF as a Wing Commander on 29 September 1958.

CHAPTER NINETEEN

The 'Invalids'

Any candidate for pilot training in the RAF has always been required to pass a rigorous medical examination to prove himself 'A1' fit in every way before he could be accepted. Physically, mentally, and psychologically, every embryo pilot has had to meet the exacting standards considered paramount for such a demanding responsibility. Yet during 1914-18 and 1939-45 many men with physical disabilities which would by normal standards have barred them immediately from becoming pilots in the RFC, RNAS, or RAF not only flew in combat as operational pilots but established themselves as outstanding fighting men and leaders.

In the case of World War Two the names of Douglas Bader and Colin Hodgkinson come immediately to mind in this context, both of whom had lost both legs yet fought the Luftwaffe from the cockpit of an RAF fighter. Nevertheless these two were by no means the only 'invalids' who, pedantically speaking, were unfit for flying duties with the RAF, yet overcame their disabilities and achieved fighting reputations seldom matched by their more able-bodied contemporaries.

Take the example of Bertie Rex O'Bryen Hoare. Born in Hove, he was accepted by the RAF for a Short Service Commission on 18 May 1936, trained for pilot at 11 FTS, Wittering*, and on graduation on 10 January 1937 was first posted to No 207 Squadron at Worthy Down to fly Fairey Gordons and, a little later, Vickers Wellesleys. By the outbreak of war in 1939 he was serving with No 23 Squadron at Wittering, flying Blenheim IF 'fighters'. Within the following five years he was to become one of the RAF's greatest night fighter pilots – yet he had only one eye! By early 1941, as a Flight Lieutenant, still with 23 Squadron but

* Another pupil on the same course as Hoare was R.A.B.Learoyd, later, Wing Commander,VC.

now based at Ford, Hoare began night intruder operations over German-occupied Europe and on 3 March claimed an enemy aircraft as probably destroyed. Flying Blenheim IFs, then Douglas Havocs, Hoare steadily accumulated victories as his expertise in the specialised night intruder role increased. On 21 April he destroyed a Focke Wulf Fw 200, then probably destroyed a Ju 88 on 4 May, followed by two more victims in the latter month, one of which he destroyed at such close range that his aircraft collided with the German and Hoare returned to base with his aircraft's wings damaged by the debris. Awarded a DFC, he became a Flight commander with 23 Squadron, and on 13 September tackled two Heinkel He 111s, destroying one and damaging the other.

In April 1942, 'Sam' Hoare became CO of 23 Squadron and on 2 April damaged two Dorniers, while on 28 May he destroyed an aircraft on the ground while strafing a German airfield. The following month saw him awarded a Bar to his DFC. On 2 July the squadron received its first operational DH Mosquito II (DD670) and on 6 July Hoare flew the unit's first Mosquito intruder sortie in this machine – an uneventful patrol over Caen. The following night, however, in DD670, Hoare patrolled the airfield at Avord and spotted an aircraft with its lights on east of Chartres. Stalking this – a Dornier 217 – he gave it three bursts of 20 mm cannon shells and the Dornier crashed in flames at Montdidier – 23 Squadron's first victim of its Mosquito bite.

September brought Hoare both success and near-disaster. Flying Mosquito DD670, 'B', he had destroyed another aircraft on 30 July, and another on 10 September. Three nights later while patrolling near Twente he spotted a German aircraft with its tail light switched on. Chasing this machine Hoare flew cautiously, suspecting it was a decoy hoping to lure him over some alerted flak guns. His intended prey suddenly switched its direction but Hoare closed with it as it flew lower and lower, then saw the German fly into the ground, without Hoare firing a shot! Beginning his return flight to base, Hoare was crossing the coast near Hammstede when his starboard engine was hit by flak. Feathering the motor, his port engine then began running rough, losing power, and Hoare had to juggle with the power of both engines to keep flying. Gradually losing height in the darkness, Hoare then found that his radio was useless, but by skilful piloting he finally reached England where some marker searchlights directed him to Hunsdon where he made a bellylanding, neither crew member being injured.

Shortly after, Hoare was awarded a DSO and taken off operations with a posting as an instructor. Credited at that time with six enemy aircraft destroyed and a further eight probably destroyed or damaged, Hoare's tally was all the more remarkable in that he had achieved all his successes to date without benefit of AI radar – just relying on one eye!

After a year of non-operational duties Hoare returned to night operational flying in September 1943 as a Wing Commander, appointed to command No 605 Squadron at Castle Camps from where, with his navigator from 23 Squadron, Flying Officer J.F.Potter, DFC, he destroyed a Dornier Do 217 at Dedelsdorf on 27 September. His unit moved base to Bradwell Bay in October 1943 and it was from here on 19 January 1944 that Hoare shot down a Ju 188 at Chievres to mark up 605 Squadron's 100th claimed victim of World War Two. In February Hoare claimed three enemy aircraft as damaged, while on 24 March he destroyed a Bf 109 nightfighter, and in the following month was awarded a Bar to his DSO, promoted to Group Captain, and was succeeded in command of 605 Squadron by Wing Commander N.J.Starr, DFC. Though he was officially non-operational for the remainder of the war, Hoare continued to fly occasionally, and on 4 September 1944 strafed and damaged at least six German aircraft on the ground during a sortie.

*

Another outstanding fighter pilot whose eyesight initially rejected him for RAF pilot training was Geoffrey B. Warnes. A Yorkshireman from Leeds, Warnes learned to fly in peacetime with the Yorkshire Aeroplane Club at Yeadon where his instructor was J.H.Lacey – 'Ginger' – later to gain high honours as a fighter pilot. The day after war was declared Warnes volunteered for the RAF as a pilot, but the fact that he needed to wear spectacles was sufficient for his application to be refused on medical grounds. Still determined to enlist, Warnes persevered and within six months had been commissioned in a ground duties branch of the RAF, and in 1940 was posted to a balloon barrage unit. Here a sympathetic CO recommended Warnes for a refresher flying course and, despite another initial rejection – he still wore spectacles – he eventually became a flying instructor.

It may have been traditional Yorkshire stubbornness, but Warnes was still not satisfied – he wanted to fly on operations, not spend the war teaching 'circuits and bumps'. Since his only apparent obstacle to such an ambition was his eyesight, he consulted an eye specialist in London who recommended a fairly recent innovation in ophthalmology, contact lenses. Warnes promptly paid him £50 to make a pair and a few weeks later applied yet again for medical examination for flying fitness on operations. This time his persistence paid off and the medical examiner passed him as a 'special case'. Taking a short fighter conversion course, Warnes finally achieved his goal in mid-1942 with a posting to No 263 Squadron to fly Westland Whirlwind two-engined fighters.

In the following sixteen months Warnes flew a variety of low-level sorties, including fighter-bomber attacks against enemy shipping, rail targets, and enemy airfields, generally 'hunting' in the Brest and Cherbourg Peninsula areas and over the Western Approaches. His personal prowess brought Warnes a DSO and a DFC before he was 'rested' with a spell at No 10 Group HQ as a staff officer. In December 1943 Geoff Warnes returned to 263 Squadron, this time as its commanding officer. By then the unit had recently exchanged its Whirlwinds for Hawker Typhoons but was still engaged in its low-level fighter-bomber role. On 22 February 1944 Warnes led nine of his Typhoons on a planned sweep over northern France but the low snow-clouds and poor visibility led him to abort that intention and instead he took his men down low to search the sea around the Channel Islands area for possible enemy shipping targets.

Ten miles west of Guernsey Warnes' engine suddenly cut. Too low to bale out, Warnes told his men over his R/T, ' I'm going to ditch'. Setting the Typhoon down in icy seas, Warnes apparently managed a safe ditching because one of the circling Typhoon pilots saw him swimming towards what looked like a semi-inflated dinghy.

At that point an Australian, Flying Officer R.B.Tuff calmly announced over his radio, 'I think the CO's hurt and can't get to his dinghy. I'm going to bale out and help him.'

Then, ignoring an order from the formation's deputy leader forbidding him to do so, Tuff abandoned his Typhoon and parachuted into the sea, while his aircraft was seen to plunge vertically into the water. Visibility in the area suddenly worsened – neither Geoffrey Warnes nor Tuff were seen again. For his selfless gallantry Tuff was later awarded a 'Mentioned in Despatches'.

*

For James Archibald Findlay Maclachlan the loss of an arm in combat proved no handicap to further operational flying. Born in Styal, Cheshire, Maclachlan joined the RAF in May 1937, was eventually commissioned on 1 March 1938, and was serving in a Fairey Battle bomber unit in France, No 88 Squadron, when Germany invaded France in May 1940. On his return to England he 'remustered' to fighter pilot and served with Nos 73 and 145 Squadrons through the Battle of Britain. Awarded a DFC in August 1940, he left 73 Squadron finally on 19 October 1940 and was next posted overseas to Malta to join No 261 Squadron in defence of that beleaguered key island. By February 1941 Maclachlan had been credited officially with at least eight enemy aircraft destroyed, but on 16 February he was himself shot down by two Messerschmitt Bf 109s.

Taking to his parachute he plunged into the sea and managed to scramble aboard his dinghy – only to be deliberately strafed by the 109s and having his left forearm shattered by bullets. Eventually rescued, Maclachlan was rushed to hospital where his left arm was amputated below the elbow.

On his return to England 'Mac' visited the Queen Mary's Hospital at Roehampton and, in his own words; 'I explained the layout of a Hurricane and together with the designers we worked

(Left) Sqn Ldr J A F Maclachlan, DSO, DFC in his Hurricane. *(Right)* One of Maclachlan's victims on 29 July 1943, a Ju88.

Geoffrey Page in his Hurricane 'Little Willie', 1940.

Wg Cdr A G Page, DFC in his Spitfire IXE, France, 1944.

Trio from 56 Squadron. *Lt-rt:* Sgt Peter Hillwood, Flt Lt 'Jumbo' Gracie, DFC, Flt Sgt 'Taffy' Higginson, DFM.

out what was wanted. They designed a marvellous arm which enabled me to operate the engine throttle while taking the control column and the firing button with my right hand.'

After being fitted with this artificial, detachable left forearm and hand, Maclachlan virtually bullied the higher authorities into giving him another crack at operations, and on 1 November 1941, as a Squadron Leader recently awarded a Bar to his DFC, he arrived at Tangmere, and on 4 November officially succeeded Squadron Leader R.E.P. Brooker, DFC as CO of No 1 Squadron.

Flying all-black painted Hurricane IICs, No 1 Squadron's role at that time was night intrusion, and Maclachlan selected Hurricane BD983 as his personal machine and had his ground crew paint a personal insigne on its nose panel – an arm being drilled by a cannon shell, with two fingers of the hand giving a two-finger 'salute' – a gesture universally, if mildly, expressive of the Service injunction to 'Get stuffed' ... His prime task on taking up his command was to train his pilots in the night intrusion task, and though one or two trial sorties were flown during the winter the squadron officially commenced night sorties over Europe from 1 April 1942. Appropriately, Maclachlan, with his Czech commander of A Flight, Karel Kuttelwascher, flew the first patrols that night, leaving Tangmere at 2215 hours. Returning at 0030 hours Mac had had no success, but the Czech had opened the score-book by destroying one Ju 88 and damaging a second at Evreux. Next night Maclachlan destroyed a train near Cherbourg, but it was not until 27 April that Mac bagged his first night aircraft kills, destroying a Dornier Do 217 and damaging another at St Andre-de-L'Eure airfield. On 30 April Maclachlan's bag for the night comprised two trains and a tug on the French coast, but on 4/5 May Maclachlan was patrolling over Dinard airfield and shot up a Dornier as it was preparing to land, sending it down to crash. He next turned onto a Heinkel He 111 as it lowered its undercarriage on 'finals', fired a crisp burst of all four 20 mm cannons, and saw the He 111 dip its nose, then dive into the airfield's undershoot area with one engine blazing.

On 16 May Maclachlan was notified that he had been awarded a DSO, an honour duly celebrated by the traditional party in the Mess which also honoured Kuttelwascher's award of his first

DFC. On 4 June Maclachlan managed to infiltrate his Hurricane into a group of orbiting Dorniers over St Andre airfield and proceeded to destroy two within a mere 14 seconds of close firing, then damaged two others before the ground flak gunners woke up to the fact. These were to be his last victories with 1 Squadron, which he led from Tangmere to Acklington on 8 July where it was soon to exchange its Hurricanes for Typhoons.

Then, on 22 July Maclachlan left the squadron, being posted to No 59 OTU for instructional duties. This post was followed by a lecture tour of the USA, but in mid-1943 Maclachlan returned to operations with a posting to No 132 Squadron at Gravesend, later Newchurch, to fly Spitfire Vs. Though off operations for almost a year, the one-armed 'Mac' quickly proved he had not lost his touch. Accompanied by one of his Flight commanders, Flight Lieutenant Geoffrey Page, DFC, Maclachlan undertook a daylight prowl on June 29 in the area south of Paris, and within just ten minutes of furious action he and Page shot down four Henschel Hs 126s and two Ju 88s; Mac's share in the tally being three of the Henschels and a half-share in one Ju 88.

In July came the award of a second Bar to his DFC, but in the same month, while flying over northern France, his Spitfire was hit by flak. His Spitfire was seen to go into a steep dive, level out at some 2,000 feet, then flick-roll viciously and dive into the ground and burst into flames. His No 2 circled the crash for several minutes but there was no sign of life, and he flew home to report Mac as presumed dead. In fact, Maclachlan was still alive and was later reported by the Germans to be a prisoner of war, but by the time this notification reached England James Maclachlan had died of his injuries.

As a fighting leader Maclachlan had been an inspiring figure to his subordinates, one of whom, Andre Jubelin, a French pilot who had served under Mac in No 1 Squadron, said of him:

Maclachlan was a born leader ... of all the single-minded men, Mac seemed to me the purest and loftiest I had ever met. Slender, with an obstinate expression in his triangular countenance, he exhibited a broad black line round the irises of his luminous eyes and wore a slight reddish moustache under a sharply pointed nose ... on return from a successful patrol he would unscrew his leather arm [*sic*] and throw it up in the air for the others to play ball with, whooping with joy.*

*

Maclachlan's companion on his last high-scoring sortie near Paris in June 1943, Geoffrey Page, was just one of many young fighter pilots who had 'earned' the unsought honour of belonging to the very exclusive Guinea Pigs Club; men who had suffered the agonies of being extensively burned in action and subsequently restored to a normality via the skills, patience, and deep understanding of the New Zealand-born plastic surgeon Archibald McIndoe and his team of dedicated men and women at the Queen Victoria Hospital at East Grinstead. Eventually to have a membership roll well in excess of 600, the Guinea Pigs Club was (is) largely an air crew community, including in its ranks such men as Tom Gleave, George Bennions, Jo Capka, Pat Wells and Jack Mann – pilots who had passed through a crucible of fire, endured years of pain and continual surgery, yet had returned to fly again. Alan Geoffrey Page's story exemplified the Guinea Pigs: in many ways a mini-epic of courage and self-determination – and a triumph for the human spirit.

Born on 16 May 1920, Page was commissioned as a Pilot Officer on 3 October 1939 and joined No 56 Squadron in June 1940 at North Weald to fly Hurricanes. His baptism of combat came quickly, and on 13 July he shot down a Bf 109, then shared the destruction of a Ju 88 with two other pilots on 20 July, and on 25 July shot a Ju 87 Stuka out of the sky. On 12 August Page and his fellow squadron pilots were scrambled shortly before 1 p.m. to meet a German bombing force attacking Manston but arrived on the scene too late to catch the raiders. Landing at Rochford, near Southend to refuel and await further orders, the 56 Squadron pilots lounged in the hot sunshine at their dispersal through the remaining afternoon until a telephone call sent them racing to their Hurricanes, into the cockpits, and taxying out for

---

* *The Flying Sailor* by A. Jubelin; Hurst & Blackett, 1953

a fast take-off. With Flight Lieutenant 'Jumbo' Gracie in the lead, and Michael Constable Maxwell flying as Gracie's No 2, Geoffrey Page, flying Hurricane P2970, US-X, bearing his personal title 'Little Willie', slotted in as Gracie's No 3. Over the Thames Estuary the ten Hurricanes* sighted their targets – three neat Vics, each of nine Dorniers, of KG2, in excellent formation which gave the Dorniers' gunners superb crossfire coverage.

Putting his men into Echelon Right formation, Gracie led them at the Dorniers from the left side, eased behind the bombers, dived slightly below them, then climbed fast for the attack. The German gunners began firing, their tracers focussing on Gracie's leading Hurricane. Gracie fired, then broke away. Maxwell and Page followed in, firing at the bombers, then a yellow-nosed Messerschmitt Bf 109 flashed past between them aiming at Page's machine. As Maxwell turned swiftly to deal with the 109, Geoffrey Page's Hurricane rocked violently as the Dornier gunners' crossfire took toll of his aircraft, blowing a ragged hole in its starboard wing and simultaneously rupturing the petrol header tank immediately in front of Page.

The tank exploded like a fire-bomb, feeding torch-intensity flames back into the cockpit. With his flying goggles pushed up on his helmet and no flying gloves covering his bare hands, Page took the full blast of terrifying heat in his face and arms. Seeing in horror the skin of his hands shrivelling in the heat, Page frantically struggled to get out of his cockpit and away from the inferno, finally – he knew not how – tumbling into space and falling headlong. Trying to pull the ripcord of his parachute brought agony from his mutilated fingers, but it opened with a loud crack and as his descent slowed Page nearly vomited as he smelt his burnt flesh.

Hitting the sea – he had fallen some two miles off Epple Bay – his next problem was divesting himself of his parachute and harness before these dragged him to a drowning death. With hands and fingers drooping with strips of burnt flesh and open bleeding wounds, Page somehow twisted the harness release disc. He then discovered he could not inflate his 'Mae West'

---

* An 11th Hurricane had aborted the sortie earlier with engine defects.

life-preserver waistcoat – the cockpit fire had burned a gaping hole in it. With no alternative, Page began to swim the two miles to shore, each movement of his body a lancing agony, then secondary shock began bemusing his consciousness and his utter despair at his predicament finally gave way to uncontrollable tears of sheer misery; he was just a boy of barely twenty years – a hell of a way to die with so much life as yet unfulfilled ...

The following hours and days slid by in a mist of pain and dream-like confusion. A passing merchant ship's crew retrieved him from the sea and transferred him to the Margate lifeboat. Once ashore a waiting ambulance sped him to Margate General Hospital, and later he was moved to the Royal Masonic Hospital in Hammersmith. Weeks later Page was visited by Archie McIndoe and a few days later was taken to East Grinstead to join fellow burns patients such as Tom Gleave and Richard Hillary, the latter having been shot down in flames on 3 September.

In the following two and more years Geoffrey Page underwent fifteen major surgical operations and numerous minor ones, each one a painful but progressive step towards his avowed intention not merely to rejoin the RAF for fulltime service but to fly on operations again. His iron-willed determination to achieve that goal amazed even McIndoe who wrote in his private minute-book, 'The bloody fool wants to fly again. He'll never be able to do it, of course, but fancy thinking of it, after all he's been through'. Yet by early 1943 Geoffrey Page, by then promoted to Flight Lieutenant, had not only returned to firstline flying but was serving with No 132 Squadron as a Flight commander, flying Spitfire Vs.

In company with Squadron Leader J.A.F.Maclachlan, Page re-opened his personal vendetta with the Luftwaffe by sharing the shooting down of four Henschel Hs 126s and two Ju 88s in a single sortie. Awarded a DFC, Page was further promoted to Squadron Leader and became 132 Squadron's commander in January 1944. As part of the recently formed 2nd Tactical Air Force (2nd TAF) preparing for the Allied invasion of Europe, Page's squadron spent most of its days sweeping over France, and on 26 April Page shared the destruction of a German communications aircraft, while three days later he destroyed a

Bf 110. On 5 June, the eve of D-Day, 132 Squadron was based at Ford as one of 125 Wing's three Spitfire units – the others being Nos 453 and 602 Squadrons – and on 23 June Page added a Fw 190 to his tally. On 25 June, however, the Wing moved to B.11 airfield in France, and on 7 July Page became Wing Leader with promotion to Wing Commander, a day which saw him destroy a Fw 190 to mark the occasion. On 20 July he shot down a Bf 109, followed by another on 26 September, but on 29 September, due to a re-organisation of 2nd TAF's Spitfire elements, 132 Squadron exchanged its Spitfire IXEs for older Marks and flew back to Hawkinge to revert to bomber escort duties and, later, to embark for overseas operations in the Burma campaign.

Page, already awarded a Bar to his DFC in mid-1944, was later awarded a DSO, but on leaving 132 Squadron returned to hospital for further surgery. He finally retired from the RAF in December 1948 to become a sales executive with the aircraft firm of Vickers-Armstrong at Weybridge. In effect, Geoffrey Page had fought two wars; one in which all fighter pilots faced the distinct possibility of swift death on every operational sortie, and a second private war to overcome mutilation and pain. He had triumphed in each.

CHAPTER TWENTY

Vignettes

What kind of man was the fighter pilot? How different was he from the bomber skipper, coastal captain, photo-recce 'loner'? Certainly, the fighter pilot attracted an aura of glamour to the lay eye which was denied to his fellow pilots in any other facet of aerial warfare; a view perhaps reflected and sustained by the description in a 1969 American journal:*

> Say what you will about him: arrogant, cocky, boisterous, and a fun-loving fool to boot – he has earned his place in the sun. Across the span of 50 years he has given this country some of its proudest moments and most cherished military traditions ... So here's a "nickel on the grass" to you, my friend, for your spirit, enthusiasm, sacrifice, and courage – but most of all to your friendship. Yours is a dying breed and when you are gone – the world will be a lesser place.

Though in the main a view which would evoke derision from most World War Two RAF fighter pilots, that fulsome tribute nevertheless contained elements of truth. During the years 1939-45 the prime tenor of fighter warfare was teamwork, interdependence on fellow pilots in the same section, Flight, or squadron; the halcyon days of the 1916-18 lone ace were no longer viable if a fighter pilot was to survive. Yet once combat ensued, formations became scattered to the winds and each pilot fought an individual battle, relying almost entirely on his own skills, instincts, and courage to conquer – and to live to fight another day.

In Bomber and Coastal Command pilots needed equal virtues of individual ability, but bore the additional responsibility of the

* *Grumman Horizons*

lives of their faithful crews who looked to their skippers for all ultimate decisions. The fighter pilot's responsibilities in such a context were no jot less to his fellow pilots, but his parameters for individual decision and action were so much broader. Such 'freedom' of decision called for men of self-sufficiency, capable of lightning reactions and cool-headed yet explosive aggression. Time was rarely available for reasoned consideration – split-second judgment was the razor's edge between life or death in the air.

It was perhaps inevitable that the extreme contrasts of an operational fighter pilot's life – nerve-exhausting peaks of action, followed by the constant need to re-adjust mind and body to a normality if sanity was to be preserved – induced attitudes of near-fatalism in many; to live for the moment seemed the only rational means of coping – tomorrow might never dawn. Add the universal natural exhilaration, verve, self-assured conceit, and unconscious arrogance of extreme youth, and it was hardly surprising that most off-duty pleasures were pursued with a gaiety and vigour of high pitch. And it should be remembered that a vast majority of fighter pilots *were* very young when they first flew to battle; any man in his late 20s or early 30s was good-humouredly dubbed an 'old man' for the fighter war. To a nineteen- or twenty-year-old youngster life could offer nothing more attractive than the excitement and personal challenge of fighter combat, or finer comradeship than the esoteric community of a fighter squadron; while such a status, with its overt appeal to the lay public in general (and the opposite sex in particular) provided balm to any immature ego.

Young or 'old', once a fighter pilot had emerged from his initial baptism of combat his outlook on his job swiftly matured. The hitherto conviction 'it won't happen to me' had been abruptly dispelled – it had become only too apparent that the Reaper played no favourites in his grisly selection. Further experience hardened his resolve, self-discipline increased, tactical know-how broadened, instinctive skills were honed. With rising rank and therefore increased responsibilities, his mental horizons widened; no longer simply concerned with his own problems, he became a leader, shepherding, guarding, guiding his flock; be it six, sixty or six hundred fighter pilots, all now looked to him for decision and inspiration. Still young in years, perhaps no more than 23, 24 or 25 years old, these men who had survived to become Squadron Leaders and Wing Commanders now wore the mantle of veteran maturity in the arena of the skies. In the army and navy such responsibilities in war were usually borne by men of an older generation, often of higher equivalent rank and many years Service seniority, but aerial fighting has always been a young man's game, needing youth at the helm.

It is a measure of the intensity and toll of the air war in the years 1939-41 that those who led the fighter formations of 1942-45 were mainly men who had begun their operational careers after the Battle of Britain. With the relatively rare exceptions of such early veterans as Sailor Malan, Bader, Deere, Jameson, Walker, Hanks, and others, the 'new' leaders of the latter war years in effect filled gaps created in Fighter Command's ranks by the deaths in action of such potential future commanders as Caesar Hull, Eric Lock, Geoffrey Allard, John Mungo-Park, Marmaduke Pattle, Archie McKellar, and dozens of others who had shown hugely their fitness for future high command.

Other casualties of those early years may or may not have proved eligible for eventual leading roles had they survived, but their all-too brief fighting careers would have put them at least in the forefront of fighter 'greats'. One such indefatigable fighter was Leslie Redford Clisby, an Australian born in McLaren Vale in South Australia on 26 June 1914, who came to England to join the RAF and was destined to die in the skies of France. Joining the RAF with a Short Service Commission on 26 August 1937, Clisby completed his pilot training and was posted to No 1 Squadron on 19 December 1937, initially flying Hawker Fury biplanes but converting to Hurricanes as these began arriving on the unit in February 1939.

In April 1939 No 1 Squadron received a new CO, Squadron Leader P.J.H. 'Bull' Halahan, an Irishman and Old Cranwellian, who was to lead his unit through probably its 'finest hour' just over a year later. From 30 August that year the squadron stood by at one hour's notice to proceed to France, its twelve Hurricanes and their pilots on constant call, and on 8 September the aircraft finally left Tangmere to fly to Octeville airfield, near Le Havre, where the pilots were accommodated in the single cells of an adjacent nunnery! By 9 October the squadron had established itself at Vassincourt airfield, near Bar-le-Duc, from where it claimed its first combat victory of the war on 31 October when Pilot Officer 'Boy' Mould shot down a reconnaissance Dornier. It was one of only a few actual contacts with the Luftwaffe during the winter of 1939-40 – the so-termed 'Phoney War' or *Sitzkrieg* period which proved to be merely the lull before the storm.

Clisby, known as 'Digger' to his colleagues from his Australian origin and his insistence on wearing his deep blue RAAF uniform even though this was showing distinct signs of wear and tear, was among the unit pilots to claim victories prior to the May 1940 onslaught. On 1 April 1940 he and Mould were led by Flight Lieutenant Peter 'Prosser' Hanks on a patrol of the front near Luxembourg when they ran into a formation of nine Bf 110s some 4,000 feet higher and immediately climbed to attack. Despite Hanks' Hurricane being so damaged that he had to forceland at Etain, all three Hurricane pilots claimed a Bf 110 apiece, with Clisby's victim spiralling to earth in flames.

Next day Clisby led both sections of A Flight on a patrol over Metz and had just begun chasing a lone Dornier when three Bf 109s were spotted diving towards the Hurricanes from behind. The leading Messerschmitt fired at pointblank range at Flying Officer 'Pussy' Palmer and shot his Hurricane down in flames, though Palmer was able to take to his parachute safely. Latching on to this Bf 109's tail, Clisby too closed to such short range that his fire almost disintegrated the Bf 109. No further chances for combat came Clisby's way until the German assault on 10 May, from which date No 1 Squadron, in common with every other RAF unit based in France, commenced fast, furious, and continuous action.

On 11 May Clisby accounted for at least two Dorniers, and the following morning he flew as wing-man to 'Bull' Halahan when the squadron put up eight Hurricanes to provide escort for some Fairey Battles from No 12 Squadron attempting to destroy two bridges over the Maas.* Over the target area the Hurricanes became embroiled with a host of Bf 109s from the elite *Jagdgeschwader* JG27 and had to fight for their lives. In the mêlée which ensued Clisby destroyed three Bf 109s for certain, then as he was returning to base encountered a loose formation of Arado biplanes. A fellow Hurricane pilot heard Clisby 'whooping with delight over his R/T (*sic*)' as he lined up behind the Arados and rapidly shot down three within seconds before his ammunition ran out. This six-in-a-day success led to an award of a DFC to the Australian.

May 13 was a relatively 'quiet' day for No 1 Squadron, though several brief combats resulted in three claims at the cost of one pilot wounded, but next day brought Clisby back into action. At 0600 hours B Flight was scrambled to intercept a large formation of He 111s escorted by at least two *Staffeln* of Bf 110s first, Clisby, Hanks and Mould each accounted for one of these before the remaining Bf 110s fled eastwards. Turning their attentions now to the Heinkels, the five Hurricanes tackled these in a classic stern assault. Clisby selected two Heinkels as his targets and his savage onslaught sent one down to forceland in a large field. Seeing its crew climb out of the wreck the aggressive 'Digger' immediately landed alongside and gave chase to the Germans, waving his Service revolver! The Germans promptly surrendered and were handed over to some nearby French troops, after which Clisby took off and returned to base.

This episode was entirely in keeping with Clisby's character; tough, uncompromising, and taking on any odds without hesitation with a determination that, in the opinion of his fellow pilots, could only result in his eventual death. Not given to boasting or exaggeration, Clisby confided to his closest friend on the unit, Halahan, in the evening of 14 May that by then he had destroyed or probably destroyed nineteen German aircraft – fourteen of these in the past three days. Regrettably, the squadron's official records for that period were lost thereby leaving only the recollections of his contemporaries to verify Clisby's actual combat record; those positively known victories quoted hereto being merely those confirmed in personal diaries

* An action which resulted in Fg Off D.Garland and Sgt T.Gray of 12 Squadron later being awarded posthumous VCs.

and notes written at the time by other pilots.

On 15 May the squadron had probably its greatest battle of the campaign to date. Throughout the day it fought successive combats with German formations of 100 or more aircraft, and during the early evening Clisby was one of six pilots from B Flight who took off on an unscheduled scramble hoping to intercept some twenty Bf 110s reported over Laon. Somewhere in the eventual combat Leslie Clisby died. His companions accounted for at least five Bf 110s, and one unconfirmed report credited the Australian with two Bf 110s destroyed before his Hurricane was seen to fall out of control, with flames coming from its engine.

Another survivor of the 1940 French debacle destined to be killed in action later before his ultimate potential as a leading RAF pilot had been fully realised was Newell Orton. Born in Warwick in 1915, Orton was educated at King's High School, Warwick and Leamington Technical College before he enlisted in the RAF Volunteer Reserve in 1935. Promoted to Sergeant and given pilot training, he was granted an SSC and at the outbreak of war was a Flying Officer serving with No 73 Squadron, and flew to France with this unit.

A married man, and known to his squadron colleagues as 'Fanny', Orton was a skilful but not a spectacular pilot, and though he was eventually to emerge from the French campaign as 73 Squadron's highest-scoring pilot, he received little of the sort of publicity foisted upon his friend Edgar 'Cobber' Kain of the same squadron. Gaining experience in several isolated combats during the pre-*blitz* period, Orton was leading the rear section of three Hurricanes in a nine aircraft patrol in March 1940 when all nine began chasing two German aircraft. Orton then noticed three BF 109s intent on tackling the Hurricanes from astern, so turned and engaged these, shooting one 109 down in flames. Later, in the same sortie, the Hurricanes were attacked by twelve Bf 110s, and Orton destroyed one of these.

Prior to 10 May Orton added at least two more to his 'score' and was awarded a DFC later for his prowess, but once the German advance into France gained momentum, Orton was in action daily; sending one German down on the first day of the *blitzkrieg* but having to bale out of his damaged Hurricane minutes later. Returning safely to his squadron, Orton destroyed two bombers next day. The following four days of non-stop fighting brought Orton at least nine more confirmed combat victories, apart from a further three probably destroyed. Two of these fell to his guns when – *single-handed* – he calmly attacked a formation of nearly thirty Bf 109s. On 15 May Orton was piloting one of six Hurricanes from 73 Squadron which engaged a dozen Bf 110s at very low height. Orton shot down two Bf 110s but was in turn shot down in flames. Taking to his parachute at a mere 600 feet the injured and badly burned Orton plunged into some trees, and was rescued from his precarious dangling position by a passing RAF officer and taken to hospital for treatment to his burns and a shoulder wound. Awarded a Bar to his DFC, Orton was evacuated to England for further hospitalisation and eventual convalescence, sharing part of the latter period in the company of another 'burns case', Flight Lieutenant E.J.B.Nicolson, VC. On his return to flying duties, with promotion to Flight Lieutenant, Orton was posted to 59 OTU as a fighter instructor along with several other ex-France campaign veterans.

In July 1941, by then further promoted to Squadron Leader, 'Fanny' Orton joined No 242 Squadron at Manston in a supernumerary capacity to 'ease' himself back onto the latest operational scene, and demonstrated that he had not lost any shooting acumen by probably destroying a Bf 109 on 4 July. By the end of the same month Orton took up his appointment as CO of No 54 Squadron at Hornchurch (later, Martlesham Heath from August), and on 12 August shot down two Bf 109s. A month later, on 17 September, he led his Spitfires into a sprawling engagement with a number of Bf 109s, was seen to shoot one down, but was then seen to fall away from the fight and crash to his death.

The French campaign of 1939-40 proved to be the 'breeding ground' of many future RAF leaders, among them a pilot who was several years older than most of his fellows, having risen through the ranks of the Service the 'hard way'. Born in Mexborough, Yorkshire on 26 November 1913, Royce Clifford Wilkinson initially joined the RAF as an Aircraft Apprentice at Halton in January 1930 to train as an aero-engine fitter, passed out as an LAC, and was posted to Aboukir, Egypt in 1933. Returning to England in 1936 he commenced pilot training in July that year and graduated with the rank of Sergeant, and in 1939 was serving with No 3 Squadron. In May 1940, still a Sergeant with 3 Squadron, he went with his unit to Merville in France to help stem the German advance and quickly established himself as one of his squadron's foremost fighters. On 12 May he shared the shooting down of two Henschel Hs 126s, destroyed a Heinkel He 111 next day, followed by the destruction of two Bf 109s on 14 May.

Within the next seven days Wilkinson claimed a further six enemy aircraft destroyed in the air, often leading his Flight and, on occasion, even leading the whole squadron. In between aerial combats he took part in various ground-strafes of German troops and transports, usually in the teeth of thick and highly efficient flak opposition. When further operations by 3 Squadron became virtually impossible, and evacuation to England began, Wilkinson was detailed to reach the coast by road, there being no 'serviceable' aircraft left for him to fly back. With German troops expected at almost any hour, Wilkinson decided against a road journey and inspected an abandoned Hurricane which had about one foot of its two-bladed wooden propeller shot away at one tip. He promptly sawed one foot off the tip of its other blade, then flew it home …!

On his return to England Wilkinson was awarded a DFM and Bar at the end of May 1940, then commissioned as a Pilot Officer with almost immediate promotion to Flight Lieutenant. As such he was then posted in October to Kirton-in-Lindsey as a Flight commander with the newly-forming No 71 Squadron – the first American Eagle squadron – under the command of Squadron Leader Walter Churchill, DSO,DFC, his former boss on 3 Squadron in May-June 1940. Initial equipment for the 'Eagles' was intended to be American-designed Brewster Buffalo fighters, but the arrival of its first three examples on 24 October soon dismayed the pilots as to the Buffalo's potential for operational flying, being too slow, ill-armed, of poor performance, and dangerously unstable in certain facets of manoeuvrability – in Churchill's view, deathtraps. Accordingly, Churchill quietly detailed Wilkinson and his two most experienced Americans to take off, then land again *without* locking the tail wheels. Each man obeyed 'orders' – resulting in three ground-looped, thoroughly wrecked aircraft. No more deathtraps were foisted upon the squadron, instead on 7 November its first nine Hurricane Is were ferried in by air.

To the Americans, most of whose 'pictures' of Englishmen were derived from Hollywood caricatures, Wilkinson's thick Yorkshire brogue was almost a foreign language initially, but they soon warmed to his overtly friendly approach and, especially, his expert tutelage. Their respect for his aerial skills was soon extended to his deadly mastery in the nightly poker games and crap shooting in the Mess!

Wilkinson remained with 71 Squadron for nearly seven months, teaching, guiding, then helping to lead them into battle. Then, on 14 May 1941, the second Eagle squadron, No 121, came into being, and Wilkinson was transferred to it as a Flight commander to continue his excellent work, this time under the command of Squadron Leader Robin P.R.Powell, DFC, a pre-war pilot and Battle of Britain veteran. Wilkinson's sojourn with 121 Squadron lasted until March 1942 when, with promotion to Squadron Leader, he became the first CO of the newly-formed No 174 Squadron based at Manston.

Equipped with Hurricane IIB fighter-bombers, 174's role was in the main ground attacks against German airfields, transportation, installations in France, with occasional 'sideshow' sorties against enemy shipping. After four months with 174, he was next posted to command No 1 Squadron, taking up his appointment from 31 July 1942 at Acklington. His latest unit was in the process of working up on Hawker Typhoons, and apart from an occasional interception sortie against individual Luftwaffe aircraft appearing along the east coast the following months were taken up with 'ironing out the bugs' in the squadron's Typhoons; a task of no small magnitutde for both air and ground crews.

On 9 February 1943 the squadron moved south to Biggin Hill, from where it undertook standing defensive patrols around Beachy Head and Dungeness which produced virtually no direct combat; then on 15 March the squadron completed a further move of base, this time to Lympne. Here it more or less continued its defensive patrol tasks but, being now ostensibly in the front line, began despatching offensive sorties over France, usually to strafe and bomb enemy trains and other forms of transport.

Further promotion to Wing Commander on 23 May 1943 gave Royce Wilkinson command of the Gravesend Wing, by which time he had added an OBE to his DFM & Bar, awarded in recognition of his sterling services with the first two Eagle squadrons. He remained in that post until March 1944, when he was given command of No 149 Airfield HQ in No 11 Group, then in the following August was sent to Australia on special duties, where he remained until December 1945 saw him return to an Air Ministry staff appointment until his eventual release from the RAF in April 1946.

Another pilot who rose through the lowest airman ranks to become an outstanding fighter leader, and indeed ultimately climbed to the dizzy heights of RAF hierarchy, was William Vernon Crawford – 'Bill' – Compton. A New Zealander, born on 2 March 1916 in Invercargill, Compton, along with three other youngsters of equally adventurous spirit, set sail for England in a ketch in 1938 with the object of joining the RAF. Wrecked on a reef off New Guinea, the boys spent six weeks with the local natives before leaving in a canoe to return to civilisation. Undeterred, Compton next signed as ship's carpenter on a tramp steamer and thus worked his passage to England, arriving days after the outbreak of war in September 1939 and joining the RAF in the following month as a ground tradesman with the lowest possible classification of AC2 (Aircraftman 2nd Class). Volunteering for pilot training almost immediately, he was accepted and trained in 1940, graduating as a Sergeant with an initial posting to No 603 Squadron in early 1941. His stay with 603 was brief because on 1 March No 485 Squadron was formed at Driffield – the first New Zealand fighter unit to be formed in England – and Compton was transferred to this 'native' squadron and commissioned as Pilot Officer. The Kiwi squadron flew its first operational patrols on 13 April, and had its first clashes with the Luftwaffe on 2 June.

As far as combat victories were concerned Compton was a slow

(Left) Fg Off Leslie Clisby, DFC. *(Right)* Fg Off (later, Sqn Ldr) N Orton, DFC.

Two veterans of France, 1940, with 85 Squadron. Sqn Ldr R H A Lee, DSO, DFC *(lt)* & Plt Off A G Lewis, DFC.

Lt-rt: Wg Cdr R C Wilkinson, DFM; Col C Peterson, DSO, DFC; Mrs Peterson; Wg Cdr A Linney (OC 276 Sqn). Occasion was presentation by Peterson of a cheque for 100 US Dollars to 276 Squadron's Fund, and a 'personal' Supermarine Walrus model to Peterson for his 'future convenience' . . . .

Men of No. 121 American 'Eagle' Squadron.

starter, gaining his first 'probably destroyed' in late September followed by a Bf 109 'confirmed' in October. By 12 February 1942 he had been promoted to Flight Lieutenant, and on that day took part in the notorious 'Channel Dash' operations, probably destroying one Bf 109 and destroying a second. The award of a DFC followed a few weeks later, and in the following three months Compton registered several more victories before breaking his wrist in a crashlanding after combat and becoming hospitalised.

By August 1942 Compton was back on operations, this time as a Flight commander with No 611 Squadron, and claimed a Fw 190 'damaged' during the aerial struggle over Dieppe on 19 August. By November 1942 he had been credited with at least eight enemy aircraft confirmed as destroyed, and early in that month added another to his total: 'We had just turned back into France after being warned that enemy aircraft were approaching from St Omer when I spotted eight Focke Wulfs about 4,000 feet below us. Warned the squadron and we dived on them. They split up in all directions. One Focke Wulf shot up almost vertically and as it turned off the top of the climb I opened fire; the elevators and part of the rudder came away, the machine turned over on its back, flew like this for a few seconds, and then dived towards the ground. Saw the pilot bale out as it went down.'

Awarded a Bar to his DFC and promoted to Squadron Leader, Compton succeeded a fellow Kiwi, Colin Gray, as commander of No 64 Squadron at Fairlop, satellite airfield to Hornchurch, in December 1942. As part of the Hornchurch Wing, 64 Squadron flew frequent sorties over France and the Low Countries, either as fighter sweeps or as escorts to bombing formations, and Compton almost invariably led his squadron on each occasion. During one escort mission to some USAAF Liberators raiding Rouen in March 1943 Compton destroyed two Fw 190s in a series of vicious combats but finished the sortie in company with one other Spitfire being chased by eight Fw 190s all the way back to the Channel coast. On another occasion off the French coast he was again embroiled with Fw 190s:

While leading 64 Squadron we were informed by Operations

of two to three enemy aircraft over a ship off Calais. I dived down under a layer of cloud about 7,000 feet and searched for these for two to three minutes. I could not see them so called up to say we would attack the ship. I had started my dive when I saw seven Fw 190s about two miles away coming from Cap Gris Nez. I pulled up sharply and managed to get above and behind without being seen. I fired a very short burst at the No 4 but they went into cloud and I saw no hits. I was then attacked and broke away. One Fw 190 then closed in on my port and did not see me. I fired a second burst and saw hits on the fuselage and wing root. I was using armour-piercing incendiary which, when they hit, left a streak of flame about 18 inches long. The enemy aircraft began smoking furiously and headed for the coast. I fired another short burst and saw hits. The enemy aircraft caught fire and hit the water about 100 yards offshore west of Calais.

In June 1943, with promotion to Wing Commander, Bill Compton became leader of the Hornchurch Wing and was frequently in action throughout that summer. His superb leadership brought him the award of a DSO in September, as well as an American Silver Star for his many escort sorties protecting USAAF Fortress and Liberator bomb missions. He was then rested from operations from December 1943 until April 1944 by touring the USA on a lecture trip, returning to the operational scene as Wing Leader of No 145 Wing, 2nd TAF in time for the Allied invasion of Normandy on 6 June. In constant action with his Wing, Compton eventually raised his officially credited victory tally to 21 destroyed, a share in one more destroyed, and various probables and damaged before finally coming off operations on 6 January 1945 and being posted to No 11 Group HQ as a staff officer for the remainder of the war. Awarded a Bar to his DSO and the French *Légion d'Honneur* and *Croix de Guerre*, Compton later rose to Air rank in the postwar RAF and added a CBE to his many honours.

CHAPTER TWENTY-ONE

From the Cockpit

No man who has not flown a fighter aircraft in life-or-death combat can fully recount the emotions, actions and reactions felt by the men who did. Only the men in the cockpits knew the myriad forms of individual experience which constituted a fighter pilot's life during war. Considering the many thousands who fought in fighters during 1939-45, relatively few have told their singular stories in published forms, usually after several decades' time-lag from the events described; only a tiny handful of such accounts are unvarnished *contemporary* descriptions, devoid of hindsight and reflecting the writer's actual feelings at the time in question. The following reports and accounts by various fighter pilots were recorded immediately after the events, and each is representative in very broad terms of differing periods and varying roles or tasks throughout the war; a cross-section of the fighter pilots' particular forms of warfare.

The German invasion of Poland in September 1939 which, in effect, precipitated war between Britain and Germany, led to many Polish pilots fleeing to Britain to continue their blood-vendetta against Nazidom, and harbouring a hatred for all things German which became legendary in RAF circles. During 1940 three 'all-Polish' fighter squadrons were officially formed i:e Nos 302 (13 July), 303 (2 August), and 306 (28 August) in date sequence of formation, but additionally a total of 89 Poles were serving in other 'British' squadrons by November.

Probably the most famous Polish fighter unit was No 303 '*Kosciuszko*' Squadron which, though still officially non-operational, claimed its first German aircraft on 30 August 1940 during a training flight. Immediately declared operational as a result, 31 August saw the squadron record its first 'proper' victories when six of its Hurricanes claimed four Bf 109s destroyed and two others damaged in a single combat. Two of the pilots involved wrote down their accounts in the unit's private diary that evening:

The date was 31st August 1940. The eve of the day of our first dog-fights over Warsaw. A good time for a fight. We took off and waited in the air for orders. It did not take long to find the enemy. There was a moment of joy as we saw them. I went ahead, pointing their direction to the Flight. We put on speed and chased them. Revenge was coming. The three Huns ahead of us split up their formation and dived. We dived after them and I gave one a burst in the dive. He pulled up – that was what I wanted. A new burst. Fire and smoke broke out in the white belly of the Me 109. It went down like a flaming torch. I fired another burst just in case.

Sergeant S Karubin

After a few minutes chase I caught up with four Me109s, going towards the Channel. They broke formation and one of them swung away to one side. I went after him, keeping an eye on the others. I had to hurry as the three Jerries were already behind me and above me to the port side. I opened fire at 300 yards. After the first burst he put out smoke. I gave him another two bursts and the Jerry went down with a big trail of grey smoke. It was high time to scram because of the other three Me 109s behind my back. I noticed a white smudge on the water about seven miles south of Newhaven.

Flying Officer Z K Henneberg

*

Another European 'exile' who came to England to continue his fight against Germany was the Frenchman René Mouchotte. Arriving in England, via Gibraltar in late June 1940, Mouchotte became the A Flight commander of the first Free French fighter squadron, No 340 nearly two years later. His private diary* entry for 11 June 1942 reads:

* Eventually published in France 1949 as *Les Carnets de Rene Mouchotte*; then in English, 1956 by Staples Press. Reproduced by permission of Granada Publishing.

A bit of excitement this afternoon. Took off with my number two, young Sergeant Bouguen, to patrol to St Catherine's Point, southern bastion of the Isle of Wight. 'Get up as fast as you can, bandits at 16,000 feet'. I put the nose of my Spitfire at the clouds and climb like hell to 20,000 feet. There I saw two suspicious black specks, which I chased. They disappeared ... barely back in my patrol area, the radio sent me due south. My heart leapt. I cocked my guns, lighted up my sight again, cut in my camera. I heard 'Steer 170', then shortly afterwards, '190', then '200', and finally '240'. I scanned the sky ... four planes appeared a few miles away, coming from the south-west ... I was already above them, they were in pairs. Attacked one of the rear pair immediately, manoeuvring to put my number two in a good position to open up at his. My adversary saw me just before I could fire and turned steeply to port. I pressed the button, without hope, for my speed took me past behind him. To catch him again I gave myself one of the finest black-outs of my career. Blind, I went on making the turn.

When my sight came back, I saw one of the Focke Wulfs going up vertically in front of me ... was it the first one? ... I don't know ... my high speed enabled me to follow him in a vertical climb and to see him with his big black crosses quite close. Fixed well in my red circle, I let him have it with my four machine guns and two cannons. Tiny luminous points lighted up in his wings, followed by little plumes of smoke. He tilted over to starboard and seemed to stop, immobile in space. A horrible feeling attacked me: I could feel the Boche, visibly out of control, falling back on me from above ... I remember the rest very vaguely. After a sideslip, I recall a whirlwind of planes, lots of black crosses. I attacked again but did well not to fire – it was young Bouguen. Then a shout hit me, 'Look out behind!' I disengaged without seeing my adversary. Then I found myself in a vertical death-dive behind an apparently disabled Fw 190. At full speed I had trouble keeping the nose of my plane strictly vertical. The noise becoming intense, the vibration alarming, while I thrust with both hands on the stick. My ears hurt horribly. A shot in the cockpit ... the perspex at my side was torn away ... the altimeter needle whizzed round the dial ... three thousand feet ... I had to pull out, get the stick back gently or it would be all up and the old man with it ... I climbed again, going like a bullet. Once my controls had lost some of their stiffness, I tried to turn to port to find my Boche again. I turned and looked everywhere without success ... I can only claim one Fw 190 damaged.

On 27 August 1943 René Mouchotte, while leading the Biggin Hill Wing, was killed in action. Seven days later his body was washed ashore on a beach near the Hotel Bellevue, Westende-Plage (Middelkerke), and was eventually interred in his family's vault in Père-Lachaise, Paris on 3 November 1949 after an impressive military ceremony.

*

Wing Commander John Checketts, DSO,DFC from Invercargill, New Zealand, was a Squadron Leader serving with No 485 (NZ) Squadron in September 1943 as its commander. While leading his unit as top cover for a Marauder bombing raid on Cambrai, he was jumped by some twenty Fw 190s from out of the sun, and in the ensuing dogfight shot one down in flames. His record of the occasion continued:

Suddenly flak bursts appeared all around me and I started to weave and twist to avoid them. I then saw five Fw 190s at three o'clock above me coming down to attack us and called my No 2 to break. We fought for altitude and finally got it, when to my surprise saw two more Fw 190s above me. One of them came for me in a port turn, the same as mine, and the other took the other turn and attacked head-on. The first enemy aircraft could not get me and I thought the other one could not either. His first attack was miles out and I thought I would get a shot at him next time round, but we both missed. His third attack was terrific and I saw all his cannon firing, also his spinner and engine cowlings. There was a terrific explosion at my feet and my cockpit filled with flames. I frantically clutched my hood release and dragged the hood open. The flames gushed round my face and I released my harness and stood out in the slipstream. The stench of burning flesh was sickening and I seemed to be hours trying to escape this inferno. At last my body was wholly out but the toe of my flying boot caught on my windscreen catch and I was being dragged swiftly down; a terrific kick and I was hurtling head over heels down and down. I clutched my ripcord and pulled and a hard jerk stayed my fall. The Fw 190 flew close to me and I was terribly afraid – would he shoot me? No. I saw my No 2 fly away home to dinner as I drifted slowly down with the white canopy billowing above me and my friend the enemy watching me.

Badly burned on face, arms, and legs, Checketts was saved from capture by some local Frenchmen, then was nursed and fed in bed for two weeks, and within a month had been smuggled back to England where he resumed operations shortly after his release from hospitalisation.

*

On 6 May 1943 Flying Officer G. 'Peter' Panitz and his navigator Pilot Officer R.S.Williams, both Australians, of No 456 Squadron RAAF set out in a Mosquito for a Day Ranger sortie. Panitz's report afterwards read:

Set course for Portland Bill which was crossed at 1439 hours. Crossed French coast at Mont St Michel at zero feet. Picked up railway near La Boussac west of Pontorson. Followed line and found moving goods train on line about two miles south-east of Dol. One attack made with cannon and machine gun and nearly all strikes were seen to be on target. The train stopped, issuing steam. Single engine seen on line leaving Combourg. Made dummy run, engine stopped fireman and driver ran into woods. Two attacks made with cannon and machine gun on engine. Many strikes seen and steam to above 100 feet. Returned to Combourg and set course for Montfort railway, picked up at St Uniac. Followed railway and saw goods train on branch line St Meen. Two attacks made with cannon and machine gun. Few strikes seen first attack and good many strikes and steam after second attack. Turned starboard to main railway which was picked up at Caulnes where goods train was found stationary just clear of station. Attack made using machine guns only. Strikes low on boiler and plenty of steam seen. Continued down line, cloud cover then breaking. Found train about five miles east of Lamballe. Short attack made with cannon and machine gun. Attack most effective and large column of steam and smoke seen. West on to Lamballe where three goods trains seen in yard, one moving west; attacked moving train from port quarter, many strikes seen in fire-box, cloud of smoke, then steam, train stopped ... crossed French coast at Pleneuf at 1,500 feet, climbing into cloud at 1535 hours ... crossed English coast about five miles west of Start Point at 1610 hours. Weather over Channel 10/10ths at 800/1200 feet – over France 10/10ths at 1,000 feet breaking to 7/10ths at 2,000 feet at Lamballe.

On 22 August 1944, Wing Commander G. Panitz, DFC, OC No 464 Squadron RAAF, and his navigator Flight Lieutenant R.S.Williams, DFC were lost in Mosquito NT229 during a squadron attack on railway marshalling yards at Chagny, near Dijon.

*

In October 1943 No 401 Squadron RCAF – nicknamed the 'Rams' from its mountain sheep's head motif on its official badge – began receiving new Spitfire Mk IXbs, and the unit's first successes in combat with these came on 26 November, while protecting Marauder bombers raiding Cambrai-Epinoy airfield. Flight Lieutenant J.Sheppard led his own Section down low to tackle several German fighters seen taking off from Achiet, west of Cambrai:

We came down behind the EA (enemy aircraft) in line astern closing fast at 450 mph. Throttling down, I fired a short burst

(Right) 'Bill' Compton, when a Flt Lt serving with No. 485 Sqn RNZAF.

(Below) Wg Cdr Compton (seated on Spitfire's engine) with No. 64 Sqn at Fairlop, March 1943.

They came from every corner [of] the Empire . . . . . Flt Sgt Vin[cent] Bunting from Jamaica *(lt)* talking with the South Afric[an] Group Captain A G 'Sailor' Malan, DSO, DFC at Biggin [Hill].

Sqn Ldr R E Morrow, DFC, RCAF, who commanded N[o] 402 Sqn RCAF from Decem[ber] 1941 until August 1942. Se[en] here at Rochford as a Flt Lt [on] 27 September 1941.

Fighting Poles. *Lt-rt:* Sqn L[dr] Witold Urbanowicz; Fg Off [Jan] Zumbach; Fg Off Miroslaw Feric; Flt Lt Zdzislaw Henneberg. Photo taken 15 December 1940 after all ha[d] received DFC awards for th[eir] prowess during the Battle o[f] Britain.

(Above) No. 65 Sqn group, including Fg Off (later, Wg Cdr) B Finucane *(3rd from lt)* and the New Zealander Fg Off R G Wigg *(4th from lt)*.

(Left) Rene Mouchotte (in French uniform) with *(lt-rt)* Sqn Ldr Jack Charles, DFC; Grp Capt A G Malan, DSO, DFC; Wg Cdr A Deere, DSO, DFC. Occasion was Biggin Hill's 1000th claimed combat victory on 15 May 1943.

A pair of Tigers. Sqn Ldr J
Mungo-Park, DFC *(lt)* and
Off H. M. Stephens, DSO (
No. 74 ('Tiger') Squadron,
1940-41.

Belgian pilots of No. 609 S
with Charles de Moulin
supporting the unit masco
Cdr William the Goat'.

Spitfire IX, DU-L, of No. 3
(Czechoslovakian) Squad
snapped as it was about to
off to help cover the Allied
invasion of Normandy, 6 J
1944.

from dead astern and overshot; EA which had not seen us until then commenced violent evasive action. I pulled up to 200 feet and dived again firing a short burst and observed some strikes on wings and fuselage. The EA was then using all available ground cover, and jinking furiously. He led us over the aerodrome from north-east to south-west where I had to skid violently to avoid light flak bursting all around my aircraft. I then chased the EA down the railway towards Albert, giving him another short burst and observing strikes. Hopping over trees and hedges the pilot was taking such violent evasive action that he hit the ground three times with his propeller sending up dust. He then led us over Albert at roof height. Turning starboard, I gave him a long burst from 200 to 75 yards and observed strikes in the fuselage and wings. The cockpit cover came off in two jagged pieces. I swung into line astern, then over to the port side of EA, seeing flames surrounding the pilot's cockpit. A few seconds later he flew into the deck and blew up.

Sheppard's determination to destroy his opponent despite the hazards of flak and ultra-low level pursuit exemplified most fighter pilots' attitudes, probably never more so than in the case of the night fighters and intruders. Having shot the port wing off a Junkers Ju 188 on the night of 31 August 1944, Squadron Leader J.D.Somerville, DSO,DFC, and his navigator Flying Officer G.D.Robinson, DFC of No 410 'Cougar' Squadron RCAF bagged the unit's 40th victory the following night. In Somerville's own words:

I closed in to 1,000 feet and identified a Do 217 by pulling off to starboard and getting a silhouette against the bright northern sky. I pulled back into line astern and opened fire at approximately 800 feet. It appeared the EA must have seen me at the exact split-second that I opened fire, for it started a fairly hard starboard turn. On the first burst half of the EA port tail plane and rudder flew off and evidently I must have holed his oil tank, because my windscreen became smothered in oil. EA started doing a steady starboard turn, losing height rapidly as if the pilot had been killed or was having difficulty in controlling his aircraft. After the first burst the combat developed into a dogfight as return fire was experienced from the dorsal and ventral guns of the EA. No hits appeared to register although the fire seemed uncomfortably close. I re-opened fire every time I got close enough to see the EA through the oil, which was gradually clearing due to the slipstream; all the time the EA kept firing back at me. It appeared that the EA dived vertically into the ground at the precise moment that I used up all my ammunition. I orbited port and saw the EA strike the ground and burn furiously, position approximately eight miles north-west of Pontorson.

Such determined aggression, a vital facet of all successful fighter pilots' characters, remained as sharp even when such pilots were not officially 'operational'. Flying Officer H.W.'Bud' Bowker, RCAF, after his first operational spell, was officially 'resting' as a test pilot with an RCAF repair and salvage unit on 22 May 1944, and was flying a repaired fighter out over the Channel to test its cannons. The test proved somewhat livelier than he had anticipated:

At 700 feet, south of Selsey Bill, I sighted two Fw 190s on a bearing of 250-260 degrees magnetic at literally zero feet, below and slightly in front. I dived and turned starboard to 300 yards astern. The EA were flying in close formation, line abreast. They pulled up to about 30 feet and turned slowly to port, closing in even more. I fired a long burst with 15 degrees deflection, hitting the port wing of the port aircraft, midway along, where a bulge which I thought to be a bomb, rocket, or tank, had previously been observed. An explosion occurred and the aircraft was blown to starboard with its right wing down. The second aircraft flew into the first, which exploded and hit the deck. I expended the remainder of my ammunition on the second which had a buckled port mainplane and fuselage. Two strikes were observed – on tail and starboard wing-tip. Aircraft was now out of control and hit the deck almost vertically. I orbited position and gave fixes, but saw only a few pieces of wreckage.

For very many fighter pilots their war was comprised of years of training and flying without contact with the Luftwaffe, or opportunities to make a kill. Luck and circumstance played a huge part in whether a man became an ace or even managed to account for at least one opponent to justify his purpose. Richard Joseph – 'Dick' – Audet was a case in point. Born in Lethbridge, Alberta, Audet joined the RCAF in 1941 and served with several units from 1942-44 without even meeting a German aircraft. In October 1944 he was a Flight Lieutenant serving with No 411 Squadron RCAF based at B.88 Airfield, Heesch with the 2nd TAF, flying Spitfire IXes, still without any form of victory registered in his log book, but on 29 December he finally made his mark by destroying five German fighters in five minutes of wheeling combat. His report testifies to his accumulated flying and shooting skills:

I was leading Yellow Section of 411 Squadron in the Rheine-Osnabruck area when Control reported Huns at Rheine and the squadron turned in that direction. An Me 262 was sighted and just at that time I spotted twelve EA on our starboard side at two o'clock. These turned out to be a mixture of approximately four Me 109s and eight Fw 190s. I attacked an Me 109 which was the last aircraft in the formation all flying line astern. At approximately 200 yards and 30 degrees to starboard at 10,000 feet I opened fire and saw strikes all over the fuselage and wing roots. The 109 burst into flames on the starboard side of the fuselage only and trailed intense black smoke. I then broke off the attack. I then went round in a defensive circle at about 8,500 feet until I spotted an Fw 190 which I immediately attacked from 250 yards down to 100 yards and from 30 degrees to line astern. I saw strikes over cockpit and to the rear of the fuselage. It burst into flames from the engine back and as I passed very close over top of it I saw the pilot slumped over in the cockpit which was also in flames.

My third attack followed immediately on the second. I followed what I believed to be an Me 109 in a slight dive. He then climbed sharply and his coupé (cockpit hood) flew off at about 3-4,000 feet. I then gave a very short burst from about 300 yards and line astern and his aircraft whipped downwards in a dive. The pilot attempted or did bale out – I saw a black object on the edge of the cockpit but his 'chute ripped to shreds. I then took cine shots of his aircraft going to the ground and the bits of parachute floating around. I saw this aircraft hit and smash into many flaming pieces on the ground ... I next spotted an Fw 190 being pursued at about 5,000 feet by a Spitfire which was in turn pursued by an Fw 190. I called this Yellow Section pilot to break and attacked the Fw 190 up his rear. The fight went downward in a steep dive. When I was about 250 yards and line astern of this 190 I opened fire. There were many strikes on the length of the fuselage and it immediately burst into flames. I saw this Fw 190 go straight into the ground and burn. Several minutes later while attempting to form my Section up again I spotted an Fw 190 from 4,000 feet. He was at about 2,000 feet. I dived down on him and he turned in to me from the right. Then he flipped around in a left-hand turn and attempted a head-on attack. I slowed down to wait for the 190 to fly in range. At about 200 yards and 20 degrees I gave a very short burst, but couldn't see any strikes. This aircraft flicked violently, and continued to do so until he crashed into the ground.

Audet's five-victory feat was confirmed by other members of his section and brought him an immediate DFC award. Within the first four months of 1945 Audet added six more victories to his tally and received a Bar to his DFC, but on 3 May 1945, while engaged in shooting up a train he was shot down and killed by flak.

From mid-1944 until the final weeks of the European war RAF fighter and bomber crews became faced with a new German fighter which threatened to achieve German air superiority over the Reich – the Messerschmitt Me 262 twin-jet fighter. By the spring of 1945, however, even this menace had begun to be mastered by Allied fighter pilots, despite the obvious superior speed of the 262 to any RAF fighter design. No 133 Polish Wing, based at Andrews Field and comprised of four Polish-manned

Mustang III squadrons, spent the final months of its war on long-range escort duties for Allied bomber streams raiding what remained of the Nazi empire.

On 9 April 1945 Nos 306 and 309 Squadrons were detailed for just such a raid on Hamburg during the afternoon, in the course of which the Mustangs destroyed four Me 262s – the Wing's final combat victories – one being the victim of Flight Lieutenant M.Gorzula, who described his own victory thus:

We had barely left the target area when my earpieces vibrated and I heard, 'Hello, Escort Leader' ... 'Hello, Escort Leader! ... This is Bomber Leader ... some jet about ... Over'. I looked all round carefully, but couldn't see any Jerries. Then a green cartridge was fired from the bomber stream, a second one followed, and then a third. Things began to hum now. Order after order came through. Release supplementary fuel tanks! I pepped up my engine: more revs, more boost. I saw six aircraft about 2,000 yards away diving at the bombers. We headed for the attackers. When I got closer I recognised them as Me 262s, the latest German twin-jet fighter.

The Me 262s levelled out after the attack, but one of them peeled off to see about a bomber which was losing height. I increased revs and boost and approached the Me from above his tail at 500 m.p.h. My Mustang quivered in her all-out effort and the engine was whining away at top pitch. I was not more than 1,000 yards away but couldn't gain any more. Jets must be faster than props, but I boosted once again and got a little closer. Finally I gave Jerry a trial squirt. Seemed all right ... just a little correction ... then I gave him a longish burst, then another and that seemed to have some effect. The Me slowed up, I gave him a third dose and that certainly did the trick. I saw a flash and the Me broke in two. The Jerry jumped out and his 'chute began to open up, but almost immediately the fabric burst into flames ... no need to follow the debris of the Me or the Jerry to earth, so I climbed back and reported.

One common aspect of most fighter pilots' personal accounts is the lack of individual animosity towards their opponent pilots. In the majority of such recollections the pilots were primarily concerned with destroying an enemy *aircraft*, rather than its crew men. This is not to say they were totally unconscious of the human element pitted against them, but – unlike the earthbound fighting soldier – they were seldom actually to see the man or men they were deliberately intent on killing. Thus, for many, combat was a machine-versus-machine conflict overlain with considerations of tactics, weather, and other peripheral facets. For some Allied fighter pilots, however, the personal hatred of Hitler's Nazi regime was paramount. Poles, Belgians, Dutch, French, Norwegians, had all become exiles from homelands invaded and ravaged by Germany, and in almost all cases had seen or heard of relatives, families, friends killed or suffering under the Nazi heel. For them the war was a matter of revenge and retribution – a highly personal 'eye for an eye' fight. Nor was that feeling restricted to non-British pilots, because British-born men had also had homes destroyed and loved ones killed or maimed by German bombing and raiding. For one such fighter pilot* an abiding hatred of all Germans had been born when a German bomb had killed his weeks-old son and left his only other child, a two-year-old daughter, with one arm and a hideously scarred face. From that moment he had only one desire – to kill every German he met:

My first chance to assuage my hate happened during a fighter sweep over the Channel to the Abbeville area. We were supposed to be looking for trouble, hoping the German fighters known to be based in that area would come up and fight. We were about 80 strong and soon found what we were looking for when a batch of 109s jumped the tail squadron from high cloud cover.

Within seconds we were split all over the sky as another bunch of 109s attacked the lead squadron from below, and it became a case of every man for himself. My section leader gave us the 'Break!' as several Huns came at us from behind and I peeled off very smartly into a short dive, twisted to turn, then climbed

* For obvious reasons, he preferred to remain anonymous.

as fast as I could get my Spit to go. Levelling out at about 24,000 feet, I looked round me, saw nobody near, then looked downwards at the main battle milling around. Near the edge of the main brawl I spotted a 109 crawling away south. He looked to be damaged by the way he was flying, and I decided immediately that this bastard would never reach his home again, whatever it took to kill him. I dived fast behind this straggler, closed quickly behind his tail, then very carefully shortened the range until his wings overlapped the outer ring of my gunsight circle. I then gave him a burst of three seconds with cannon and Browning. His tail and rear fuselage shed pieces of metal and he staggered under the impact. Moving off to one side I saw him appear to recover and continue his flight path south. Allowing deflection, I gave him a second burst with all guns. Strikes were obvious all along his starboard fuselage extending forwards to the cockpit and engine cowling.

Seconds later his cockpit canopy fell away and I could now see the pilot clearly. He was wearing some sort of black leather fur-lined jacket and a black leather helmet, with his eye goggles pushed back on top of his head. His face turned towards me, but he made no move to leave his seat. I thought he must be wounded and unable to bale out. Such was my blind hate that I actually felt pleased to have this lame duck at my mercy. I swung slightly behind and above him, very calmly depressed my Spit's nose and lined my sight on the now open cockpit, then thumbed my firing button for the third time.

The pilot and his cockpit virtually disappeared in an explosion of cannon shells and ruptured fuel tanks as the aircraft literally fell apart into dozens of pieces. Flying through the smoke and flying debris I looked back as I turned – there was nothing now to be seen. All I could feel at that moment was pure joy, then reaction set in and I felt drained of all emotion, as if a great weight had been lifted from me.

Select Bibliography

Books about fighter pilots, their exploits and aircraft, have occupied the greatest proportion of all published aviation literature since the 1914-18 war, and this is especially true of the period 1940 to date. The following tabulation is directly relevant only to the theme of this book, and even then is simply a personal selection of titles commended by the author to those readers desiring further, deeper knowledge of the overall subject.

Officially sponsored histories
RAF Yearbook,1938 L.Bridgman; Gale & Polden, 1939
Royal Air Force,1939-45, 3 Vols Richards/Saunders, HMSO 1953-54
RCAF Overseas, 3 Vols RCAF/OUP, 1944-45
*New Zealanders with the RAF,*3 Vols H. Thompson, 1959
Air War against Germany & Italy,1939-45 J. Herington, 1954
Air Power over Europe,1944-45 J. Herington; 1954
The Defence of the United Kingdon B. Collier: HMSO,1957
Destiny can wait PAF Association; Heinemann,1949

Squadron & Unit Histories
Twice Vertical (1 Sqn) M. Shaw; Macdonald,1971
43 Squadron J. Beedle; Beaumont Aviation,1966
Fighter Squadron at War (85 Sqn) A. Brookes; Ian Allan, 1980
Tiger Squadron (74 Sqn) J.I.T. Jones; W.H. Allen,1954
I Fear No Man (74 Sqn) D. Tidy; Macdonald,1972
Eighty Private,1945
Treble One R.P.D.Sands; Private,1957
242 Squadron History & Notes A.E.M. Barton; Private
Squadron 303 A. Fiedler; P. Davies, 1942

Defence until Dawn (488 Sqn RNZAF) L. Hunt; Private, 1949
The Flying Sword (601 Sqn AAF) T. Moulson; Macdonald, 1964
Glasgow's Fighter Squadron (602 Sqn AAF) F.G. Nancarrow; Collins, 1942
603 Squadron A.S.Kennedy; Private
Under the White Rose (609 Sqn AAF) F. Ziegler; Macdonald, 1971
Twenty-One Squadrons (AAF) L.Hunt; Garnstone Press, 1972
Fighter Squadrons of the RAF J.D. Rawlings; Macdonald, 1969
RCAF Squadrons Kostenuk/Griffin; S. Stevens, 1977

Bibliography & General
Dowding and the Battle of Britain R.C. Wright; Macdonald, 1969
Years of Command S. Douglas; Collins,1966
Fighter Command P. Wykeham; Putnam, 1960
Fighter Command,1936-68 C. Bowyer; J.M. Dent, 1980
To Know the Sky P.Hill; W. Kimber, 1962
Fighter Aces of the RAF E.C.R. Baker; W. Kimber, 1962
Aces High Williams/Shores; Spearman, 1966
Raiders Approach H. Sutton; Gale & Polden, 1953
Combat Report H. Bolitho; Batsford, 1943
Fighter Pilot P. Richey; Batsford, 1942
Squadrons Up N. Monks; Gollancz, 1940
AASF C. Gardner; Hutchinson, 1940
Reach for the Sky P. Brickhill; Collins, 1954
War Eagles J. Childers; Heinemann, 1943
The Big Show P. Clostermann; Chatto & Windus, 1952
Flames in the Sky P. Clostermann; Chatto & Windus, 1953
Spitfire Pilot D.M. Crook; Faber & Faber, 1942
Spitfire B.J. Lane; J. Murray, 1942
Fly for your Life L. Forrester; Muller, 1956
Arise to Conquer I. Gleed; Gollancz, 1942
The Flying Sailor A. Jubelin; Hurst & Blackett, 1953
Against the Sun E. Lanchbery; Cassell, 1955
The Mouchotte Diaries R. Mouchotte; Staples Press, 1956
Biggin Hill G. Wallace; Putnam, 1957
Scramble J.R.D. Braham; Muller, 1961
Sailor Malan O. Walker; Cassell, 1953

Nine Lives A. Deere; Hodder & Stoughton, 1959
Wing Leader J.E. Johnson; Chatto & Windus, 1956
One of the Few J.A. Kent; W. Kimber, 1971
Ginger Lacey R.T. Bickers; R. Hale, 1962
Where no angels dwell S. Johnstone; Jarrolds, 1969
Shoulder the Sky G. Thomas; A. Barker, 1959
Duel of Eagles P.Townsend; Weidenfeld & Nicolson, 1970
Double Mission N. Franks; W. Kimber, 1976
Fighter Leader N. Franks; W. Kimber, 1978
The Greatest Air Battle N. Franks; W. Kimber, 1979
Sky Tiger N. Franks; W. Kimber, 1980
Wings of Freedom N. Franks; W. Kimber, 1980
The Air Battle of Dunkirk N. Franks; W. Kimber, 1983
Paddy Finucane D. Stokes; W. Kimber, 1983
Fighter Pilot G. Barclay; W. Kimber, 1976
The Guinea Pig Club E. Bishop; Macmillan, 1963
Eagle Day R. Collier; J.M. Dent, 1980
Night Fighter Rawnsley/Wright; Collins, 1957
Cover of Darkness R. Chisholm; Chatto & Windus, 1953
Night Flyer L. Brandon; W. Kimber, 1961
Night Intruder J. Howard-Williams; David & Charles, 1976
The Narrow Margin Wood/Dempster; Arrow, 1969
Battle over Britain F. Mason; McWhirter Twins, 1969
Hurricane at War C. Bowyer; Ian Allan, 1974
Mosquito at War C. Bowyer; Ian Allan, 1973
Beaufighter at War C. Bowyer; Ian Allan, 1976
Typhoon and Tempest at War Beamont/Reed; Ian Allan, 1974
Spitfire at War A. Price; Ian Allan, 1974
Mustang at War R. Freeman; Ian Allan, 1974
2nd Tactical Air Force C. Shores; Osprey, 1970
A Clasp for the Few K.G. Wynn; Private, 1981
Lonely Warrior V. Houart; Souvenir Press, 1956
Ten Fighter Boys Forbes/Allen; Collins, 1942
Bluey Truscott I. Southall; Angus & Robertson, 1958
Gladiators over Norway V. MacClure; W.H. Allen, 1942
Fight for the Sky Ed. D. Bader; Sidgwick & Jackson, 1973
Pilots of Fighter Command C. Orde; Harrap, 1942
RAF in Russia H. Griffith; Hammond, Hammond, 1942

Air War over Europe, 1939-45 C. Bowyer; W. Kimber, 1981
The Last Enemy R. Hillary; Macmillan, 1943
Richard Hillary L. Dickson; Macmillan, 1950
I had a row with a German T.P. Gleave; Macmillan, 1941

Index

Index

*(An index of places follows
the index of personal names)*

PLACES